THE LEGAL MIND

How does a lawyer think? Does legal intuition exist? Do lawyers need imagination? Why is legal language so abstract? It is no longer possible to answer these questions by applying philosophical analysis alone. Recent advances in the cognitive sciences have reshaped our conceptions of the human mental faculties and the tools we use to solve problems. A new picture of the functioning of the legal mind is emerging. In *The Legal Mind*, Bartosz Brożek uses philosophical arguments and insight from the cognitive sciences to depict legal thinking as a close cooperation between three cognitive mechanisms – intuition, imagination, and language – and addresses the question of how to efficiently use these mental tools. This novel and provocative approach provides a fresh perspective on legal thinking and gives rise to important questions pertaining to the limits of legal interpretation and rationality in the law.

Bartosz Brożek is a full professor at the Faculty of Law and Administration and the director of the Copernicus Center for Interdisciplinary Studies at the Jagiellonian University in Kraków. Brożek is the author of 20 book monographs, editor of 24 volumes, and author of more than 100 research papers. He has received numerous scholarships and awards, including the Humboldt Fellowship.

The Legal Mind

A NEW INTRODUCTION TO LEGAL EPISTEMOLOGY

BARTOSZ BROŻEK

Jagiellonian University (Kraków)

CAMBRIDGE
UNIVERSITY PRESS

CAMBRIDGE
UNIVERSITY PRESS

University Printing House, Cambridge CB2 8BS, United Kingdom

One Liberty Plaza, 20th Floor, New York, NY 10006, USA

477 Williamstown Road, Port Melbourne, VIC 3207, Australia

314–321, 3rd Floor, Plot 3, Splendor Forum, Jasola District Centre,
New Delhi – 110025, India

79 Anson Road, #06–04/06, Singapore 079906

Cambridge University Press is part of the University of Cambridge.

It furthers the University's mission by disseminating knowledge in the pursuit of
education, learning, and research at the highest international levels of excellence.

www.cambridge.org
Information on this title: www.cambridge.org/9781108493253
DOI: 10.1017/9781108695084

© Bartosz Brożek 2020

First published 2020

Printed in the United Kingdom by TJ International Ltd. Padstow Cornwall

A catalogue record for this publication is available from the British Library.

Library of Congress Cataloging-in-Publication Data
NAMES: Brożek, Bartosz, author.
TITLE: The legal mind : a new introduction to legal epistemology / Bartosz Brożek.
DESCRIPTION: New York : Cambridge University Press, 2019. | Includes bibliographical
references and index.
IDENTIFIERS: LCCN 2019038314 (print) | LCCN 2019038315 (ebook) | ISBN 9781108493253
(hardback) | ISBN 9781108717526 (epub)
SUBJECTS: LCSH: Law – Methodology. | Law – Philosophy.
CLASSIFICATION: LCC K212 .B79 2019 (print) | LCC K212 (ebook) | DDC 340/.1–dc23
LC record available at https://lccn.loc.gov/2019038314
LC ebook record available at https://lccn.loc.gov/2019038315

ISBN 978-1-108-49325-3 Hardback

For Atka

Contents

Acknowledgments

This book has benefited from my discussions about the nature of thinking with Michał Heller and Jerzy Stelmach. I would like to thank them both for their encouragement and support. I would also like to thank a number of colleagues and collaborators who read (parts of) the manuscript and offered their comments. They are: Jaap Hage, Marek Jakubiec, Przemysław Pałka, Łukasz Kurek, Mateusz Hohol, Bartłomiej Kucharzyk, Bartosz Janik, Łukasz Kwiatek, Michał Furman, Tomasz Zygmunt, and Maciej Próchnicki.

I thank Łukasz Wiraszka, who translated from Polish a part of the text that now comprises much of Chapters 1–3, as well as Aeddan Shaw, who proofread the entire manuscript.

I would like to express my gratitude to Matt Gallaway of Cambridge University Press for his help and encouragement in the process of writing this book, as well as Becky Jackaman and the entire production team at CUP for their professionalism and assistance.

This book has been written with the support of research grant no. 2017/27/B/HS5/01407 funded by the National Science Center.

Last but not least, I would like to thank Atka for her constant support and inspiration.

Introduction

The Architecture of the Legal Mind

The Harvard law professor Thomas Reid Powell is credited with saying: "If you can think about something that is related to something else without thinking about the thing to which it is related, then you have a legal mind."[1] Once our amusement caused by this sarcastic comment fades, we should realize that Powell is referring here to something more than a stereotypical picture of a boring, abstraction-loving lawyer. It may well transpire that it is not a stereotype, but rather a standard that we are laughing at, while fully embracing it at the same time.

Let us consider some of the classical textbooks on legal methodology. In a typical work belonging to German jurisprudence and revolving around the so-called *juristische Methodenlehre* one finds a detailed analysis of the structure of legal provisions, considerations of legal syllogism, a set of rules for linguistic, systemic, and teleological interpretation, definitions and classifications of legal loopholes, the so-called collision rules or a description of the structure of the legal system.[2] Similar problems are dealt with in the textbooks written from the perspective of the common law tradition: the stare decisis doctrine, procedures for separating ratio decidendi from obiter dictum, vertical and horizontal dimensions of the precedent, distinguishing and overruling, literal meaning, functional interpretation, the burden of proof, etc.[3] These are all very abstract issues. Moreover, the methodological textbooks clearly suggest that the legal mind is mainly preoccupied with reasoning: the establishment of the valid law, the interpretation of legal provisions, their application to concrete cases, or proving facts. They are mental operations that require language. When one needs to know what is the valid law, it must be checked – in the continental tradition – which statutory provisions have been properly enacted or – in the common law tradition – what are the rationes decidendi in the existing precedents. When one interprets the law, one is concerned with linguistic expressions, considering their literal or functional meaning. The application of law is often depicted as a logical procedure,

[1]   Quoted after Fuller, 1969, p. 4.
[2]   Cf. Larenz, 1991.
[3]   Cf. McLeod, 2013; Schauer, 2009.

1

consisting in "subsuming" the given facts under a general legal norm. Finally, establishing facts boils down to determining which set of sentences represents a true, or best supported by evidence, description of real events. It seems that the legal world is linguistic and that lawyers are excellent text analyzers.

A moment of unbiased reflection must lead to the conclusion that this view of the legal mind involves a monstrous mistake. Is it true that lawyers are (almost) exclusively preoccupied with text analysis? Is there no place in their thinking for intuition? Are they, as implied by the authors of lawyer jokes, completely devoid of imagination? This neither sits nor sounds right; even mathematicians cannot limit themselves to manipulating abstract symbols, since no one has ever proved a new theorem in this way. As J. B. Roberts observes,

> the scheme in mathematical thinking is to divine and demonstrate. There are no set patterns of procedure. We try this and that. We guess. We try to generalize the result in order to make the proof easier. We try special cases to see if any insight can be gained in this way. Finally – who knows how? – a proof is obtained.[4]

Mathematicians, physicists, biologists, psychologists, artists, novelists, even the average Joe Bloggs, do not think exclusively in language.[5] They rely on their intuition, explore the fantasy worlds developed by imagination, and do other things to deal with the problems they encounter. Why should lawyers be different?

Of course, it may be argued that the accusation I have formulated is exaggerated. From the fact that the legal methodology textbooks are focused on linguistic and formal aspects of reasoning, it does not follow that all the mental efforts of lawyers are restricted to textual analysis. However, the formal tools are what is characteristic of legal thinking. True, lawyers certainly use nonlinguistic methods of problem-solving, but these are highly idiosyncratic and hence cannot be subject to a systematic methodological reflection. Whatever happens in the legal mind leads to one, and only one, publicly visible and debatable outcome: linguistic expressions. Therefore, only they deserve our conscious effort and attention. Everything else, whatever it happens to be, must remain in the invisible background.

We pay a high price for this relegation of the nonlinguistic cognitive mechanisms to the peripheries of methodological reflection over the law. The point is not only that we too easily abandon the opportunity to jointly develop tools that may be extremely efficient in dealing with legal problems; we change the problems themselves and generate new ones that could easily be avoided. Again, let us use mathematics here as an illustration. The overemphasis on linguistic precision and the formalization of thinking may lead to outright nonsense. A particularly telling example is provided by the "new mathematics" movement, which had a huge influence on mathematical education in the United States in the 1960s. This approach was masterfully, although anecdotally rather than systematically,

---

[4] Quoted after Feynman, 1965, p. 10.
[5] Cf. Brożek, 2016b, p. 6off; Magee, 1997, p. 76ff.

criticized by the great physicist Richard Feynman, who happened to be evaluating mathematical textbooks written at this period. According to Feynman, the idea that children should learn exact definitions and precise language leads to confusion and misunderstanding. Let us consider a task from one of the textbooks: "Colour the picture of the ball red." Why not simply say "Colour the ball red"? As Feynman observes:

> the increase in precision to "colour the picture of the ball" begins to produce doubts, whereas, before that, there was no difficulty. The picture of a ball includes a circle and includes a background. Should we colour the entire square area in which the ball image appears or just the part inside the circle of the ball? Colouring the ball red is clear. Colouring the picture of the ball red has become somewhat more confused.[6]

Let us turn to another of Feynman's examples: "we can and do say, 'The answer is a whole number less than 9 and bigger than 6,' but we do not have to say, 'The answer is a member of the set which is the intersection of the set of those numbers which are larger than 6 and the set of numbers which are smaller than 9'."[7] Such a complication is useless: it does not contribute to a better understanding of mathematics, but only generates unwelcome confusion. Why would one say "Find out if the set of the lollypops is equal in number to the set of girls," when the question is if there are just enough lollypops for the girls?[8] The tools for thinking we have at our disposal, both in mathematics and in law, should be adapted to the problems they help to solve, and not be as precise as possible.

Legal thinking is by no means special;[9] anyway, it is no more special than problem-solving in other fields of reflection. The reason for this is simple: a lawyer is only a human being and has nothing more than human cognitive tools. There is nothing exceptional in legal syllogism, *a simile* and *a contrario* arguments, or in the theories developed by legal doctrine to aid judges and advocates in their job. These are creations of normal minds, with all their strengths and weaknesses. What distinguishes the mind of a lawyer from that of a mathematician is the kind of problems they encounter: a lawyer is experienced in interpretation and the application of law, while a mathematician is experienced in proving theorems. They both have similar brains and minds, but ones that are trained in answering different kinds of questions. A lawyer will intuitively assess whether Smith's claim has any chance of success in court; a mathematician will be helpless in this matter, but at the same time will have a strong intuition regarding the truth or falsehood of a theorem belonging to noncommutative geometry. A lawyer is well-versed in many complex doctrinal theories, as well as accustomed to numerous precedents, but has only

---

[6] Feynman, 1965, p. 14.
[7] Ibid., p. 15.
[8] Ibid., p. 14.
[9] Cf. Alexander & Sherwin, 2008.

a small fraction of the mathematician's knowledge about the world of algebraic structures. Both legal and mathematical minds are based on the same cognitive mechanism, but are however fed with different contents.[10]

How should the architecture of the legal mind be described? In the context of the spectacular advancements in the cognitive sciences (neuroscience, experimental psychology, research in artificial intelligence)[11] that has taken place in recent decades, there seems to be no other option but to take into account the data and theories developed in these disciplines. A continued trust in extreme antinaturalism, a stance hostile to any empirical research, combined with the belief that legal thinking can be reconstructed by someone sitting in a comfortable armchair and employing complex linguistic and logical analysis, is a symptom of fear rather than a well-considered research strategy.[12] The fear is easy to explain: we feel safe sticking to often tested reasoning habits and known, commonly accepted theories.[13] A view of legal thinking embodied in the classical textbooks and often rehearsed by the most respected jurists is an oasis of certainty and safety. It is difficult to abandon it, while rethinking the foundations of legal epistemology in light of the developments in the cognitive sciences may require doing precisely that. An attempt to look at the legal mind afresh is impossible without killing, or at least silencing, our inner epistemological conservative.

The use of empirical theories in legal philosophy is connected to one more danger. After breaking off with tradition, we tend to become revolutionaries. Like neophytes, we see the need for change everywhere, even if there are no reasons to do so. Yet, it is impossible for the cognitive science to completely alter our understanding of legal thinking.[14] Moreover, empirical research usually pertains to precisely determined cognitive mechanisms, which are tested in a very peculiar way. Psychologists come up with a research paradigm (e.g. some kind of a cognitive task), which is then performed by the experiment's participants in the controlled conditions of a laboratory.[15] The outcomes obtained by following such a procedure cannot be easily generalized; they are also subject to different interpretations. Experimental psychology and neuroscience do not provide us with a coherent picture of cognitive mechanisms, but rather with a hugely fragmented one. A more coherent view is constructed by employing theoretical argumentation, which requires a high dose of methodological caution. As a result, there exists no single, commonly accepted explanation of the human cognitive capacities, but a number of competing explanations. These facts must be well remembered when an attempt is made to reconstruct

[10]   Cf. Brożek & Hohol, 2015.
[11]   Cf. Eckhardt, 1996; Thagard, 2005.
[12]   Cf. Stelmach et al., 2017.
[13]   Cf. Brożek, 2016b, pp. 136–138.
[14]   Cf. Pardo & Patterson, 2013.
[15]   Cf. Danziger, 1990.

the architecture of the legal mind. Our inner epistemological revolutionary cannot be given too much freedom.

In the following considerations I will take advantage not only of the findings of the cognitive sciences but also of philosophical argument. Further, I will be relying on the view of mental mechanisms emerging simultaneously from a few research paradigms in neuroscience and experimental psychology. I will take into account the research pertaining to unconscious decision-making,[16] insight,[17] mental simulation (as understood in the embodied cognition paradigm),[18] and the evolution of language.[19] I believe that these conceptions form a coherent picture of the functioning of the human mind. However, it is not a psychological but a philosophical theory. Although it is deeply rooted in empirical findings, it cannot be tested through a series of simple experiments. I think that it should be accepted, or at least seriously considered, not because the empirical data suggest so, but because it is in many respects better than alternative philosophical theories. Only one of the strengths of the philosophical conception I am developing in this book is that it is coherent with many important findings of the cognitive sciences.[20]

The main thesis defended in this book can be succinctly stated as follows: *legal thinking consists in a simultaneous use and cooperation of three cognitive mechanisms – intuition, imagination, and thinking in language.* Let us have a closer look at this statement. First, as I have already indicated, it is a brief slogan. When I say that intuition is one of the forms of legal cognition, I have in mind all of the unconscious processes of decision-making, including what psychologists call intuition and insight. The claim that the legal mind takes advantage of imagination will be developed against the backdrop of the theory of mental simulation, which can be a conscious process (and then it deserves the label "imagination"), as well as an unconscious one. By saying that lawyers think in language, I do not refer to the application of logically valid schemes of reasoning alone, but to all the ways in which linguistic constructions aid legal thinking.

Second, my thesis is that legal thinking consists of the *simultaneous* use of the three above-mentioned cognitive mechanisms. By stressing this fact, I express a strong conviction that without any of those abilities – intuition, imagination, or language – legal thinking would be impossible. The legal mind cannot exist as an intuitive oracle, a generator of images, or a syntactic machine only.

Third and finally, I want to underline that the three building blocks of the architecture of the legal mind do not work in isolation but cooperate closely through various interactions. Intuition provides us with automatic solutions to the encountered problems; but through the use of imagination and language we can ignore or

---

[16] Cf. Kahneman, 2011; Gigerenzer & Gaissmaier, 2011.
[17] Cf. Weisberg, 2006.
[18] Cf. Bergen, 2012; Barsalou, 1999; Barsalou, 2008; Barsalou, 2009.
[19] Cf. Tomasello, 1999; Tomasello, 2003; Tomasello, 2008.
[20] Cf. Brożek, 2013a.

modify these intuitive hints. Imagination evokes intuitions and paves the way for insights, but also enables us to understand linguistic expressions. In turn, conceptual constructions and formal arguments constitute a framework, which we fill in with the help of intuition and imagination. All these issues will be discussed in Chapters 1–3. At this stage, I need to emphasize one thing: The following chapters will be devoted to the analysis of the structural elements of the legal mind. I will address, in turn, intuition, imagination, and thinking in language, as if their workings could easily be separated. However, it is merely an analytic maneuver. When we concentrate on one of the mechanisms, the other two – although relegated to the background – will be constantly present. The main thesis of the book should, therefore, accompany us in all the stages of the analysis.

I will begin my reconstruction of the architecture of the legal mind with a more detailed look at the unconscious processes of decision-making. In Chapter 1, I will analyze the famous paper by J. C. Hutcheson, "Judgment Intuitive,"[21] where Judge Hutcheson defends the claim that good lawyers are characterized by the ability to solve legal problems through a hunch – a kind of feeling that helps to identify the best solution to the considered problem. On my interpretation, hunch is an effect of the functioning of two different cognitive mechanisms: intuition and insight, which are addressed in the following parts of the chapter. I define intuition as an experience-based mechanism, which operates at the unconscious level and is fast and automatic. It continuously provides us with suggestions of how to solve the problems we face. Intuition has serious limitations, which are best exposed in the research over the so-called heuristics. The anchoring effect, the (over)reliance on the representativeness heuristics or the availability heuristics, as well as other "mental shortcuts" may lead – also in legal thinking – to systematic mistakes. These errors, as I will argue, are a fair price to pay for relatively dependable and easy-to-apply thinking tools. In Chapter 1, I also pose the question pertaining to the role of insights in legal thinking. An insight may be defined as an unexpected solution to a problem, which consists in restructuring it or looking at it from a new perspective. Neuroscientific research suggests that insights have a lot in common with intuition: in both cases roughly the same brain regions are activated; regions, it should be stressed, that have nothing to do with thinking in language. However, while intuition is a "heavy duty" mechanism, constantly delivering potential solutions to the encountered problems, insight is a "special task force" – it is used only when there is no clear intuition. Moreover, both intuition and insight are largely based on emotions. From this point of view, one may argue that the legal mind at its unconscious foundations is an emotional mind.

In Chapter 2 I deal with imagination. My point of departure will be the conceptions of Leon Petrażycki, although not his famous theories pertaining to the role of emotions in the law but his less well-known, perhaps even more intriguing,

---

[21] Hutcheson, 1929.

considerations of the place of representations ("mental pictures") in legal thinking. According to my interpretation, Petrażycki provides us with an insightful conception of the structure of the legal mind, where imagination constitutes a bridge between emotional reactions and discursive thinking in language. I develop this idea in the remaining part of the chapter. First, I make an attempt to interpret the concept of imagination in light of the contemporary cognitive sciences. I claim that imagining a thing or an event is possible thanks to the ability of mental simulation. Mental simulations – which use the same brain circuits that are activated when an actual object is observed or action undertaken – may be unconscious or conscious (and then they may be called the products of imagination). Their most important feature is that they are multimodal: they may involve visual, auditory, kinaesthetic, motoric, olfactory, and other modalities.[22] At the same time, it is argued that mental simulations play an essential role in concrete language understanding; it is less clear what their function is in abstract language processing.[23] A number of solutions to this puzzle have been proposed (e.g. the theory of conceptual metaphors);[24] I posit, however, that the best explanation is offered by the so-called dual-coding theory, which emphasizes the concrete-abstract nature of thinking in language. At the end of Chapter 2, a more thorough analysis of two functions of mental simulations in legal thinking – the heuristic and the hermeneutic – is carried out. On the one hand, a lawyer may use mental simulations to evoke intuitions and generate insights; on the other, mental simulations help to better understand linguistic expressions. From this perspective, imagination is the missing link between two other building blocks of the legal mind: intuition and thinking in language.

As a prologue to the considerations of Chapter 3, which is devoted to language, I carry out a short analysis of a paper by Alf Ross, "Tû-tû."[25] Ross poses the question pertaining to the nature of legal concepts and arrives at a surprising conclusion: that many of those concepts, including such essential ones as "property," are semantically empty. Their sole role is to better structure legal knowledge. I believe that Ross commits a number of mistakes en route to this controversial thesis, disregarding the real influence abstract language has on legal thinking. In order to determine the extent of this influence I try to show how language makes thinking objective, enriches it with new levels of abstraction, enables the construction of unified theories, and opens the way for dialogization (i.e. the consideration of alternative solutions to the given problem). On the one hand, it means that by using a linguistic conceptual scheme we are in a position to better understand the world we inhabit and the problems we are dealing with; on the other, language changes the nature of human cognition in a radical way, bringing us into a new cognitive niche.[26] The

---

[22] Cf. Barsalou, 2008.
[23] Cf. Bergen, 2012; Borghi et al., 2017.
[24] Cf. Lakoff & Johnson, 1980; Lakoff & Johnson, 1999.
[25] Ross, 1957.
[26] Cf. Clark, 2006; Pinker, 2003.

niche generates new kinds of problems (theoretical, interpretational, persuasive), but also equips us with a set of extraordinary instruments for thinking – theories, argument types, reasoning schemes, etc. It is in this way that legal thinking goes beyond the concrete and reaches abstraction.

The next two chapters are devoted to the question of how to use intuition, imagination, and linguistic constructions. Chapter 4 revolves around the structural aspects of legal thinking. I begin by describing a debate on the role of logic in the law, which took place in the US jurisprudence in the first half of the twentieth century. Legal realists such as Holmes, Pound, Dewey, and Llewellyn launched an attack on the idea that lawyers and, in particular, judges make their decisions applying logically valid schemes of reasoning. They claimed that the world regulated by the law is too complex to be captured in a perfect, ordered system of legal rules. The realist assault was quite powerful. In the chapter I argue, however, that even though – in accordance with the realist view – lawyers cannot rely exclusively on the "deductive" or top-down strategy (i.e. they cannot base their decisions on abstract rules only), the opposite strategy, bottom-up, is similarly inefficient. It can be demonstrated by formulating relatively simple arguments of logical and semantic nature. It transpires that the legal mind cannot be limited to the use of abstract linguistic tools; but it will also fail to solve legal problems if confined to particular cases only. Lawyers need to combine the two strategies – top-down and bottom-up – using intuition, imagination, and language to accomplish it. Their cognitive efforts will be more effective if they follow six principles: of experience, caution, exemplification, variation, unification and contrast, which I describe in detail in the following part of the chapter. Finally, I consider the concept of justification. I posit that the very idea of justification emerged together with the development of language and inherited two features of language-based thinking: the dialogical and the formal. In consequence, one can speak of two dimensions of justification: dialogue based (a belief is justified if it is acceptable to the parties of a discussion) and theory based (a belief is justified if it "fits" into a broader theory). These two general criteria determine the legal justification space.

Finally, Chapter 5 is devoted to two aspects of substantive rationality: the constructivist and the ecological. Before introducing these two concepts, I provide an outline of Immanuel Kant's practical philosophy, which constitutes a perfect background for discussing both the ideal and the factual dimensions of rational thinking. Then, I proceed to discuss various views of constructive rationality. I observe that these standards are ideal in the sense that they can never be fully realized by the legal mind; rather, they serve as "signposts," which organize and direct our cognitive efforts, and in the actual legal practice can only be approximated. I contrast this understanding of substantive rationality with a different view, which measures the quality of legal decisions and institutions by how they "fit" into the social environment. This ecological approach sheds some light on the ongoing debates in legal philosophy; in particular, it provides an interesting interpretation of the conceptions of rationality and normativity, which are based on the "Reason First" principle. Finally, I analyze the relationship between constructive and ecological rationality. I come to the conclusion that the former provides variation, while the latter provides selection. By constructing various often mutually incompatible theories of rational thought and action, we are able to generate a broad pool of conceptual constructions and exemplary solutions, which may be used to deal with particular problems. However, it is the social environment that remains the ultimate judge in deciding whether a given solution is useful of not.

At the end of this Introduction, four reservations need to be made. First, the structure of the legal mind that I attempt to reconstruct is independent of the role the lawyer plays in legal controversies. I do not provide a picture of the judicial mind or that of an advocate; I do not place any emphasis on the use of mental mechanisms characteristic of the legislative process; also, I do not try to develop a methodology of doctrinal research. I believe that the conclusions I formulate are applicable to all legal roles and all types of legal problems. Of course, there are important differences between the thinking of a judge and of an advocate: they have different goals and responsibilities, and operate in quite different institutional frameworks. However, it does not change the fact that both the judge and the advocate (or any person taking part in legal discourse: a legislator, a mediator, a doctrinal scholar) use the same tools for thinking: intuition, imagination, and language.

Second, one needs to remember that legal thinking takes place "in the shadow of the valid law." This expression may be understood in many ways. In the common law tradition the existing or valid law (in large part, at least) may be identified with the rationes decidendi of the past precedents; in the continental legal systems, on the other hand, valid law is constituted by legal provisions, which have been properly introduced (according to a procedure prescribed by the constitution) and have not been derogated from the legal system.[27] But legal philosophy provides us with a plethora of other criteria of the validity of law: being the (potential) outcome of rational practical discourse,[28] being in compliance with natural law,[29] being issued on the basis of the Basic Norm,[30] being a good prediction of the behavior of the court,[31] etc. In legal thinking the idea of the valid law manifests itself at two levels: intuitive and theoretical. On the one hand, a lawyer trained in the continental tradition, with some practical experience, will have an "intuition of the valid law" in the following sense: they will be able to automatically assess in most cases whether the given provisions of a statute belong to the legal system. Their common law counterpart will have the corresponding, intuitive knowledge pertaining to binding precedents. On the other hand, both will have theories of legal validity at their

[27] Cf. Grabowski, 2013.
[28] Cf. Alexy, 2009.
[29] Cf. Fuller, 1969.
[30] Cf. Kelsen, 1967.
[31] Cf. Holmes, 1897.

disposal that can be called for and used in solving legal problems, whenever it transpires that there are doubts as to which legal norms are binding.

Third, in order to emphasize the universal character of the conception I develop in this book, I have decided to illustrate my analyses with material from different legal systems. I make extensive use of historical examples (Roman law, Hammurabi's code); I also take into consideration cases and conceptual constructions drawn from European, Polish, and German, as well as English and US law. I believe that it is essential to understand what constitutes the common ground for any type of legal thinking and in which way different legal traditions and particular legal systems shape and otherwise influence the basic mechanisms for solving legal problems.

Fourth, the subtitle of this book reads: "A New Introduction to Legal Epistemology." In connection to it, I would like to make two observations. The theory I develop in the book is not "new" in the sense that it introduces ideas no one has considered before; also, it is not based on unpublished empirical research. It is "new" because it offers a novel approach to understanding the structure of legal thinking and the interactions between various mechanisms of the legal mind. I strongly believe that this fresh perspective – even if not completely new – opens up a number of new research fields in legal philosophy and contributes to our understanding of the functioning of the legal mind. When I claim that the book is "an introduction" I am also referring to an important issue. Contemporary legal philosophy, and science in general, tends to be very specialized and detail-oriented. In this spirit, I should have written about "the role of unconscious insight in the English law of the first half of the nineteenth century" or "the use of auditory mental simulations in dealing with intellectual property law cases." I believe, however, that there can be no real progress without more synthesizing and general theoretical proposals. Of course, this comes at a price. Writing a general introduction to legal thinking, one cannot offer much detail and engage in direct discussions with other points of view. I leave it to the Reader to decide whether the price is worth paying.

1

Intuition

The last few decades can rightly be termed the age of intuition. While the traditional approach to human cognition revolved around conscious thinking and investigated such problems as logically valid reasoning schemes, standards for belief revision, formal justification criteria, or ramifications of the rational choice, more recent contributions to the field have enjoyed a somewhat different focus. Psychologists, economists, and philosophers are more inclined to speak about the unconscious decision-making processes, the role of heuristics in human thinking, or the importance of emotions for our cognitive efforts.[1] The image of the human mind that has emerged as a result is one which has been completely transformed. No longer are they a bundle of rational powers, with intuition and other unconscious mechanisms constituting only an irrational nuisance; our minds are increasingly seen as operating largely at the unconscious level and as emotion-driven, with the rational faculties only constituting an addition or overlay of sorts. The goal of this chapter is to consider how this fundamental theoretical shift influences our reflections upon the very nature of legal thinking.

Of course, the question pertaining to the role of intuition or other unconscious processes in legal decision-making is not one that is completely alien to legal philosophy. Representatives of the realist movement, most notably Leon Petrażycki and Joseph Hutcheson, devoted considerable effort to elucidating the place of intuitive judgment in the law.[2] However, their positions, while doubtless interesting and filled with striking observations, were developed against a relatively poor theoretical background: the picture of the human mind available in the first half of the twentieth century was quite different from the one that is being sketched out by the contemporary cognitive sciences. Therefore, it is only reasonable to rethink the role and place of unconscious processes in legal thinking in light of the latest experiments and theories.

---

[1]   See e.g. Damasio, 2006; Damasio, 2018; Kahneman, 2011.
[2]   Cf. Petrażycki, 2011; Hutcheson, 1929.

There is no common agreement as to the exact shape and nature of the mechanisms comprising the unconscious mind. However, two such mechanisms are usually brought to the fore: intuition and insight. The former is a fast, automatic, and experience-based faculty, one which provides immediate answers to the encountered problem. The latter, in turn, is connected to a situation when no immediate answer is available or the potential answers are in conflict. Under such circumstances, it is possible that a sudden, unexpected, and novel solution to a problem comes to one's mind. Importantly, intuition and insight seem to share the same neural infrastructure; they are linked at the structural and functional level. In this chapter, I will try to show how the interplay between them can help solve legal problems.

The psychological literature places considerable emphasis on the typical and systematic mistakes people tend to commit when they rely on intuitive judgments. This research paradigm was initiated by the groundbreaking experiments of Daniel Kahneman and Amos Tversky in the 1970s.[3] Since then, it has been demonstrated that these mistakes (e.g. anchoring effect) are also made in the context of legal thinking.[4] It is a serious challenge to the claim that intuition, together with other unconscious mechanisms, is an important tool in the lawyer's mental toolbox: if it produces so many mistakes, one should avoid it at any cost. I shall argue, however, that the dangers connected with intuition are considerably exaggerated. Under typical circumstances, our intuitive judgments are quite reliable; they only become questionable when we encounter an abstract and atypical problem.

The discussion of the role of intuition and other unconscious mechanisms in legal decision-making may be seen as a part of a larger debate pertaining to the place of reason and emotions in legal and, more generally, practical reasoning. The picture of the human mind being developed by contemporary cognitive sciences may be somewhat alien to one accustomed to more traditional conceptions. It transpires that we are driven by our emotions not only in social interactions but also in our cognitive efforts. Reason has a relatively smaller, but still important, role to play in this context. From this perspective, lawyers are far more emotional creatures than is usually assumed. I will address this issue in some detail at the end of this chapter.

1.1 HUNCH

In 1929, US judge J. C. Hutcheson published a lecture entitled "The Judgment Intuitive: The Role of the 'Hunch' in Judicial Decision."[5] It is an enormously engaging, few-page long defense of the role of intuition (Hutcheson calls it *hunch*) in judicial reasoning. Hutcheson admits that he came to appreciate its role quite late, when he himself became a judge. After graduating from university, he

---

[3]   Cf. Tversky & Kahneman, 1974.
[4]   Guthrie et al., 2000; Enough & Mussweiler, 2001.
[5]   Hutcheson, 1929.

entertained a different view of the application of law, in which a judge's intellect is a "cold logic engine," and the law is seen as a "system of rules and precedents, of categories and concepts," which could be "administered" correctly to arrive at a solution to any legal problem.[6] Actually, however, things are quite different:

> While when the case is difficult or involved, and turns upon a hairsbreadth of law or of fact ..., I, after canvassing all the available material at my command, and duly cogitating upon it, give my imagination play, and brooding over the cause, wait for the feeling, the hunch – that intuitive flash of understanding which makes the jump-spark connection between question and decision, and at the point where the path is darkest for the judicial feet, sheds its light along the way.[7]

Hutcheson is quick to add that the hunch is not only at the disposal of extraordinary judges – all good lawyers utilize it, although attorneys will intuitively seek solutions beneficial for their clients, while the judge will aim at a just and legally acceptable decision. Moreover, the role of intuition is not limited to the sphere of law:

> that tiptoe faculty of the mind which can feel and follow a hunch makes not only the best gamblers, the best detectives, the best lawyers, the best judges, the materials of whose trades are the most chancey because most human, and the results of whose activities are for the same cause the most subject to uncertainty and the best attained by approximation, but it is that same faculty which has guided and will continue to guide the great scientists of the world, and even those august dealers in certitude, the mathematicians themselves, to their most difficult solutions, which have opened and will continue to open hidden doors; which have widened and will ever widen man's horizon.[8]

Hunch is therefore much more than a vague ability to solve hard cases in law; it is rather a capacity allowing the best experts to reach a state of mind in which the "flash of understanding" helps to solve the most difficult problems in any area of experience. A detective, a mathematician, or a lawyer, if they are really good at what they do, may hope for a hunch. A detective will connect apparently unrelated pieces of information to explain a murder mystery. A mathematician will suddenly spot a similarity between an algebraic problem to be solved and a well-known theorem in category theory, which will lead to the sought-after proof. An experienced judge, facing a hard case, will come up with a decision that is both compatible with the sense of justice and defendable according to the methodological precepts of jurisprudence.

These considerations are still quite sketchy. One would easily agree that some detectives, mathematicians, or judges are better than other representatives of their professions; that they are often able to find a surprising, if not brilliant, solution to a problem they face. One may also admit, after Hutcheson, that any such display of

[6] Ibid., pp. 274–276.
[7] Ibid., p. 278.
[8] Ibid., p. 279.

amazing ingenuity should be attributed to the workings of a hunch, a kind of feeling, which is a characteristic feature of the best experts only. However, we will not achieve too deep an understanding of intuition in law if we stop here: a more thorough analysis of hunch is called for.

The first step is to answer the question of whether hunch is indeed a uniform capacity or rather an outcome of the operations of several different mechanisms. In order to consider this problem, it is reasonable to look at a few concrete legal cases that required something more than the use of typical intellectual tools for dealing with legal questions. For many years, Hutcheson served as a federal judge in Houston, Texas. In 1928, only a year before publishing "The Judgment Intuitive," he presided over the *Hornby Castle* case. "Hornby Castle was streaming up the Houston ship channel. Ahead of the *Castle* were two vessels, a barge traveling slowly in the same direction as the *Castle*, and the streamer *Cody* traveling down the channel toward the barge and the *Castle*. Following customary practice, the *Castle* signalled that it would pass the barge on the left and then cross the channel to pass the *Cody* on the right. However, the *Castle* swung too wide in passing the barge and, in danger of grounding itself upon the bank, collided with the *Cody*."[9] The facts of the case were not disputed, but the parties adopted different legal qualifications of the facts. The *Cody*'s counsel argued that the cause of the accident was negligence on the part of the *Castle*'s pilot, who failed to abide by the given signals. The *Castle*'s attorney, on the other hand, claimed that according to custom once a ship was in danger the preexisting agreement was voided and avoiding the collision became the duty of a ship not in danger (i.e. the *Cody*).[10]

Considering this case, Hutcheson concluded that when there is a conflict of rights, the fault lies with the party that – through acting irresponsibly – caused the danger in the first place, and he entered a judgment for the plaintiff.[11] If one assumes that this decision was based on a hunch, it may be defined as an ability to find a solution to a complicated case that respects a rudimentary sense of justice. Such an understanding of hunch is compatible with Hutcheson's explicit declarations. He observes that "the judge really decides by feeling, and not by judgment; by 'hunching' and not by ratiocination, and that the ratiocination appears only in the opinion."[12] And he adds: "all of us have known judges who can make the soundest judgments and write the dullest opinions on them; whose decisions were hardly ever affirmed for the reasons which they gave. Their difficulty was that while they had the flash, the intuitive power of judgment, they could not show it forth."[13] From this perspective, the use of hunch consists in waiting for a clue from the unconscious; when we are considering a complex legal case, we can finally say: the answer has appeared from

9   Cf. Zelden, 1989, p. 87.
10   Ibid., p. 87.
11   Cf. ibid., p. 87.
12   Hutcheson, 1929, p. 285.
13   Ibid., p. 287.

nowhere and we're certain it is the right one as it "feels right." Such an answer does not need to be rational; it need not come with a ready-made justification. It is rather based on the feeling that "this should be so" although it does not have to be accompanied by the knowledge why this is the right solution.

Hunch can be understood in yet another way. Let us consider a well-known precedent from English law.[14] On September 26, 1928, Mrs Donoghue was spending the evening with a friend of hers in Wellmeadow Café in Paisley, where the other woman ordered a Scotsman ice cream float, that is ginger beer with ice cream, which were served separately. Mrs Donoghue poured half of the beer over her ice cream and ate some of it. Then, while she was pouring the remaining beer onto the ice cream, a decomposed snail emerged from the bottle. The event caused health problems in Mrs Donoghue: she was in a shock for a period of time and suffered from gastritis. For that reason, she decided to file a claim against the producer of the ginger beer, Mr Stevenson, demanding £500 in compensation. From the legal point of view, the situation was complicated since Mrs Donoghue was not bound by a contract with the owner of Wellmeadow Café (it was her friend who bought her the Scotsman ice cream float) or with the beer manufacturer, and in accordance with the law at the time, compensation for injury caused by defective products could only be claimed on the basis of a legally binding commercial contract. Ultimately, the case was heard by the House of Lords, where a decision was made, in a 3 to 2 vote, in favor of Mrs Donoghue and she was awarded the compensation. Lord Atkin, one of the judges, justified the decision as follows:

> in English law there must be, and is, some general conception of relations giving rise to a duty of care, of which the particular cases found in the books are but instances. The liability for negligence . . . is no doubt based upon a general public sentiment of moral wrongdoing for which the offender must pay. But acts or omissions which any moral code would censure cannot, in a practical world, be treated so as to give a right to every person injured by them to demand relief. In this way rules of law arise which limit the range of complainants and the extent of their remedy. The rule that you are to love your neighbour becomes in law, you must not injure your neighbour; and the lawyer's question, Who is my neighbour? receives a restricted reply. You must take reasonable care to avoid acts or omissions which you can reasonably foresee would be likely to injure your neighbour. Who, then, in law, is my neighbour? The answer seems to be – persons who are so closely and directly affected by my act that I ought reasonably to have them in contemplation as being so affected when I am directing my mind to the acts or omissions which are called in question.[15]

Thus, Lord Atkin argues that Mr Stevenson's *ex delicto* liability toward Mrs Donoghue is deeply rooted in the principles of English law, and more precisely, in the (unwritten) rule that requires us to take proper care of persons who can be

---

[14] *Donoghue* v. *Stevenson* [1932] AC 562.
[15] Ibid.

affected by our actions. What role could hunch have played in deciding the *Donoghue* v. *Stevenson* case? The judges must have felt that someone should be held responsible for Mrs Donoghue's injury. It is worth noting, however, that something else was of crucial importance in the decision made by the House of Lords: the argument that Mr Stevenson's liability was grounded in the structure of English law; that the decision in Mrs Donoghue's favor "fitted into" the larger puzzle of the legal principles, rules, and precedents. That was also a kind of feeling, or hunch: the sense of congruity between a particular decision and broadly defined legal knowledge. A similar course of reasoning must be entertained by a great mathematician or a smart detective: it is not enough to "feel" that a claim is true; it must also "fit in" with the previously proved hypothesis; it is not enough to have a strong feeling that person X is the murderer – such a hypothesis must bring the available bits of information into proper order so that it creates a feeling of a consistent whole. It must be added that such a feeling does not yet constitute a justification for the decision made. Like any other feeling, it is subjective in nature, which is why it must be integrated into the structure of rational argumentation to have any public or objective weight.

Let us summarize the discussion. When Hutcheson speaks of a hunch, what he has in mind is a capacity typical of brilliant experts: lawyers, mathematicians, gamblers, detectives, etc. However, it seems that everyone can be assumed to have *a kind* of hunch: even the least talented judge or mathematician, faced with a problem, will "feel" that it is worth considering a particular solution. Ingenious experts will simply have better "feelings." What is more, the quality of a hunch must depend on a person's education and experience. Even a most talented mathematician is never born with the ability to prove complex theorems of noncommutative geometry; similarly, a talented student of law – perhaps a future judge of the Supreme Court – cannot answer difficult legal questions without some consideration. Hunch is something we gradually develop. Finally, when Hutcheson describes the ways in which hunch works, he seems to be speaking of two different, though related, abilities. One is the ability to make a quick, almost automatic judgment concerning a given situation (e.g. which of the two parties in a legal case is right); the other one is the capacity for finding an unexpected solution that "fits in" with the already established facts, theories, or normative systems (i.e. with the available knowledge). Psychologists use the term "intuition" to refer to the first ability, while the latter is called "insight."[16]

1.2 WHAT IS INTUITION?

"Intuition" is a word with a turbulent history. It comes from the Latin *intueri*, "examine," "consider." Up until the eighteenth century, it was used to denote

---

[16] Cf. Dorfman et al., 1996, p. 257.

a mental take on a given situation, examining things in one's "mind's eye." In the course of time, however, its use shifted away from the etymological source, first in philosophy and theology, and then in other disciplines.[17] Today, the word is used with reference to the ability to understand something instinctively, without the need for conscious reasoning.[18] This semantic development of "intuition" can easily become the cause of serious misunderstanding or conceptual confusion. For example, there is so-called analytical (rational) intuition,[19] especially in such disciplines as mathematics and logic. The question of how we know that in a plane, given a line and a point not on it, at most one line parallel to the given line can be drawn through the point, can only be answered: "one can see it" or "it is evident." The same mechanism seems to be at work in more complex problems, though. Let us consider the proof that is usually given at school for the Pythagorean theorem: a diagram is usually drawn on which one can "see" that the square of the length of the hypotenuse is equal to the sum of the squares of the lengths of the other two sides. There is no complex mathematical argumentation here or any moving step by step from premises to conclusions (even if the construction of the diagram that is used in the proof takes several steps). The truthfulness of the claim that in every triangle the sum of the lengths of any two sides is greater than the length of the other side and the truth of the Pythagorean theorem are discovered by intuition in the sense that we can "see" that they are correct; these propositions are "evident."

Some also speak of phenomenological intuition.[20] In simple terms, it can be defined as the ability to grasp that which is essential in phenomena, i.e. in the objects of a person's conscious perception, whether it be an item of furniture (e.g. a three-legged table), a relation between people (e.g. love), or a legal institution (e.g. a car sales contract between person X and person Y). According to phenomenologists, one can discover a priori elements in every phenomenon, i.e. ones that are independent of experience. We recognize an object as a table because it fits in with the a priori form of a table: if it did not have a table top, we would categorize it as something else. Similarly, a relation between two people that is based on egoism and reluctance to make sacrifices for another person can hardly be considered love, as this feeling has its particular a priori form too. A legal contract also has such a form: if person Y was only playing a joke on person X by saying that they will sell them their Porsche for $500, we would not conclude that a promise has been made, and hence there would be no binding contract. Well-trained phenomenological intuition helps us to discover that which is a priori in phenomena, which constitutes their invariant forms.[21]

The meanings of analytical and phenomenological intuitions are based on the etymological source of the word; in this sense, intuition is the ability to perceive

[17] Cf. Simpson & Weiner, 1989.
[18] Cf. Stevenson & Soanes, 2006.
[19] Cf. Tieszen, 1989.
[20] Cf. Levinas, 1973.
[21] Cf. Kaufmann, 1986; Stelmach, 1991.

something with one's mind's eye, whether it is about the truthfulness (evident nature) of a claim or the a priori structures of phenomena. However, such an approach is unfamiliar to a psychologist or even a "naturalized" philosopher. Although they may admit that the phenomenon of analytical intuition is real, they will contend that it should be given a different, less confusing name; perhaps, they could even concede that there is phenomenological intuition, but – they will argue – it is a somewhat mysterious ability, just as the a priori structures that phenomenologists talk about. Still, we can respond to these reactions by saying that psychologists and more empirically inclined philosophers had better treat their opponents' views with more caution and look at them with greater sympathy. After all, both the advocates of analytical intuition and phenomenologists want to account for certain aspects of our everyday experience, even if they approach the task with sophisticated and slightly artificial conceptual frameworks. They may be doing that in a rather hasty manner, without due respect for the principles of empirical methodology, and hence without proper justification. However, the fact is that they employ the concepts of analytical and phenomenological intuitions in order to discover some truths about human cognitive processing.

On the other hand, the conceptual confusion cannot be regarded as a property of a well-constructed theory. The claim that a lawyer can employ different kinds of intuition – analytical, phenomenological, and psychological ones – may be justifiable at the level of metatheoretical considerations but not in developing a coherent conception of legal reasoning. Therefore, in the discussion that follows I will employ the term in its psychological sense, albeit without losing sight of those capacities of the human mind that are often referred to as analytical or phenomenological intuition (though I will not use these terms).[22]

What is, therefore, intuition in the psychological sense? In view of the multiplicity of approaches to intuitive cognition in contemporary cognitive science, we should not expect to formulate one uncontroversial definition of "intuition." What is more, that would be a short-sighted approach that would lead to oversimplifying the problem and incorrect conclusions. What seems more reasonable is to seek a more general characterization of intuitive cognition by indicating some of its characteristic properties. Such an approach should enable us to incorporate various, sometimes quite different, understandings of intuition in our model.

Psychologists seem to agree that intuition is an unconscious mechanism.[23] However, "unconsciousness" is an ambiguous term, and it is Sigmund Freud who is, in a large measure, to be blamed for that. In his early texts, he used two terms – "the subconscious" (*das Unterbewusste*) and "the unconscious" (*das Unbewusste*) – interchangeably to refer to memories, feelings, and other mental phenomena that are beyond a person's conscious control, claiming that they represent the main

---

[22] Cf. Chapter 2, where I discuss the role of imagination in legal reasoning.
[23] Cf. Gigerenzer, 2007.

source of psychological disorders. With time, in order to prevent confusion, he abandoned the first one and only used the concept of unconsciousness.[24] Of course, when psychologists speak of the unconscious nature of intuition, they do not refer to Freud's theory. The feeling that enables a mathematician to solve a complex arithmetic problem and that helps a judge to decide a difficult legal case has little to do with deeply hidden memories that haunt our nightmares.

Another understanding of unconscious mechanisms, and one which is commonly adopted in the cognitive sciences, sees them as operating on subliminal stimuli.[25] Those stimuli are too weak, too short, and lack the intensity to be perceived and become the object of conscious reflection, but they can influence our behavior. Unconscious cognition has been the subject of discussion since 1957, when James Vicary, a marketing specialist, announced that he had managed to increase the sales of Coca-Cola and popcorn at the cinema in Fort Dix (New Jersey) by displaying the texts "Drink Coca-Cola" and "Eat popcorn" for a very short time.[26] Today, Vicary's "study" is widely recognized as a fraud; at the same time, though, numerous replicable experiments show that – under special circumstances – subliminal stimuli can influence the decisions people make.[27] However, intuition cannot operate exclusively on such stimuli. The nature of the problems that talented judges or brilliant mathematicians intuitively solve does not allow much room for the occurrence of subliminal signals. Considering a difficult legal case, such as the *Hornby Castle* case, is a far cry from watching a film in which a smart marketing expert displays a subliminal message such as "Drink Coca-Cola." Thus, even if some intuitive judgments are (partly) based on subliminal signals, it is not the source of recognizing intuition as an unconscious mental mechanism.

According to a third understanding of unconscious processes, these are processes that we are not aware of, but that could – at least potentially – become the object of our conscious reflection. In his well-known book *The User Illusion*, Tor Nørretranders claims that in every second we only process 16 bits of information out of the 11 million bits that reach our brains from the senses.[28] Even if these estimates are based on unconfirmed experimental data and on creative simplification, it is commonly accepted that we are conscious of very few of the processes that constantly take place in our brains.[29] This fact is borne out by numerous studies and theories which show that the unconscious mind has a ubiquitous and powerful influence on the human psyche, from learning to decision-making.[30] It is precisely in this sense that intuition is an unconscious mechanism: it is beyond our control, although what it does for us could potentially (at least in large part) be effected

[24] Cf. Bargh & Morsella, 2008.
[25] Cf. ibid. See also Lakoff & Johnson, 1999.
[26] Karremans et al., 2006, p. 792.
[27] Cf. ibid., p. 793f.
[28] Cf. Nørretranders, 1999.
[29] Cf. Bargh, 2017.
[30] Cf. Bargh & Morsella, 2008.

consciously. As a rule, intuition does not operate on stimuli that cannot become conscious but on ones that have not become conscious. It is not a mysterious ability that surpasses sophisticated reasoning; it is quite an ordinary process that takes place at the backstage of our conscious thinking and supports it with clues in our problem-solving activities.

There are crucial differences between intuition and meticulous reasoning. Conscious thinking is relatively slow and it requires concentration, but it offers a sense of free choice.[31] By contrast, intuition "operates automatically and quickly, with little or no effort and no sense of voluntary control."[32] Let us use the so-called Wason selection task to illustrate these differences.[33] There are four cards on the table. Each of them has a word printed on one side, specifying whether a given person is an adult or a minor, while the word on the other side informs us whether the person drinks beer or lemonade. The cards are shown in such a way the we can only see one side of each card:

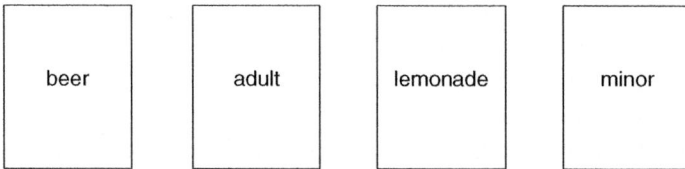

| beer | adult | lemonade | minor |

Now, let us consider the following rule: "If a person drinks beer, he or she should be adult." Which one(s) of the four cards should be turned over to check if the rule was broken? One would answer,[34] without much hesitation, that the cards with the words "beer" and "minor" should be turned over. One would not be concerned with adults and those who drink lemonade, but would want to check whether the beer drinker is an adult and whether the minor drinks lemonade rather than beer.

It is worth noting that this is a logical problem and, in order to solve it, we need to understand the nature of the so-called material implication: "If p, then q." The implication is false in only one case: if its antecedent (p) is true and its consequent (q) is false. If the rule says, "If a person drinks beer, he or she should be adult," it will be false (broken) only when on one side there is information that the person drinks beer and, on the other side, information that the person is a minor. That is why, in this task, we should look at the other side of the card that says "beer" (since if the word on the other side is not "adult," then the rule is broken) and at the other side of the card with the word "minor" (since if the word on the other side is "beer," then the rule is broken).

---

[31] Kahneman, 2011, p. 21.
[32] Ibid., p. 20.
[33] Cf. Wason & Shapiro, 1971.
[34] Statistically speaking; cf. Wason & Shapiro, 1971.

The point is that we do not engage in any conscious reasoning while solving this version of the Wason selection task! We do not start by observing that the rule "If a person drinks beer, he or she should be adult" has the form of a material implication; we do not determine what is the antecedent and what is the consequent here; we do not reflect on when the implication is false; and finally, we do not conclude that the rule is broken only when its antecedent ("The person drinks beer") is true and the consequent ("The person is an adult") false. The conviction that the cards with the words "beer" and "minor" should be turned over is not a result of reasoning: it appears quickly and automatically, beyond our conscious control, almost with no mental effort on our part. It is an intuitive judgment.[35]

Let us now consider an alternative version of the selection task. Suppose the cards have the word "yellow" or "brown" on one side, while the other side has an odd or even number printed on it, and the cards are arranged as follows:

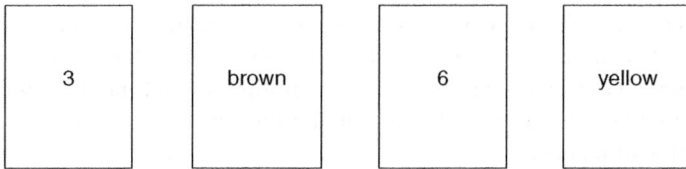

3	brown	6	yellow

The rule governing this example says: "If a card has the word 'brown' on one side, then there is an even number on the other side." In this case, intuition will also provide us with an immediate answer. The problem is that in about 90 percent of cases the answer is wrong.[36] Most of us will say that we should turn over the card with the word "brown" or perhaps two cards: the one with the word "brown" and the one with the number 6. However, the correct answer to this problem, which is analogous to the first version of the Wason selection task, is that we should check the cards with the word "brown" and with the number 3, since the rule will prove false only if a card has the word "brown" on one side and an odd number on the other. The mistake produced by intuition can, obviously, be corrected but that can only be done by means of slow and focused reasoning.

The speed of intuition can be ascribed to the fact that it is based in large part on affective processes.[37] An intuitive judgment is an emotional reaction to a state of affairs, such as a problem that we face. Although there is no common agreement as to the form of the mechanism responsible for such reactions, there are compelling theories to account for it. The most famous one is the somatic marker hypothesis put forth by Antonio Damasio.[38] Damasio's hypothesis was formulated in the context of

---

[35] Naturally, this description does not apply univocally to every single person. Someone who has had the opportunity to consider similar tasks in the past or is a well-trained logician may approach the problem in a different way.

[36] Cf. Wason & Shapiro, 1971.

[37] Cf. Zajonc, 1980.

[38] Cf. Damasio et al., 1996.

research into the process of making social decisions by patients with injuries to the ventromedial prefrontal cortex. Such patients often manifest "asocial" behavior despite the fact that they are normal in terms of intellectual functioning (such abilities as memory, language, and perception remain within normal limits). They cannot make proper use of emotions and feelings to guide their behavior. According to Damasio, the cause of the disorder lies with the fact that such patients have a disrupted access to so-called somatic markers. In a situation that calls for a complex decision-making process, a normal brain activates somatic states that "categorize" the possible ways of behaving as good or bad. This information is (consciously or unconsciously) used by the organism to take a favorable course of action.[39] Importantly, somatic markers develop with experience, which we acquire in social interactions: they are learned rather than innate. They help us to make unconscious, intuitive decisions that can be rational:

> The quality of one's intuition depends on how well we have reasoned in the past; on how well we have classified the events of our experience in relation to the emotions that preceded and followed them; and also on how well we have reflected on the successes and failures of our past intuitions. Intuition is simply rapid cognition with the required knowledge partially swept under the carpet, all courtesy of emotion and much past practice.[40]

Damasio highlights an important fact here: good intuition is an effect of training. Most people give a correct answer immediately in the version of the Wason selection task that is based on the rule "If a person drinks beer, he or she should be adult." This can be explained by the fact that they use well-trained intuition. After all, it is from our earliest years that we have to deal with the social norm that prohibits the consumption of alcohol by underage individuals, which is why we can "automatically" understand it and decide whether it is violated. By contrast, the rule "If a card has the word 'brown' on one side, then there is an even number on the other side" has little to do with our everyday experience. Our knowledge of the world, which we have acquired over the course of many years, simply does not include information about the relationship between color and number parity; but it does include information about the link between age and drinking alcohol.

The fact that our intuition is based on our previous experience has an important bearing on the discussion on intuitive decisions in such disciplines as law. An average person who has not gone through proper legal training is not able to make quick and correct decisions even in relatively simple legal problems. From that person's perspective, such problems are more or less like a Wason selection task based on the rule "If a card has the word 'brown' on one side, then there is an even number on the other side." Of course, just as in the case of the selection task, intuition will provide that individual with *some* clue, but they cannot expect it to be

[39]   Cf. Damasio et al., 1991.
[40]   Damasio, 2006, p. xix.

the right answer. By contrast, an experienced lawyer, who has not only obtained adequate education but has also engaged in legal practice for many years, is in a far better situation here: intuition will usually provide them with the correct solution. In other words, an experienced lawyer is an expert in their discipline, just like a physician with adequate experience or a carpenter who has made items of wood for many years. In each case, their expert knowledge concerning, respectively, legal issues, diagnosing and treating patients, and making wooden objects has, as a result of a long-term training, been "swept under the carpet," thereby becoming intuitive.[41]

This analysis shows that intuition is *unconscious* (the processes that lead to providing an answer to a given problem take place beyond one's consciousness, with the answer appearing out of "nowhere"), *fast* (in comparison with conscious reasoning), *automatic* (intuitive judgments emerge spontaneously; they cannot be intentionally controlled), and *based on experience* (intuition draws on the knowledge that we have acquired in our interactions with the environment). The two versions of the Wason selection task suggest one other thing: intuition can be wrong. Nevertheless, it is hardly surprising that intuition can suggest incorrect answers concerning issues in which we have not acquired adequate experience, for example when we deal with the rule "If a card has the word 'brown' on one side, then there is an even number on the other side" or when a lay person is faced with a complex legal problem. The fact that our intuition leads us astray regarding issues that we have little knowledge or experience in is rather natural. However, studies show that even experts' intuitive judgments can be wrong in certain circumstances. Let us consider this phenomenon now.

1.3 INTUITION'S MISTAKES

The human mind is a device that has to deal with an extremely complex world, something of a tough challenge for two reasons: on the one hand, it is impossible in a decision-making process to take into consideration all of the relevant items of information that we have managed to acquire. On the other hand, we can always assume that we have no access to numerous facts that should have a bearing on the decision we are making. In other words, there are two respects in which we are quite different from Laplace's omniscient demon: neither can we know everything, nor can we actively take advantage of everything we know or could know.[42] That would simply be beyond our cognitive capacity.

For example, let us imagine a judge who is to decide upon a simple case concerning compensation liability resulting from a failure to comply with a contract. The judge would have to answer the question of whether the contract was concluded in the first place. This may seem to be a simple task, especially when

[41] Cf. Kahneman & Klein, 2009.
[42] Cf. Heller, 2013.

the plaintiff presents a copy of the contract that is signed by both parties. However, Laplace's inquisitive judge should ascertain whether the defendant's signature is authentic. To this end, the court has to call in an expert witness with adequate expertise to examine the signature. The problem is that expert witnesses are sometimes wrong; after all, they are also human beings, who are susceptible to error, have their own weaknesses, and employ imperfect theories and technologies. Laplace's judge would have to take this fact into consideration; yet, it would be of little help to call in an infinite number of expert witnesses and to conduct a thorough analysis of the available graphological theories, with all their underlying assumptions. The kind of certainty that this judge seeks is unattainable. Even if the plaintiff and the defendant both admitted that they had concluded the contract, Laplace's judge would still have to allow for the fact that the defendant's declaration could be a result of psychological coercion. This time too, the judge could call in an expert witness, but again with a similar result. The same is true about the other issues that the judge would have to consider: determining the full contents of the contract, confirming that it has not been fulfilled, estimating the extent of the loss, etc. None of these questions, whether factual or normative, can be answered with absolute certainty; there will always be additional items of information that have not been acquired but that might prove relevant to the problem under consideration.[43]

Although real judges have little to do with Laplace's demon, they are in a fairly good situation as no one expects them to make instant decisions. Of course, we would prefer quick legal proceedings, but it would be unreasonable to expect instantaneous court decisions made without evidentiary hearing or adequate deliberation. By contrast, most of the decisions we make on a daily basis are different. Nobody engages in a several-days long, meticulous analysis that would require gathering a lot of data while doing the shopping at a store, choosing a restaurant for a dinner with friends, deciding whether to go there by tram or on foot, or evaluating the credibility of a passerby asked about the way. Such decisions must be taken relatively quickly, since it is only in this way that we can effectively function in a social environment.

Evolution has coped with this problem by providing our minds with heuristics, a kind of "mental shortcut." Instead of taking into consideration all the information that could prove relevant to solving a given problem, thereby wasting time on gathering and analyzing it, in our decisions we rely on a few selected facts.[44] We use this strategy very frequently, both consciously and unconsciously. It is also employed in law, and in a much institutionalized manner at that: after all, legal presumptions are examples of heuristics. For example, in Polish law the presumption of paternity leads to the acceptance of a given claim without determining all of the potentially relevant facts (e.g. no DNA paternity testing is done), based on only

---

[43] Laplace's judge is different from Dworkin's Judge Hercules: the former knows everything about facts, while the latter knows everything about the law. Cf. Dworkin, 2013, p. 132ff.

[44] Cf. Simon, 1956; Gigerenzer, 2001.

some of the facts (e.g. the fact that the child is born within nine months after the termination of the marriage). However, these are examples of highly abstract and consciously applied heuristics. And the human mind, whose time and energy resources are limited, also needs to employ heuristics at a more elementary level of experience in unconscious decision-making.

For example, from the evolutionary point of view, it is reasonable to make decisions on the basis of data that can be easily retrieved from memory. Studies show that what we remember particularly well is, inter alia, recurring events (whether we only witnessed them or were their participants) and those associated with strong emotional reactions.[45] It is easy to observe that such events must be particularly important for the organism. We have to cope with recurring events much more frequently than with untypical situations, while the circumstances that trigger strong emotional reactions are by definition relevant to our well-being. It can be argued then that information that can be easily recalled should play a significant role in our fast and unconscious decision-making as it relates either to the problems we face most frequently or to problems that are particularly crucial to our survival. In the psychological literature, this decision-making mechanism is referred to as the availability heuristic.[46] Another mechanism that the evolutionary perspective can shed light upon is our reliance on that which is representative of a certain type of action or object in our unconscious decision-making. Again, by definition, we usually deal with typical situations. Therefore, from a statistical point of view, our first, unconscious reaction to any problem should be based on the assumption that the problem is typical or very similar to a prototypical situation. In psychology, this decision-making mechanism is known as the representativeness heuristic.[47] Finally, it can be argued that quick and unconscious decisions cannot ignore the "immediate surroundings" of a given problem. Such contextual information will, most probably, turn out to be important in our search for the solution. If particular items of information reach the brain (almost) at the same time, it must be assumed that this is not a coincidence. A special type of this mechanism is often referred to as the anchoring and adjustment heuristic.[48]

Intuition is based on (availability, representativeness, and anchoring and adjustment) heuristics, which is why it can provide us with quick solutions to our problems. However, there is a price that we have to pay for this speed. Psychological studies – in particular those of Kahneman and Tversky – have demonstrated that our trust in intuitive judgments may result in systematic errors.[49] One of them is the so-called anchoring effect: while making quantitative estimates, people unconsciously rely on the "anchor," i.e. a readily available number

---

[45] Cf. Kensinger, 2009.
[46] Cf. Kahneman, 2011.
[47] Cf. ibid.
[48] Cf. ibid.
[49] Cf. Tversky & Kahneman, 1974, p. 1974.

that does not have anything to do with the problem at hand. In their classic experiments, Kahneman and Tversky asked the participants to estimate what percentage of the UN members were African countries. First, however, the participants were to decide whether the figure was greater or smaller than the number indicated by a spinning wheel. The spinning wheel was "tweaked" to indicate either 10 or 65. It turned out that the participants who had drawn 10 on the spinning wheel made the average estimate that about 25 percent of the UN members were African countries; by contrast, those who had drawn 65 averaged out at a much higher estimate, about 45 percent. This and other studies suggest that our intuitive judgments may highly rely on irrelevant, random quantitative data.[50]

The anchoring effect can also be observed in law. Chris Guthrie, Jeffrey Rachlinski, and Andrew Wistrich had a group of judges consider the following case. The plaintiff was hit by a truck belonging to the defendant company. It was determined that the cause of the accident was the truck's faulty brakes; what is more, the defendant company had not performed the obligatory periodical technical checkups of the truck. Following the accident, the plaintiff was hospitalized for several months and had been confined to a wheelchair ever since. Prior to the event, he had been an electrician of good repute and had a large number of regular clients. In court, he claimed damages for the lost income, in addition to the costs of the medical care and the harm he had suffered. However, he did not specify the amount he wished to claim from the defendant. The judges who participated in the experiment were to decide on the amount of the compensation that the plaintiff should receive. They were divided into two groups: judges in one group were provided with the above description of the facts; in the other group, the description additionally included the information that the defendant had filed a motion to dismiss the claim on the grounds that the losses incurred by the plaintiff did not exceed US$75,000 and that the claim should therefore be considered by a different court of law. The defendant company's motion was obviously unfounded since the losses incurred by the plaintiff with all certainty exceeded the amount of $75,000. Yet, it turned out that adding the information with this number to the description of the facts had a significant impact on the participants' average estimate of the due compensation. Whereas the judges in the first group were inclined to award the plaintiff an average amount of $1,249,000, those in the second group must have been "anchored" to the figure 75,000 and decided to award him only $882,000 on average.[51]

In their classic 1974 study "Judgment under certainty: Heuristics and biases," Kahneman and Tversky discuss two other types of systematic errors that can result from reliance on intuitive judgment.[52] One of them is connected to the use of the representativeness heuristic. The participants of an experiment conducted by

[50] Cf. ibid., p. 1128.
[51] Cf. Guthrie et al., 2000, p. 2018.
[52] Cf. Tversky & Kahneman, 1974.

Kahneman and Tversky were to order, from the least to the most probable, several scenarios of the future of a young woman named Linda, who was 31, single, talkative, and very intelligent. The woman was a philosophy graduate who had been an activist against discrimination and for social justice and had taken part in demonstrations against nuclear power. The scenarios to be arranged included: (a) Linda is an activist in the feminist movement; (b) Linda is a social security worker who helps people with mental disorders; (c) Linda is a member of the League of Women Voters; (d) Linda is a bank teller; (e) Linda is an insurance salesperson; (f) Linda is a bank teller and an activist in the feminist movement.[53] Kahneman and Tversky were shocked to find out that *all* the participants considered it more probable that Linda would be a bank teller and an activist in the feminist movement than that she would be a bank teller only. This is an obvious fallacy since the probability of two independent events occurring together is lower than the probability of either one of them occurring alone. This fallacy can be accounted for with the hypothesis that intuition is based on the use of the representativeness heuristic: Linda's traits are representative of a feminist activist, and not of a bank teller, which is why the scenario of her future life in which she is active in the feminist movement appears so overwhelming that we ignore the fundamental laws of probability.

Errors of this type are also committed by lawyers in connection with legal problems. In one study, attorneys were asked to estimate the chances that a given legal case (*Jones* v. *Clinton*) would end in a particular way: with judicial verdict, dismissal, settlement, withdrawal of the legal action, etc. One of the other options was "other than a judicial verdict." It turned out that the subjects considered the probability of a settlement between the two parties to be higher than that of an outcome "other than a judicial verdict," although the latter option includes the former one, along with several others (dismissal, withdrawal, etc.).[54] It can be argued that this error stemmed from the fact that some of the characteristics of the *Jones* v. *Clinton* case were representative of cases that usually end in settlement; by contrast, there are no features that would be representative of cases whose typical outcome is "other than a judicial verdict."

Another type of fallacy in the use of intuition that Kahneman and Tversky demonstrated in their study is a consequence of the application of the availability heuristic. As already mentioned, it consists in estimating the probability of a certain type of event on the basis of how easy it is for us to recall its instances. For example, when speakers of English are asked whether there are more English words beginning with the letter "r" or more with "r" as the third letter, they usually choose the first answer, which is incorrect, most probably because it is easier to recall words beginning with the letter "r" than those in which "r" is the third letter.[55] Lawyers are also susceptible to this type of error in their legal practice. Let us consider the

---

[53] Cf. Kahneman, 2011, p. 211.
[54] Peer & Gamliel, 2013, p. 116.
[55] Cf. Tversky & Kahneman, 1974, p. 1127.

following example.[56] The participants of an experiment were given a description of a legal case concerning a car accident caused by an intoxicated driver. The description included both the prosecutor's and the attorney's lines of argumentation. One half of the subjects received the description of the attorney's argumentation written in vivid and concrete language, with the attorney's argumentation described in a more abstract way, while the other half of the subjects received descriptions of the opposite kind. It turned out that the two groups of subjects gave similar verdicts immediately after reading the files; however, when they were asked to deliver a verdict again after 48 hours, the participants had a tendency to favor the party whose argumentation was written in a more vivid and concrete language. In other words, those who received a vivid version of the prosecutor's line of argumentation tended to find the defendant guilty, while those who read a more concrete description of the attorney's reasoning were more inclined to find the driver not guilty.[57] The source of this effect is often ascribed to the availability heuristic: it is easier to recall a more vivid and concrete description of an event than one using abstract language, full of technical terms and statistics.

Besides these three types of error – associated with the anchoring effect and the representativeness and availability heuristics – the literature describes other phenomena where intuitive judgments go awry, and also in the legal context. They include: the hindsight bias, the framing effect, and the egocentric bias.[58] Does this mean that a lawyer cannot trust their intuition? An affirmative answer to this question would be a gross misunderstanding. It can be hypothesized that the errors in deciding legal cases reported in the literature, committed by both lay persons and individuals with a legal education and long experience in legal professions, are more indicative of the nature of the tasks given to experiment participants than of the (un)reliability of intuitive cognition. Let us consider the cognitive mechanisms described by Kahneman and Tversky (e.g. the availability heuristic). When we are asked the question as to which city is larger, Chicago or Baltimore, we will immediately choose the first. The reason is simple: Chicago is more "available" as we have heard a lot about it and we know that it is a great metropolis with long traditions, while for most of us "Baltimore" is only a label associated with little or no knowledge. It is worth repeating: such a mental shortcut – that the city which we have heard more about and which is often dubbed the capital of blues and jazz, and associated with Al Capone, the Sears Tower, and Michael Jordan's Chicago Bulls is larger – is quite reasonable. In other words, it is easier for us to retrieve from memory that which is more vivid in our experience and more important for our actions in the world.

There is a similar situation with the other mental shortcuts that we employ in our intuitive reasoning. For instance, the representativeness heuristic provides

---

[56] Reyes et al., 1980.
[57] Cf. ibid.
[58] Cf. Hastie et al., 1999; McCaffery et al., 1995; Langevoort, 1998.

us with suggestions on the basis of certain schemas or prototypes: if a given situation is sufficiently similar to the typical circumstances in which we are in danger, intuition will tell us that we should be particularly careful.[59] If a person has traits that are typical of nice and friendly people – they smile a lot, tend to offer help, and are polite – we will draw the intuitive conclusion that there is nothing dangerous about them. Of course, we can be wrong in both cases. A "dangerous" situation may prove to be a joke played on us by our friends (who play on our intuitive reactions), while a friendly stranger may turn out to be a psychopath killer. The point is that such mistakes are relatively infrequent; they are frequent and systematic only in relation to problems that are themselves untypical, at least from the perspective of the evolution of the human mind (e.g. when we face a problem that calls for statistical analysis or one that has little to do with our everyday problems). In other words, intuition is a very useful cognitive ability that usually provides us with useful, if not perfect, suggestions on how to tackle a particular problem.

Once more, it must be stressed that good intuition is a result of experience and training. We cannot expect correct intuitive judgments concerning legal matters from a person who has had little to do with law; in a similar vein, a person with almost no experience in carpentry cannot count on useful intuitions regarding the restoration of an old wooden staircase. Given this, we can conclude that legal intuition is a real phenomenon; however, it is not a mysterious ability: a lawyer has legal intuition just as a mathematician has mathematical intuition and a physician medical intuition. Their intuitions use the same neural architecture, which is, however, filled with different contents as a result of a long process of training and experience.

1.4 INSIGHT

"Eureka!" This is perhaps the most famous exclamation in history. Everyone knows the story from school: King Hiero of Syracuse had commissioned his goldsmith to make a votive crown. The goldsmith, however, was accused of stealing some of the king's gold and replacing it with silver. "Furious that he may have been cheated, Hiero ordered Archimedes to investigate the matter. To ponder over the problem, Archimedes went to the public baths, where he noted that the more his body sank into the water, the more water was displaced. . . . Overwhelmed with joy, he leaped out of the bath and rushed home naked, shouting: 'Eureka! Eureka!'"[60] Once at home, he made two objects – one of gold and one of silver – of the same weight as the king's votive crown and observed how much water was displaced by each. It turned out that the volume of water displaced by the new crown was greater than the

---

[59] Cf. Kahneman & Tversky, 1972.
[60] Smólski, 2001, p. 45.

volume of water displaced by the golden object and smaller than the volume displaced by the silver object. Here was definitive proof of fraud.

It is easy to prove that nothing like this could have happened. A typical ancient Greek votive crown had an average volume of about 37 cm^3. When placed in a container of 20 cm in diameter, it would have raised the level of water by about 1.2 mm. A crown of the same weight but comprising 80 percent gold and 20 percent silver would have a volume of about 43 cm^3 and would raise the level of water by about 1.4 mm. If we allow for the meniscus (the curve at the surface of the water), the difference between these volumes does not exceed the measurement error. Simply, Archimedes could not have applied this method to prove that any fraud had taken place; as argued by historians, he had much better methods at his disposal to do so anyway.[61]

Thus, it is more than probable that the story which has Archimedes running naked in Syracuse and crying "Eureka!" never actually took place. This fact is of little importance, however, since Archimedes crying "Eureka!" is a beautiful metaphor describing the situations in which we unravel nature's greatest mysteries. Archimedes may not have run naked in Syracuse, and Isaac Newton may not have been struck by a falling apple; yet, there are numerous verified stories in the history of science describing how innovative ideas suddenly arose in the minds of thinkers in an illuminating moment of understanding. It suffices to recall how Friedrich August Kekulé discovered the structure of benzene after having a dream of a snake eating its own tail; how Henri Poincaré found the solution to a vexing mathematical problem when he put his foot on the step of a horse-drawn omnibus; or how Werner Heisenberg, plagued with hay fever, formulated the theory of quantum mechanics during his trip to the island of Helgoland.

Such moments of illumination or insight are also experienced by lawyers. At the beginning of the chapter, we made reference to the *Donoghue* v. *Stevenson* case, in which, despite the lack of explicit legal regulations, the House of Lords decided to hold Mr Stevenson responsible for the losses incurred by Mrs Donoghue on the grounds that such a decision was compliant with the broader context of English law. The verdict broke with a long tradition according to which liability for defective products could only follow from a legal contract between two parties. But that would not have been possible if it had not been for a fundamental revision of the existing pattern of reasoning, which in turn must have required adopting a completely new perspective on the problem under consideration. In psychological terms, the judges who considered the case must have had an intuitive feeling that rejecting Mrs Donoghue's claim would be unjust. However, something else was needed for the moral judgment to become a law: an insight that would incorporate such a verdict into the complex legal "puzzle" of principles, rules, and precedents.

---

[61] Cf. ibid., p. 46.

Almost all groundbreaking judicial verdicts can serve as examples of the mechanics of insight in legal reasoning. Let us consider the *Van Gend en Loos* case of 1963, which was a landmark case in the development of European law.[62] The Dutch company Van Gend en Loos imported urea formaldehyde from Germany to the Netherlands. The Dutch customs charged the company a higher tariff due to a change in the classification of the substance. The company paid the increased customs but, at the same time, took legal steps in order to obtain a refund. In court, Van Gend en Loos argued that the Dutch customs regulations were contrary to Article 12 of the Treaty of Rome, according to which "Member States shall refrain from introducing between themselves any new customs duties on imports or exports or any charges having equivalent effect, and from increasing those which they already apply in their trade with each other."

The European Court of Justice (ECJ) was faced with a serious problem when it considered the case. In accordance with the long-accepted traditional doctrine, international treaties were binding for member states only and did not apply to the citizens of the states. On the other hand, if Article 12 of the Treaty of Rome could only be cited by European Economic Community (EEC) member states in cases against other member states, the regulation would, in many cases, turn out to be an empty phrase. In psychological terms, it can be argued that the judges of the ECJ must have experienced two opposing intuitions: one following from their legal education, which suggested that Van Gend en Loos could not directly cite Article 12, and a moral one, which suggested that the Dutch authorities' behavior was unjust.

It would be difficult to ascertain the actual reasoning on the part of the judges of the ECJ in this case; the best that we can do is to attempt to reconstruct it on the basis of the grounds provided along with the verdict. The first point raised in the grounds is that in order to answer the question whether Article 12 of the Treaty is directly effective in national laws, "it is necessary to consider the spirit, the general schema and the wording of [the Treaty]."[63] What is intriguing here is the order of the sources of evidence adduced by the Court, the reverse of the usual hierarchy, according to which the point of departure in interpreting the law is the language, followed by systematic arguments, cited when in doubt, and only then those pertaining to "the spirit." This suggests that the Court decided to adopt a novel, revolutionary perspective. Further passages of the judgment seem to corroborate this hypothesis, stating that the "objective of the EEC Treaty . . . implies that [it] is more than an agreement which merely creates mutual obligations between the contracting parties."[64] The Court's argumentation leads to the conclusion that the "European Economic Community constitutes a new legal order of international law for the benefit of

---

[62] Cf. ECJ February 5, 1963, Case 26/62, *Van Gend en Loos v. Nederlandse Administratie der Belastingen* [1963] ECR 1.

[63] Ibid.

[64] Ibid.

which the states have limited their sovereign rights, albeit within limited fields, and the subjects of which comprise not only Member States but also their nationals," which is why "Article 12 must be interpreted as producing direct effects and creating individual rights which national courts must protect."[65] This argumentation must have been preceded by an adequate insight that enabled the judges to discern the possibility of reconciling the intuitive sense of justice with the requirements following from Western European legal culture. That insight led to a fundamental revision of the understanding of European Community law.

These examples may suggest that insight is only experienced by those who make great discoveries or groundbreaking decisions. Such a view would be far from the truth though. After all, it would be strange to claim that a particular psychological phenomenon only occurred in some people and in very rare situations at that. It should rather be assumed that insights are very common, but only some of them – those concerning particularly important problems or suggesting revolutionary solutions – find their place in history books. In other words, the mental mechanisms employed so effectively by the judges in the *Donoghue* v. *Stevenson* and *Van Gend en Loos* cases must also be used in attempts to solve much less spectacular, mundane problems. A student who is considering a civil law case as part of an examination might suddenly realize that the plaintiff's claim should be based on regulations concerning unjust enrichment instead of those covering breach of contract. There is no reason why such a "flash of understanding" should not be called an insight, even if the decision to cite unjust enrichment would be obvious for an experienced lawyer. An insight can apply to any type of problem: mathematical question, crossword puzzles, writing an essay, understanding clever jokes, or even how to tackle an unruly dog. Such small "Eureka moments" are part of our everyday experience.

What is an insight then? How to define it? Just as with intuition, we could refer to the various, not always compatible, understandings of the concept. Most, though not all, psychologists agree that an insight has, to a greater or lesser extent, three characteristics. First of all, it appears suddenly and is accompanied by a subjective experience of surprise or amazement. Secondly, a typical insight occurs in a dead-end situation (after a period of unsuccessful attempts to solve a problem). Thirdly, solving a problem on the basis of an insight consists in its restructuring, or viewing it from a new perspective.[66] It must be noted, however, that this characterization is sometimes questioned as it excludes certain important psychological phenomena, especially those that do not involve a cognitive impasse. For example, let us suppose that the solution to a problem suddenly appears in your mind although you are not focused on looking for it at the moment; or that you realize how a problem could be solved during the process of analyzing it, even before reaching an impasse; or that you hit upon an idea in a situation that does not involve any definite problem.[67] In

[65]   Ibid.
[66]   Shettleworth, 2012, pp. 217–218.
[67]   Cf. Kounios & Beeman, 2014, p. 73.

fact, such situations are quite frequent, and we would probably have no doubts as to whether they could be considered insights. Moreover, there are compelling arguments to assume that such situations activate the same neural structures as other, more typical instances of insight.[68]

For methodological reasons, neurobiological research on insight – or any other mental mechanisms – cannot focus on rare or unique phenomena. Such research typically involves relatively simple tasks which, however, raise no doubts as to whether they require an insight. A good example is the remote associates test (RAT), which consists in showing the participants a list of three words; the participants' task is to think of a fourth word associated with the other three. When we consider the series: "cottage – Swiss – cake," we will reach the conclusion that all three words are associated with the word "cheese," while a moment of reflection on the words "measure – video – worm" will suffice to decide that they evoke the word "tape." It is clear, then, that solving a RAT must be based on insight since the situation involves a cognitive impasse, while the answer appears suddenly and gives rise to contentment or other positive emotions; at the same time, it can be argued that this type of problem also involves some cognitive restructuring as the insight makes us aware of conceptual relations that were not clear at first glance.[69]

Studies based on brain imaging techniques, especially functional magnetic resonance imaging (fMRI), have demonstrated that insight is associated with a sudden increase in neural activity in the right anterior temporal lobe.[70] Furthermore, direct stimulation of the right frontotemporal cortex combined with inhibition of activity in the left frontotemporal cortex enhances the ability to solve such problems as RATs. Studies on patients with brain injuries also clearly indicate that insight is mostly based on the neural structures of the right prefrontal cortex. This is a particularly interesting set of observations, mainly because the right hemisphere, as opposed to the left one, plays a minor role in the use of language in the normally (in the statistical sense) lateralized brain. At the same time, the right hemisphere is associated with the dominant role in such cognitive domains as creativity, artistic activity (such as music or visual arts), space perception, and facial mimicry.[71] In other words, despite the fact that it leads to a reconceptualization of the problem, insight is a mechanism that largely works beyond linguistic categorization of the world.

Similar remarks can be made with regard to intuition: it has also been shown to draw mainly on the resources of the right hemisphere of the brain, especially the neural path that runs from the orbitofrontal to the inferior temporal cortex and uses the inferior occipitofrontal fasciculus.[72] For decades, studies on intuition and insight

---

[68] Cf. Kounios & Beeman, 2014.
[69] Cf. Mednick, 1962.
[70] Jung-Beeman et al., 2004.
[71] Cf. Kounios & Beeman, 2014.
[72] Cf. McCrea, 2010; Volz & Cramon, 2006.

have represented two separate lines of investigation, with their own methodologies and conceptual frameworks. Recently, however, it has been hypothesized that there must be structural and functional relations between them. It seems that the inter-action mainly takes place in the caudate nucleus and the occipitofrontal cortex.[73] An insight does not give us a new view of a problem ex nihilo; it uses or alters the perceptual-motor schemas that intuitive judgments are based on. The so-called incubation phase, which comes before the conceptual recombination that leads to an insight, probably involves unconscious "testing" of various solutions to a given problem on the basis of existing intuition-related schemas. An insight occurs when any of the schemas, used in an untypical or properly modified way, provides an answer.[74]

If these considerations are true, intuition and insight can be regarded as two fundamental and mutually cooperating unconscious problem-solving mechanisms. Of the two, intuition is the "laborer," an extremely efficient and constantly used tool, providing quick and relatively reliable answers to typical problems. But intuition does not halt in the face of a nonstandard problem; it is also in such cases that it provides us with clues; however, those clues may be mutually contradictory or so weak that there arises a cognitive impasse. Then comes insight, a "special-purpose mechanism," something that allows us to break away from the rigid patterns of well-trained intuitive reactions and to implement a sometimes considerable restructuring of the existing perceptual-motor schemas. Complex legal problems where "trained" intuition proves inadequate, such as the *Donoghue* v. *Stevenson* and *Van Gend en Loos* cases, call for the use of insight.

1.5 THE EMOTIONAL LAWYER

Everyone would probably agree that law is one of the spheres of social life that should be characterized by objectivity and rationality. Philosophers have pointed out for centuries that we cannot construct a fair social order without breaking away from our emotions. This "deaffectization" is to be a recipe for rational and balanced opinions and for right actions. The ability to look at our legal and moral obligations in an objective and emotionless way has even been proclaimed a virtue by major philosophical schools, in particular those following the course set by Immanuel Kant. Of course, there is some simplification here: if we carefully examine the works of the greatest thinkers, it turns out that they do not ignore or underestimate the role of affect in human life. However, many of them view rationality as the opposite of emotionality, even if the opposition is not a strict one. Unfortunately, the more popular or less nuanced approaches portray this opposition as even more clear and definite, thereby turning it into a kind of dogma according to which the reason and

---

[73]   Cf. Zander et al., 2016.
[74]   Cf. ibid., 2016.

emotions are totally incompatible, with rationality being valuable and emotionality leading us astray in our cognitive efforts.

In the meantime, modern psychological research suggests a totally different scenario. Underlying the two cognitive mechanisms of intuition and insight are, to a large extent, the neural structures responsible for emotional reactions. They are not merely "additions" to the sophisticated ability of abstract thinking based on the rules of logic. On the contrary, it can be argued that those "higher" cognitive functions not only developed from the evolutionarily older emotional mechanisms; they quite literally still serve them.[75]

In order to be able to look at the architecture of the human mind from this novel perspective, we must first realize that intuition and insight are not the only manifestations of the role of emotions in human cognition. Solving problems, whether theoretical or practical in nature, is connected with considerable effort (in biological terms, it requires the organism to expend a lot of energy), while the positive effects of this activity are often uncertain and delayed in time. This is an extremely interesting issue: how is it possible that we can overcome exhaustion and boredom in order to renew our efforts to gain cognitive mastery over the world? Evolutionary scientists claim that this is possible by virtue of epistemic emotions.[76] Contradiction or any other inconsistency that arises in our experience – whether it be the observation that the actual motion of Mercury is minimally different from that posited by Newton, the feeling that "it would be wrong" to decide the *Van Gend en Loos* case in the standard way, or the inconsistency between what we see (a dog) and what we hear (miaowing) – tends to arouse our interest or even trigger anxiety and disorientation. It motivates us to undertake some action and to attempt to explain the cause of the cognitive dissonance. The feeling that "something is wrong here" and that something should be done about it is the major driving force in the process that led Albert Einstein to formulate the theory of general relativity; the same force makes us strive to find a more satisfying solution to the *Van Gend en Loos* case or leads us to discover that the "miaowing dog" is our nephew's latest toy. If it were not for epistemic emotions, there would be no – more or less significant – discoveries; getting rid of anxiety and disorientation or satiating our curiosity, and sometimes even a moment of amusement or illumination, are the awards that we receive for making our view of the world more coherent.[77]

It would be wrong to assume that emotions only have a positive effect on cognitive processes, motivating us to search for ever-better solutions to the problems that we encounter. Emotions can also significantly disrupt the process of thinking; and what I mean here is not extreme situations in which strong affective reactions prevent us from "clear thinking." What I am referring to here are the ordinary decision-making processes that occur under optimal cognitive conditions. For example, it is difficult

[75] Cf. Hurley et al., 2011, p. 63ff.
[76] Cf. ibid., p. 66ff.
[77] Cf. Gopnik, 2000.

to work with two alternative, mutually contradictory hypotheses for a longer time; the mind tends to resolve such conflicts rather quickly instead of examining and systematically comparing the consequences that each hypothesis leads to. This is connected with the fact that we emotionally strive for certainty and award ourselves for it. It is hard to admit that our judgments and actions are based on more or less justified speculations rather than on firm foundations; it is easier to believe that we have achieved certainty even when, objectively, we are far from it.[78]

One of the more comprehensive accounts of this phenomenon is the theory of the need for cognitive closure, first proposed by Arie Kruglanski.[79] This theory concerns our desire to obtain the ultimate answer in a given situation – it could be any answer as long as it helps us to avoid uncertainty. Kruglanski argues that individuals with a high need for cognitive closure seek order and structure in their lives, shy away from chaotic situations, desire knowledge that is reliable regardless of the circumstances, and experience sudden need for closure, which is manifested in the categorical nature of their decisions and choices; they experience discomfort in situations without closure and do not desire to confront their knowledge with alternative explanations.[80]

By way of an example, let us suppose a group of subjects who are to decide the penalty for a person convicted of a petty crime are provided with information on both the aggravating and the mitigating circumstances. Half of them, however, first hear about the aggravating factors and then about the mitigating ones, while the other half receive the information in the opposite order. Those of the participants of such a study who have a high need for cognitive closure would probably be quick to form their opinions on the penalty; if they first heard about the aggravating circumstances, the mitigating factors would not affect their decisions. By contrast, those with a lower need for closure would be able to evaluate the evidence in a more balanced manner, taking into consideration all available information.[81] It can also be hypothesized that individuals with a high need for cognitive closure would be more likely to apply a literal interpretation of legal regulations, without attempting to adjust their interpretations of the law to the changing social reality.[82]

In an attempt to provide a theoretical account of such phenomena, Kruglanski and Webster point to the workings of two mechanisms: seizing and freezing. Seizing leads to accepting the first unambiguous explanation of a given situation but without

---

[78]   Cf. Kossowska, 2005, and the literature referenced therein.
[79]   Kruglanski, 1989.
[80]   Webster & Kruglanski, 1994.
[81]   Unfortunately, Webster and Kruglanski did not conduct this experiment, but they did carry out a similar one. They presented the participants with recordings of job interviews. The conversations that the participants heard included information on both positive and negative characteristics of the candidates, with the recordings having been edited in such a way that one group of subjects first heard about the negative characteristics and then about the positive ones, while the other group received the information in the opposite order. Cf. Webster & Kruglanski, 1994, p. 1060.
[82]   This is partly corroborated by studies demonstrating a link between strongly conservative views and a high need for cognitive closure. Cf. Kossowska & Hiel, 2003.

evaluating its quality. Freezing consists in a rapid incorporation of such an explanation into the existing structure of knowledge, which makes it resistant to change; as a result, any data obtained at a later stage, which could suggest an alternative explanation, are simply ignored.[83] It should not take long to conclude, therefore, that a high need for cognitive closure is a trait that makes it more difficult to make the right decisions; moreover, it can result in making systematic errors and strengthening one's belief in the correctness of one's decisions. As already mentioned, systematic errors may stem from too great a confidence in heuristic-based judgments. It must be noted, however, that heuristics lead to errors in non-typical situations (i.e. ones where heuristics are not the right tool, such as those requiring statistical analysis or the application of formal logic). A high need for cognitive closure is conducive to error in a much broader scope: it can also lead to making incorrect judgments in typical situations, while at the same increasing the likelihood of reinforcing such errors.

Legal reasoning, just as any other kind of thinking, is deeply rooted in our emotionality. It is because of our epistemic emotions that we engage in cognitive effort as they whet our curiosity and award us for successful attempts to solve problems. Yet, emotions can also disturb our reasoning, especially when our "need for certitude" makes us accept claims that have not been thoroughly examined. Emotions also underlie two fundamental cognitive mechanisms that work beyond our consciousness: intuition and insight. Acquired with experience, intuition can provide us with quick and usually correct suggestions in typical problems. By contrast, insight is useful when we face special challenges; it is applied when we have to deal with a non-typical problem whose solution requires a restructuring of the existing cognitive-behavioral schemas. We can also speak of legal intuition and legal insight, but only in the sense that they are contingent upon knowledge, resulting from experience, on how to address legal problems.

Finally, we should consider one more issue. There is no doubt that emotion-based mechanisms, especially intuition, have a considerable influence on legal reasoning. The extent of that influence, however, is open to debate. Some seem to claim that we are so dependent on emotions that rational thinking is only an ornament that has little effect on our decisions. This view is endorsed by Jonathan Haidt, with the caveat that he adopts this approach with regard to moral, rather than legal, decision-making. Given the similarities between moral and legal thinking, it can be argued that Haidt's claims are applicable to legal epistemology. In his well-known essay "The emotional dog and its rational tail," Haidt argues against the view that "moral knowledge and moral judgment are reached primarily by a process of reasoning and reflection."[84] Instead, he claims that a moral judgment arises in one's consciousness in an automatic and effortless way, as a product of moral intuition, while moral

---

[83] Webster & Kruglanski, 1994, pp. 1060–1062.
[84] Cf. Haidt, 2001, p. 815.

reasoning processes are associated with effort and usually take place when the decision has already been made, only to support it ex post. Importantly, the aim of such reasoning is to try to offer a justification of a previously accepted, intuitive moral judgment. Of course, Haidt concedes that genuine moral reasoning can lead to the emergence of a moral judgment. Nevertheless, he contends that this is only possible in those rare situations where the original intuition is weak and the circumstances make it possible to engage in long and strenuous deliberations.[85]

If Haidt were to be right, then all of the weighty tomes on the models and forms of reasoning and on the structure of legal discourse would not include any information about the methods of reasoning in law; instead they would only discuss a set of rhetorical devices that could help lawyers to defend their intuitive judgments and to influence other lawyers' – also intuitive – decisions. However, Haidt seems to go too far. It is often argued that quick and automatic moral intuitions are often informed by one's previous reasoning processes, while in situations of real moral or legal dilemmas people usually engage in deep reflection.[86] It has also been pointed out that the fact that the processes that lead to the formation of a moral (or legal) judgment are normally arational does not mean that the moral (or legal) judgment itself ought to be considered arational because it is open to debate.[87] Finally, it is claimed – in contrast to what Haidt suggests – that people are often capable of correcting their previous intuitive judgments on the basis of conscious deliberation.[88]

The following chapters will focus on those means of legal reasoning that allow us to move beyond the realm of unconscious, intuitive decisions – imagination and thinking in language.

---

[85]   Cf. ibid., p. 816ff.
[86]   Cf. Pizarro & Bloom, 2003.
[87]   Cf. *Levy*, 2006.
[88]   Cf. Fine, 2006.

2

Imagination

In this chapter I argue that imagination is the missing piece of the puzzle in the existing theories of legal cognition. At first glance, imagination seems too idiosyncratic and ephemeral to become an important part of any account of legal reasoning or argumentation. The two words used in the previous sentence are worth emphasizing: "reasoning" and "argumentation." Neither of them can easily be associated with picturing something in one's mind. Reasoning, according to the *Oxford English Dictionary*, is "the action of thinking about something in a logical, sensible way";[1] argumentation, in turn, is "the action or process of reasoning systematically in support of an idea, action, or theory."[2] Imagination, on the other hand, is not governed by logic; nor can it be described as a systematic process. This illustrates the extent of the difficulties we are confronted with when trying to return imagination to its rightful place. Legal thinking is usually referred to as the process of reasoning or argumentation,[3] and hence there seems to be no role for imagination to play in the legal context. Yet, my claim is precisely the opposite. Imagination is not only useful for lawyers; it is an indispensable tool they use on regular basis. It is simply not possible to solve legal problems without imagination.

Legal philosophers have never paid much attention to imagination. In fact, there are just a few major contributions to this topic, usually taking the perspective of the "law and literature" research paradigm,[4] which sees legal text as a literary genre and investigates it with the methods used in literary criticism. The one exception I know of is the theory of Leon Petrażycki, who at the beginning of the twentieth century developed a comprehensive view of legal thinking, where imagined objects or events (or, as Petrażycki puts it, "mental representations") have an important role to play. Moreover, he described the link between imagination and emotional and intuitive mental processes. However, his theory was embedded in a philosophical framework, which seems outdated if not ancient, at least from today's perspective. The question,

[1] Stevenson & Soanes, 2006.
[2] Ibid., 2006.
[3] Cf. Stelmach & Brożek, 2006.
[4] Cf. White, 1985.

therefore, is how to speak about imagination against the background of the contemporary cognitive sciences.

The key maneuver is to realize that psychologists working in the embodied cognition paradigm have identified a mental mechanism that can easily be equated with imagination. I am speaking about the mechanism enabling mental simulations. Mental simulations – picturing objects or "playing out" events in one's mind – have two intriguing features. On the one hand, they are multimodal: they have visual, auditory, olfactory, kinesthetic, emotional, and other aspects. Because of that, they may evoke intuitions or even serve to (re)educate them. On the other hand, it has been demonstrated that mental simulations are used in processing language: to understand an expression referring to a concrete object or an event, one unconsciously simulates the relevant thing or situation.[5] Of course, not everything in this cognitive structure is entirely clear. In particular, the processing of abstract language, which is so important in law, is quite puzzling. It may involve some mental simulations, but not in such a straightforward way as in the case of concrete expressions. Nevertheless, there is strong evidence that mental simulations provide a connection between unconscious intuition and thinking in language.

This observation has far-reaching consequences for our understanding of the legal mind. A very peculiar task of the lawyer is to apply an abstract legal rule to a concrete set of circumstances. In order to do so, one needs to work one's way back and forth from the general to the particular, taking advantage of both complex theoretical constructions and the intuitive knowledge embodied during individual experience. The possibility of such a feedback loop is conditioned by the use of the imagination, or so I argue in this chapter.

2.1 PETRAŻYCKI

Leon Petrażycki was undoubtedly one of the most interesting legal theoreticians of the turn of the twentieth century. Polish by birth and educated at German universities, he wrote his major treatises in Russian during the period of his professorship at Saint Petersburg University. However, it is not Petrażycki's life – quite typical of an educated citizen of Central Europe in those times – but rather his theories that should be the focus of our considerations.

Petrażycki was one of the first theoreticians who argued for the crucial role of the emotions in legal cognition, thirty years before Joseph Hutcheson and several decades before modern psychologists. This fact may not be surprising in itself – after all a bit of unbiased introspection should enable everyone to arrive at the conclusion that legal decisions must be conditioned by complex emotional reactions. What deserves admiration is the breadth of Petrażycki's theories and, even more so, the boldness and outstanding perspicacity of his claims.

---

[5] Cf. Barsalou, 2008; Bergen, 2016.

Petrażycki sought to redefine the foundations of the psychology known to him, which was an extraordinary enterprise, especially in view of the fact that he did it in order to understand the nature of law.[6] The revolution in psychology that he set out to instigate by placing emotions (which he called "impulsions") at the center of human psychological life was, then, only a means to an end. His most scathing criticism was directed at the division of mental phenomena into three categories, which had prevailed in philosophy at least since Kant: sensations (or cognitive impressions), feelings, and will. According to Petrażycki, this classification was the principal source of various theoretical misunderstandings that precluded an ade-quate understanding of motivational processes. He contended that sensations and feelings are often passive in character, whereas will tends to be active; by contrast, "mental life is two-sided, passive-active, sensitive-impulsive . . ., and as such cannot be accounted for in terms of solely passive or solely active 'basic elements'."[7] That is why Petrażycki argued for four, rather than three, "basic forms of inner experience": sensations, feelings, emotions (impulsions), and processes of the will.[8] Let us have a closer look at them now.

We should begin with the cognitive aspect of mental life, the simplest manifesta-tion of which are sensations. Petrażycki defines sensations as "the simplest forms of cognitive experience triggered by external and internal stimuli, i.e. physical pro-cesses which come from outside the organism and act on the external, peripheral nerve endings (e.g. sound waves, light waves, physical pressure) or which occur inside the organism (e.g. digestion, muscle contractions, secretion)."[9] Whole com-plexes of sensations that "produce images of various objects and phenomena, such as a tree, a cloud or a melody"[10] are called perceptions. Sensations and perceptions give rise to the organism's disposition to reproduce those acts, which constitutes the basis for the emergence of imaginations (i.e. experiences that are not the result of particular external or internal stimuli).

In Petrażycki's theory, another major manifestation of mental life are feelings, which are "experiences of pleasure, satisfaction or delight ('positive feelings') and experiences of sadness, displeasure or suffering."[11] Furthermore, sensations and feelings must be distinguished from will, which is "peculiar experiences that may be clearly discerned and differentiated only through careful self-examination and internal comparison; strictly active experiences," that "appear to us as active ten-dencies of one's self, aimed at instigating or producing something in the near or remote future."[12] It is not without a reason that Petrażycki so forcefully emphasizes the distinctiveness and simplicity of volitional experiences: sensations, perceptions,

[6]   Cf. Brożek, 2014b.
[7]   Petrażycki, 2002, pp. 15–16.
[8]   Ibid., p. 14.
[9]   Petrażycki, 1959, p. 215.
[10]   Ibid., p. 216.
[11]   Ibid., p. 232.
[12]   Ibid., p. 256.

imaginations, and feelings tend to come before will, which is why they can be regarded as motivations of the will. However, this close relationship between will and the other mental phenomena may easily lead to reducing will to other factors, which Petrażycki believed would be a grave mistake.

The most important forms of mental experience, according to Petrażycki, are emotions (impulsions), which have a dual, "sensitive-impulsive" character. For example, hunger cannot be reduced to a sensation only, since it also involves a certain urge (appetite). Petrażycki repeatedly points out that emotions are frequently mistaken for other phenomena. There are situations where some emotions (such as hunger, thirst, or disgust) are regarded as kinds of sensations; similarly, emotions are sometimes mistaken for a combination of imagination and feeling. Petrażycki argues, in a way that anticipates contemporary studies on epistemic emotions, that thinking has an affective dimension. He contends that "impulsive sensations, or emotions, constitute a significant element of judgements. Affirmative judgements, . . . such as 'The Earth is a sphere,' 'The Earth revolves around the Sun,' constitute appulsive emotional acts, while negative judgements, such as 'The Earth is not a sphere,' are repulsive emotional acts."[13] Emotions are also confused with feelings: the latter term is often used in reference to hunger, thirst, disgust, love, hate, anger, fury, fear, and so on. It should be remembered that, according to Petrażycki, what can be classified as feelings is only experiences of pleasure, contentment, delight, sadness, discontent, and suffering. The occurrence of certain emotions is often taken to be a manifestation of will, particularly in relation to various instincts (self-preservation, hunting, entertainment). Petrażycki argues that what drives human psychological life in all these cases is particular emotions, rather than – as most psychologists of his time claimed – sensations, feelings or will. Petrażycki summarizes the central role of emotions as follows:

> Emotions govern the physical life, movements and innumerable other physiological processes as well as the psychological life of creatures endowed with consciousness. They causally determine the direction and strength of one's attention and the associative chain of thoughts and thinking; they affect the strength, intensity and character of perceptions and traces left by cognitive processes (memory); they are causally related to the feelings of contentment and discontent; they also direct one's will, removing any of the opposing tendencies and effecting such resolutions of will that comply with their desires, in cases where such resolutions do arise (usually when a reaction is postponed in time) and trigger actions based on will rather than purely impulsive or emotional actions.[14]

It is worth examining Petrażycki's approach to the relationship between emotions and will more closely. Emotions "direct one's will, removing any of the opposing tendencies and effecting such resolutions of will that comply with their desires."

---

[13]   Ibid., p. 442.
[14]   Ibid., p. 475.

This statement must be properly understood. First of all, Petrażycki notes that not all of our actions occur with the active participation of will:[15] more often, our actions are immediately influenced by our emotions. "Will tends to play the role of an additional link between stimulus and action, but it only arises under certain conditions, mostly in cases where it is necessary to defer the action or when the action is contingent on some condition."[16] However, even where volitional processes do take place, the role of emotions remains crucial, if not decisive. Petrażycki explicitly reflects on whether free and undetermined will is possible at all. At the same time, he rejects the arguments put forward by both supporters and opponents of the free will hypothesis since he regards them as nonscientific. He acknowledges that "the universal nature of a causal relationship is likely,"[17] but it is open to dispute whether it extends onto volitional processes.

Petrażycki's perceptiveness is astounding, as is the boldness of his attempt to redefine the psychology of his time. This combination of perceptiveness and courage gave rise to a remarkable theory, which was strikingly different from the other theories of emotions from that period (e.g. those developed by Wilhelm Wundt and William James).[18] According to Petrażycki's most revolutionary hypothesis, emotions are at the center of human psychological life, influencing both our cognitive processes and that which we call the exercise of will. Some passages from Petrażycki's writings – such as those concerning the role of emotions in cognition (or epistemic emotions,[19] to use the contemporary term), the existence of free will or the critique of "affective reductionism," which reduced emotional experiences to sensations of pleasure and sorrow – read as if they were written fairly recently, possibly in the twenty-first century. Of course, an attentive (and slightly cynical) reader will immediately identify quite a number of mistakes and naiveties in his texts, including an obsolete methodology that requires scientific theories to be based on classical definitions (*per genus et differentiam*) and a rather outdated conception of intuition. Moreover, Petrażycki seems to be unaware of the fact that human cognition is mostly based on processes beyond one's conscious control.[20] And yet these criticisms, though undoubtedly adequate, turn out to be of little significance once we realize that Petrażycki developed his theories decades before the methodological revolution in science and philosophy that rejected the Aristotelean heritage, along with the classical theory of definition, and years before the concept of unconsciousness had become a commonplace in psychological theory. What remains, then, is Petrażycki's extraordinary perceptiveness, not only with regard to the role of emotions in the human psyche but also many other problems.

[15] Cf. ibid., pp. 273–274.
[16] Ibid., p. 286.
[17] Ibid., p. 284.
[18] Cf. Wundt, 1918; James, 1884.
[19] Cf. Gopnik, 2000.
[20] For a more detailed discussion of these methodological flaws in Petrażycki's writings, see Brożek, 2014b.

One of Petrażycki's observations is particularly intriguing in this context. Not only does he argue for the crucial role of emotions in decision-making, but he also shows how they are related to other psychological processes. Especially interesting are Petrażycki's views on the relationship between imaginations and emotions. Let us recall that Petrażycki uses the notion of imagination with reference to certain "mental images" that arise from the dispositions produced by the sensations and perceptions we experience. An imagination, along with the emotion it has triggered, constitutes a motivation for action. For instance, if I imagined that I was taking part in a fraud, "I would experience a mental state similar to the one I experience when I am being encouraged to eat a piece of rotten meat or to hold a spider or a snake in my hand; normally, I would have repulsive emotions, or revolting impulsions."[21]

Petrażycki presents the following line of argumentation: people have the ability to imagine certain things or situations. Those imaginations, those special "mental images," are in turn capable of triggering various emotions. Finally, those emotions are the springboard for human actions: we take a given action when an appulsive emotion makes us do so and we refrain from it due to a repulsive emotion. Importantly, Petrażycki strongly emphasizes that this mechanism applies to all aspects of human behavior, not only to morality or law (although he also notes that the emotions underlying legal behavior have certain characteristics: they are of an imperative-attributive character). He writes: "Imagine that, among a company of people you know, you say aloud certain words which are considered 'indecent,' or wipe your nose on the tablecloth or on the dress of a woman sitting next to you, or turn up without certain appropriate garments, for example without a necktie."[22] Such a violation of the "norms of decency" inevitably evokes repulsive emotions, even if those situations are only imagined. Petrażycki continues: "Imaginations of more serious 'sins' than turning up without a tie at a formal occasion, e.g. imaginations of murder, forgery, theft, etc., are associated in the human mind with repulsive emotions which become (irrespective of any theological, hedonistic, utilitarian or other considerations) more or less serious, and sometimes even totally insurmountable, psychological barriers to committing such acts."[23]

It is worth highlighting the last part of the quotation, where Petrażycki seems to be suggesting that human emotional reactions, which constitute a response to imagining certain states of affairs, are completely independent of abstract, theoretical considerations, such as the acceptance of a given ethical doctrine (hedonism, utilitarianism), the dictates of a particular religion or, arguably, knowledge of the law. On this approach, imagining one's involvement in a crime, such as robbery or murder, evokes the relevant emotions even if one does not know the adequate provisions of the Penal Code. Does Petrażycki intend to suggest that moral systems, religious doctrines, and legal regulations do not influence our behavior? Suppose

---

[21]   Cf. Petrażycki, 2002, p. 21.
[22]   Ibid., pp. 24–25.
[23]   Ibid., pp. 25–26.

I imagine that, while filling in my annual income tax declaration, I am deducting from tax certain expenses unaware of the fact that the relevant tax reduction is no longer allowed; in such a situation I would be highly unlikely to feel a "repulsive emotion." Petrażycki seems to be saying something else: under normal circumstances, in which a person is a rightful member of a given community (i.e. one properly "trained" in the behavior typical of that community), their motivations and the actions connected with them do not need to be grounded in abstract ethical theories or complex legal regulations. Put simply, the provision of the Penal Code that forbids stealing does not have to belong to the motivational chain of a person who obeys that regulation. Petrażycki is quick to add that the moral principles formulated by philosophers and legal rules introduced by the legislator do have an influence on people's behavior, but only an indirect one. They provide the foundation for constructing the relevant imaginations: "imaginations of the provisions of an act of law, of the biblical commandments or of orders from one's superior will be termed imaginations of 'normative facts.' The ethical views and convictions that involve such imaginations in their associative chains will be referred to as positive ethical views, convictions, etc., while their contents will be said to constitute positive norms."[24]

For us, the most important view that emerges from Petrażycki's theory concerns the relationship between the legal text, imaginations, and emotional reactions: legal regulations provide the basis for constructing imaginations, which in turn evoke emotions that make us carry out particular actions. This view may be expressed in a more modern language: we understand a legal text through mental simulations that trigger adequate intuitions and, as a result, lead to particular actions. Whereas intuitive thinking was the focus of the previous chapter, the ability to simulate things and events in one's mind will be discussed in Section 2.2.

2.2 MENTAL SIMULATIONS

Human beings, and most probably other animals too,[25] have the ability to imagine objects and situations and to "play" them in their minds. There is a convincing evolutionary argument for the development of this ability. Mental simulations enable us to prepare for future events, which considerably decreases the cost of acting in the world. In short, it is better to die in one's own imagination than in reality. Instead of risking your life, you can imagine several different methods of hunting a dangerous animal, thereby eliminating at least some of the mistakes you would commit in the real world. Instead of risking your good name, you can mentally "play" several versions of a speech that you are supposed to deliver before

[24] Ibid., p. 33.
[25] Cf. Byrne, 1988.

an important and demanding audience, thereby eliminating at least some of the potential causes of public humiliation.[26]

Importantly, recent studies based on the use of brain imaging techniques strongly suggest that mental simulations activate the same neural circuits that are activated when we perceive an object or carry out an activity.[27] For example, when I am imagining a hammer, the same neural circuits become activated as the ones responsible for seeing a hammer; a mental simulation of hammering a nail into a wall activates the same neural circuits as the ones that get activated when a person is actually performing that activity.[28] (Such activation may, naturally, be weaker during simulation than in actual observation or action.) Certain behavioral experiments also seem to corroborate these claims. Most of them are associated with the so-called Perky effect: imagining something may disrupt the perception of real objects. For example, when a person is imagining an object at the bottom of a blank screen, it is only after a delay that they will perceive a new picture presented in the same place; however, there will be no delay if the picture is placed at the top of the screen.[29]

An important characteristic of mental simulations is that they are multimodal in character: they can simultaneously include visual, auditory, motor, haptic, olfactory, emotional, and motivational elements.[30] When you are imagining a triangle, neuronal activation will probably occur only in those brain areas that are responsible for visual perception. By comparison, when you are mentally simulating a dog, the simulation will involve more than a static image of a Labrador or a King Charles Spaniel. Most probably, you will "see" a dog in action (wagging its tail, barking, and asking for a snack), and the whole visualization will be accompanied by positive or negative emotions.

Mental simulations have yet another important property: they can be either conscious (and then they can be termed imaginations) or unconscious. Moreover, it seems that phylogenetically Homo sapiens developed the ability for the unconscious simulation of objects and events first; what is more, in the normal human mind, unconscious simulations are much more frequent than conscious ones.[31] Based on rich experimental evidence and insightful hypotheses, cognitive scientists suggest that unconscious simulation is involved in various situations that human beings must face in their everyday lives, from simple motor activities, through social interaction, to language use and comprehension.[32]

It is also worth remembering that there are considerable individual differences in the ability to mentally simulate objects and events: even if two persons try to simulate the same thing (whether a triangle or a dog), their respective simulations may be

---

[26] In this context, Karl Popper wrote about hypotheses that "die in our stead." Cf. Popper, 1972, p. 244.
[27] See Pulvermüller et al., 2014; Dove, 2015.
[28] See Zwaan & Kaschak, 2008.
[29] See Bergen, 2012.
[30] Landriscina, 2009.
[31] Cf. ibid.
[32] Cf. Barsalou, 1999.

quite different. This issue has been most thoroughly investigated with respect to visual imagery. The first studies in this area were conducted by Francis Galton in the nineteenth century. Interested in the functioning of the "mind's eye," he asked his fellow researchers to imagine the table at which they had eaten their breakfast and to answer several questions, such as: "Is the image of the table dim or bright?," "Do the colours of the plates, cups, mustard, bread, etc. look natural?" He was astonished with the findings:

> I found that the great majority of the men of science to whom I first applied, protested that mental imagery was unknown to them, and they looked on me as fanciful and fantastic in supposing that the words "mental imagery" really expressed what I believed everybody supposed them to mean. They had no more notion of its true nature than a colour-blind man who has not discerned his defect has of the nature of colour. They had a mental deficiency of which they were unaware, and naturally enough supposed that those who were normally endowed, were romancing.[33]

Galton's later, more systematic studies conducted on a group of one hundred subjects, around half of whom were scientists, showed differences in people's descriptions of what "they see with their mind's eye." Some of them report seeing an image "[q]uite comparable to the real object," while others concluded that their "powers are zero ... I recollect the breakfast table, but do not see it."[34]

How can this be explained? Why can some of us visualize detailed images, while others have "zero powers" in this respect? Do some of us have a normally functioning brain, while others suffer from a serious defect? Let us address these questions now. For decades, psychologists have used the concept of cognitive style, understood as the way in which an individual acquires, structures, and processes information. Cognitive styles are usually characterized in terms of a quite sophisticated conceptual schema that distinguishes between different types of cognition: global vs. fragmentary, reflexive vs. impulsive, and abstract vs. concrete. It is also traditionally classified as visual and verbal: while performing a given cognitive act, "visualizers" tend to rely on visual imagination, while "verbalizers" mainly employ verbal analytical strategies. Obviously, these taxonomies can only be understood as cognitive tendencies rather than clear-cut divisions. It would be difficult to find an individual who uses this or that cognitive style only, though it cannot be denied that some of us may have a strong predilection to rely on visualizations, while others on verbalizations.

In recent years, however, psychologists have concluded that "thinking in images" is too broad a category, encompassing two fundamentally different understandings of the world. According to a theory put forward by Maria Kozhevnikov,[35] there are

---

[33] Galton, 1880, p. 301.

[34] Ibid., p. 310.

[35] Kozhevnikov et al., 2005.

object visualizers and spatial visualizers. Individuals with a tendency for object-based thinking find it easy to visualize a static image of a concrete object. They can "see" its color, shape, and texture in much detail. By contrast, individuals with spatial visualization abilities, who think in terms of patterns, devote greater attention to the spatial organization of objects; they can also mentally manipulate those structures, at the same time ignoring properties of the objects themselves. Therefore, instead of distinguishing between "visualizers" and "verbalizers," it makes more sense to talk of three cognitive styles: object-based thinking, spatial thinking, and verbal thinking. Interestingly, studies have shown that individuals with a preference for object-based thinking are not good at tasks requiring spatial imagination, and the other way around: spatial thinkers get worse results in tests in which they have to imagine a particular object in detail. As for "verbalizers," they achieved average results in both of these tasks.[36]

It is interesting to note that the distinction between the object and the spatial types of thinking may result from the structure of the human brain itself, where two distinct neural pathways are responsible for the processing of visual information: ventral and dorsal. The first is responsible for processing information pertaining to such visual properties of objects as size, shape, and color, while the latter processes the locations of objects.[37] The distinction between the two different styles of visual thinking throws important light on the already mentioned studies conducted by Galton. It can be argued that those of his subjects whose visualization included an image of a table that was "[q]uite comparable to the real object" had a tendency for object thinking, while those who could not form an image of a table in their minds must have had a better spatial thinking ability. This may be the reason why Galton's experiment caused so much confusion among the scientists he questioned as studies show that scientists tend to think in terms of relations rather than objects.[38]

Let us repeat once again: there are considerable individual differences in mental simulations of objects and events. However, such differences are a matter of degree: if a person X is an object visualizer, they find it easy to imagine what a given thing looks like in detail, but they are much worse at imagining spatial relations between things. But this does not mean they are completely unable to simulate configurations of objects or their transformations. A "verbalizer," "object visualizer," and "spatial visualizer" are just the names of certain cognitive tendencies, rather than labels attached to special, distinct abilities. It must also be borne in mind that the studies mentioned were concerned with simulations performed consciously. It may well be that the differences among the three cognitive styles are even smaller at the unconscious level.

---

[36]   Cf. Kozhevnikov, 2007.
[37]   Kozhevnikov et al., 2005, p. 711.
[38]   Ibid., pp. 720–721.

Perhaps the most interesting characteristic of mental simulations is the fact that, as demonstrated in numerous experiments, they play a significant role in language processing.[39] When we hear or produce the word "hammer," our brains activate the same areas as the ones that are responsible for seeing or using a hammer and for the ability to imagine these things. This has been demonstrated in studies based on brain imaging techniques and in behavioral tasks. Let us consider the following example. One experiment involved the use of a screen and three buttons: a grey one, a black one, and a white one. Pressing and holding the grey button showed a sentence on the screen. If the sentence made sense, the subject was supposed to release the grey button and press the black one, which was located closer to the subject; if the sentence did not make any sense, the subject was to press the white button, which was located at a greater distance from the subject. It turned out that if a meaningful sentence – whether declarative or imperative – described an action involving movement toward the body, the subjects reacted faster than in the case of sentences describing motion in the opposite direction.[40] This means that understanding the meaning of the sentences must have relied on performing an adequate simulation and if the simulation was at odds with the motion that the subject was about to make (e.g. the sentence was about a movement away from the body and it made sense, so the button closer to the body had to be pressed), the reaction was slower. The same experimental paradigm has been employed in tens of other experiments,[41] and all of them – including studies based on brain imaging or transcranial magnetic stimulation, as well as observations of individuals with injuries to certain areas of the brain – clearly show that

> [p]eople perform perceptual and motor simulation while they're processing language. They do so using the same parts of the brain they use to perceive the world and execute actions. Moreover, when specific aspects of embodied simulation are hindered, people have more trouble processing language about those specific aspects of perception or action. And finally, when brain regions dedicated to action or perception are damaged or temporarily taken offline, people have more trouble processing language about the specific perceptual or motor events it encodes. Taken together, all this evidence makes a pretty compelling case that embodied simulation plays a functional role in language understanding.[42]

What is more, it must be emphasized that mental simulations connected with language comprehension do not need to take place on the conscious level. On the contrary: behavioral studies such as the experiment just described show that mental simulations of the meanings of written sentences tend to be performed unconsciously.

---

[39] Cf. Barsalou, 1999; Bergen, 2012.
[40] Bergen, 2012, pp. 78–79.
[41] Cf. Glenberg & Kaschak, 2002.
[42] Bergen, 2012, p. 238.

However, a simulation-based approach to language comprehension faces a serious challenge, namely abstract language processing. When we read the sentence "Peter smashed Adam's iPhone," it is not difficult to imagine the situation described. It is far from clear, though, what kind of mental simulation could be performed on reading a sentence such as "Peter destroyed movable property belonging to Adam." A review of studies conducted in the last few years provides limited clues about the role of simulations in processing abstract linguistic expressions such as "movable property."[43] A number of studies have been devoted to metaphor; the conclusions of those studies are similar to the findings of research on concrete language. For instance, when subjects are asked to read the sentence "The rates climbed" and to decide if it makes sense, they tend to be faster in pressing the correct button if it is placed higher, and slower if the correct button is located lower. And even more abstract sentences, such as "You radioed the message to the policeman," interfere with motor functions, which suggests that some mental simulations involving the motor areas of the brain play a certain role in understanding such sentences. It is also argued that simulations connected with abstract language comprehension manifest significant differences from person to person. Upon reading a sentence informing that Peter destroyed a movable item belonging to Adam, a person A may imagine one object, while a person B may imagine a different thing or even some indistinct shape that is difficult to categorize. Finally, it seems highly probable that the mental simulations that accompany abstract language processing are less detailed than the simulations used in processing concrete utterances.[44]

This brief overview of issues connected with the role of mental simulation in abstract language comprehension shows that the problem is a far from trivial puzzle. On the one hand, the theory of mental simulation seems to offer a compelling account of concrete language processing; on the other hand, when we consider more abstract linguistic expressions, we are left with tentative hypotheses only. The problem of the nature and processing of abstract concepts is simply one of the greatest challenges for contemporary linguistics and cognitive philosophy.

Perhaps the most famous attempt to deal with this problem was made by George Lakoff, Mark Johnson, and their colleagues. They argue that concrete concepts constitute the basis for the formation of abstract concepts and that metaphor plays a key role in the process.[45] We say that the enemy has been caught, that someone caught the atmosphere of a moment in a photograph, or that we could not catch what someone was saying. What we have to deal with here is a more and more abstract use of language. Catching the enemy is still a physical action; it is a bit more complex than catching an object in one's hands, but very similar to it. It is an action in the world that requires the use of physical force in order to get something one has not had before. Catching the atmosphere of a given moment in a photograph is also

---

[43]   Cf. ibid., p. 209ff.
[44]   Cf. ibid., p. 210ff.
[45]   Cf. Lakoff & Johnson, 1999.

an action performed in the external world, but the thing one can get thanks to the photograph is not a physical object anymore. Finally, catching what someone says is a process that takes place in one's mind, and it resembles catching an object only in the sense that it results in a change of state: you come to understand something that you did not understand before.

Lakoff, Johnson, and their followers argue that all of these cases involve the same mechanism – metaphor – which consists in mapping the conceptual structure of one, usually more concrete, domain onto a more abstract domain. Expressions such as "catch/grasp an idea" are metaphorical because they use the conceptual structure of a physical action (catching an object) to describe an abstract event (understanding an idea). It is worth noting that the word "idea" is itself metaphorical in origin. The Greek verb *idein*, which is the etymological source of "idea," originally meant "to see." Thus, "idea," as a word denoting an object of thought, comes from the metaphor of thinking as seeing in one's mind.[46] The crucial point about conceptual metaphor is that what is mapped from the source (i.e. more concrete) domain onto the target (i.e. more abstract) domain are not single and separate concepts, but whole structures of interrelated concepts. That is why we can say that an idea (seen in one's mind's eye) is "clear," "bright," or "foggy"; and that ideas can be combined into a clear "vision" or a consistent "picture." We can say that we have grasped someone's idea and that we "see" what someone means; that we hold on to a particular set of ideas or that we have just abandoned them.

Conceptual metaphor theory undoubtedly constitutes an important contribution to the debate on the nature of abstract concepts.[47] Surely, it cannot be a coincidence that we talk about abstract phenomena with the use of conceptual inference patterns typical of discourse on concrete things. There is no doubt that metaphor gives us access to the abstract world. However, the question is whether it is the only way to understand abstract things, as Lakoff and Johnson's advocates seem to suggest. After all, with some abstract domains it would be difficult to assert that metaphor is the only key to their understanding. Consider, for example, the following passage from an EU directive:

> This obligation should not apply to branches of companies that have been struck off the register but which have a legal successor, such as in the case of any change in the legal form of the company, a merger or division, or a cross-border transfer of its registered office.[48]

Obviously, this sentence includes expressions suggesting metaphor, such as "branches of companies," being "struck off the register," or "legal successor." However, it cannot be argued that the whole sentence is based on conceptual

[46] Cf. Taylor, 1911.
[47] Cf. Borghi & Binkofsky, 2014; Jamrozik et al., 2016.
[48] Directive 2012/17/EU of the European Parliament and of the Council of June 13, 2012, L 156/1, Article 15.

metaphor. Expressions from the legal jargon, such as "branch," "division," "merger," or even "legal successor," acquire their full meanings only in the context of a vast network of abstract concepts. We can understand the expression "legal successor" not only because we know the source domain very well and we map the inferential structure of the concept "succeed somebody/something" onto the target domain (law), but primarily because we know what it means to "take over someone's rights and liabilities." Incidentally, "taking over" is metaphorical too, but the metaphor does not account for the whole meaning of the expression.[49] Similar situations abound with other abstract domains, especially in mathematics, where some aspects of meaning can be explained with recourse to metaphor; however, we will not understand mathematics unless we realize that certain mathematical concepts acquire their full meanings only within a larger conceptual structure.[50]

In cognitive science, this concrete-abstract nature of understanding is best accounted for by dual-coding theory, whose first version was developed by Allan Paivio.[51] On this approach, the human mind processes concepts in two ways: by analogue coding (with the use of so-called imagens, or units of imagery) and by symbolic coding (with so-called logogens, or verbal units). For example, the word "dog" is associated with a certain imagen (or set of imagens) that enables us to imagine a dog when we utter, hear, or read the word; however, this word is also represented in the mind by a particular logogen, which is associated with the dog imagen, on the one hand, and which interacts with various other logogens, on the other. The more abstract a given linguistic expression, the weaker and less determinate the associations among the logogens and imagens. The expressions "justice," "Hilbert space," and "statio fisci" are in various ways associated with other concepts on the level of linguistic coding, but they are unlikely to be associated with the same imagens in different people. One person may imagine justice as Themis with a pair of scales, another as a particular situation in which someone acted in a just way, and yet another person may not have any conscious imagery associated with this word.

The dual-coding theory has, in recent years, evolved in the studies of researchers who look at its fundamental concepts through the prism of the embodied simulation theory. The idea is fairly simple: the two types of mental representation, imagens and logogens, are implemented by mental simulations. Simulation of the first type has already been roughly discussed. The imagen of a "dog" is a mental image (or set of images) using more or less the same neural structures that are activated when a person is looking at a real dog. Logogens are also a type of simulation: we experience them consciously when we "talk to ourselves" in our minds. There is a considerable difference between these two types of representation: whereas imagens are embodied and multimodal, logogens are disembodied and amodal. When our mind is using the imagen of a dog, it simulates our bodies' interactions with dogs

---

[49]   Cf. Dove, 2011; Dove, 2015.
[50]   Cf. Lakoff & Núñez, 2000; Brożek & Hohol, 2014.
[51]   Cf. Paivio, 2013.

in various modalities: visual, auditory, haptic, emotional, etc.; by contrast, when we use the dog logogen, the simulation is "one-dimensional," as it does not include multiple modalities and has little to do with looking at a dog or playing with it.[52]

What is of crucial importance in this sort of "dual" coding is the fact that both types of representation interact with each other. The more concrete the logogens we use, the closer their relationships with the corresponding imagens; in other words, understanding concrete expressions is primarily based on embodied, multimodal simulations. By contrast, the more abstract the expressions, the weaker their associations with imagens and the greater the role of the relationships among the logogens. The meanings of linguistic expressions are determined by both mental simulations of events or things and the relationships among the logogens, but not to the same degree. Concrete language is more grounded in the multimodal mental representations that arise from our bodies' interaction with the environment, while abstract language mainly relies on the inference networks of linguistic symbols.[53]

This discussion leads to the conclusion that mental simulation serves two purposes. On the one hand, it is a relatively "inexpensive" solution to numerous problems: we imagine various situations in order to be better prepared for dealing with them in real life. On the other hand, mental simulation has a very important function in understanding linguistic messages: amodal linguistic symbols, unrelated to any concrete images, could only be useful in meaningless play with linguistic form. Let us now turn to how these two functions of imagination – heuristic and hermeneutic – are employed in legal thinking.

2.3 THE HEURISTIC FUNCTION

The heuristic function of mental simulations aims to produce an intuition or achieve an insight. As noted in Section 2.2, our imagery has a multimodal character: it can include visual, auditory, motor, haptic, olfactory, and emotional aspects. In a mental simulation of a particular situation – such as that of a person's behavior – intuition, shaped by years of experience, helps us evaluate that behavior. When I imagine a sane person mugging and knocking on the ground an elderly woman, my intuition makes me evaluate that act in a clearly negative way. However, when I mentally simulate the behavior of a poor mother who is stealing a loaf of bread so that her children have something to eat, my intuition will probably suggest a different judgment, which will no longer be that clear.

Intuitive judgments of this type are, naturally, moral in character: it is from a moral point of view that mugging an elderly woman deserves to be condemned, while stealing a loaf of bread in order to feed hungry children leads to a much less strict judgment. The same mechanism works in legal cognition. When a judge

---

[52] Cf. Barsalou, 2010.
[53] Cf. Dove, 2011; Dove, 2015.

reconstructs the facts on the basis of the evidence, they may, and usually do, perform (also unconsciously) a mental simulation of the situation under investigation. That simulation evokes certain intuitions, molded by a long education and experience in deciding legal cases. In this way, the judge is able to adequately classify the defendant's behavior and conclude that it fulfills – or does not fulfill – the criteria set forth in a penal act or a precedent. Naturally, it may happen that the situation under investigation gives rise to conflicting intuitions; then we have to deal with what some legal philosophers call a "hard case."[54]

For a moment, let us return to an example we discussed in the previous chapter, namely the *Van Gend en Loos* case. In this instance, the Dutch authorities, due to a change in the classification of a certain substance, levied a higher duty for importing the substance from Germany. Van Gend en Loos, a company that was charged with the higher customs duty, appealed from that decision, arguing that the imposition of a higher duty was contrary to Article 12 of the Treaty of Rome. The case had finally been handed over to the ECJ. What did the Court's process of reasoning look like in that case? Was the Court able to use mental simulation? Or, perhaps, did it have to do so? Naturally, we can only speculate on that. It is very likely, however, that the judges imagined – if only because they had read the dossier – the situation in which Van Gend and the Dutch government found themselves. In mentally simulating the company's situation, it would have been difficult for the judges to avoid a sense of astonishment and injustice. Unexpectedly, the company is charged with an additional fee that not only puts the company's financial stability at risk but also seems to be at variance with the widely proclaimed principles of a common European market: one constantly hears about the facilitation of trade among the EEC member states, while the Dutch government suddenly decides to increase the customs duty. Imagining the situation in which Van Gend en Loos had found itself must trigger an intuitive reaction (probably more moral than legal in nature) that makes the judges accept the company's complaint. On the other hand, when the judges imagined the reasoning of the Dutch government officials, they found themselves in the situation of someone who has always considered international legal norms binding only for states and not for the citizens. In its relations with the citizens, the Dutch government is only bound by domestic regulations. If the complaint had been filed by the government of Germany or some other member of the EEC, the situation would have been different; but a Dutch company is bound by the Dutch customs law. Thus, there arises a strong intuition, which is deeply rooted in the legal tradition, that tells the judges to dismiss the complaint filed by Van Gend en Loos and decide that the Dutch government is right.

It may be surmised, however, that the Court did something more than just this. It may have imagined what the situation would look like if there were no Article 12 in the Treaty of Rome. Leaving aside the fact that the case would have been beyond the

---

[54]   This is, obviously, only one of the possible understandings of a hard case in law. Cf. Dworkin, 1975.

jurisdiction of the ECJ, in that situation it would have been obvious that Van Gend en Loos's – as well as other Dutch companies' – expectations as to the stability of customs duties would not have had such strong intuitive grounds. And would that intuitive judgment have been different if the Treaty had only been binding for the Netherlands and Germany and had only applied to customs law, and not to the much wider area of economic cooperation? And what if the Treaty had been binding for more European states but it had not included regulations such as Article 2 ("The Community shall have as its task, by establishing a common market and progressively approximating the economic policies of Member States, to promote throughout the Community a harmonious development of economic activities, a continuous and balanced expansion, an increase in stability, an accelerated raising of the standard of living and closer relations between the States belonging to it"). The intuitions pertaining to each of those distinct situations – lack of Article 12, the Treaty binding two member states only, the Treaty without regulations similar to Article 2 – will most probably be different. However, by performing all those mental simulations, and by "listening to" the intuitions they gave rise to, the Court was able to better understand the problem it was facing, which is always the first step to finding a solution in a hard case. As a result, that initial step might have yielded an insight, or a series of insights, that led to the following judgment: "The Community constitutes a new legal order of international law for the benefit of which the states have limited their sovereign rights, albeit within limited fields and the subjects of which comprise not only member states but also their nationals."[55] This solution may have been found with the help of mental simulation.

Giving examples (i.e. imagining particular situations connected with the problem under consideration) might therefore be a good way of seeking out solutions to problems and identifying mistakes in the available or newly proposed solutions. Of course, the simpler and more typical the problem, the less prominent the role of mental simulations in the attempts to cope with it; after all, in such situations the intuition suggesting a way of acting is so clear and strong that lengthy considerations become pointless: everything happens almost automatically, often without conscious control. The power of examples only becomes fully apparent in more complex cases, which give rise to contradictory or very weak intuitions. Then, it is worth employing a precept that could be called a principle of variability.[56] It requires imagining many, often only slightly different, situations, which not only helps to understand the problem better, but also increases the chances of getting an insight that could lead to a solution. This was the procedure followed by the ECJ in the *Van Gend en Loos* case if it had really considered a situation in which the Treaty of Rome

---

[55] ECJ February 5, 1963, Case 26/62 *Van Gend en Loos* v. *Nederlandse Administratie der Belastingen* [1963] ECR 1.

[56] In this context, Daniel Dennett speaks of "turning the knobs of the intuition pump." Cf. Dennett, 2013.

was different (e.g. it did not include Article 2) or was only binding for the Netherlands and Germany.

Fortunately, our discussion of the significance of the principle of variability in legal thinking does not have to be limited to pure speculations and tentative reconstructions of judges' lines of reasoning. This method is often employed by lawyers, the evidence of which can be easily found in transcripts of court hearings. Let us consider the following example. In the *California* v. *Carney* case of 1985, the Supreme Court of the United States considered the case of Charles Carney, accused of trafficking in marijuana inside a camper van parked in a street of San Diego. Upon searching Carney's motor home without a warrant, the police found drugs and paraphernalia.[57] The Court had to take into account two legal norms. On the one hand, a citizen has the right to privacy in his own home and the right cannot be infringed on without a warrant; on the other hand, if the incriminating evidence is to be found in a vehicle, thereby being subject to loss, the police have the right to search the vehicle without a warrant. The question that the judges were to answer was: is a camper van a home or a vehicle?

Let us look at a longer exchange between the judge and the attorney representing the state of California:

JUDGE: What would you do with a houseboat?

ATTORNEY: A houseboat? I think that would be covered [by the legal norm allowing the police to search it without a warrant] . . .

JUDGE: It has wheels?

ATTORNEY: No, it's a vessel, and it is covered by the same rule . . .

JUDGE: Well, I want to be more specific. There is a houseboat. It's tied up to a dock that's got no motor on it at all. It's just sitting there. And it's hooked up to the sewage, electricity, et cetera, and it's right beside a house. The house is covered, and the boat is not?

ATTORNEY: That's correct. It's sort of like an automobile that is parked right next to the house in the driveway. The automobile might not be covered, and the house is.

JUDGE: But the automobile has a motor in it –

ATTORNEY: That's correct.

JUDGE: – and the houseboat does not.

ATTORNEY: No. There may be oars. There may be some way to move that from one place to another.

JUDGE: There "may be." May be. I've seen houses moved, too. [Laughter]

ATTORNEY: As have I. I've passed a few of them on the beltway.

JUDGE: You've got to get more than that.

ATTORNEY: Certainly. Again, the objective indicia of mobility would be what the officers are looking to. Perhaps in Your Honor's example, they would

---

[57] *California* v. *Carney*, 471 U.S. 386 (1985).

be looking to see if there's oars there. There's no motor. There's no way to move that thing.

JUDGE: Well, let me add one more thing. It's been tied up there for the last 36 years. [Laughter]

ATTORNEY: If the officer doesn't know that, I don't see why he should be called to that particular knowledge. One thing he does know about when he is dealing with a house –

JUDGE: The moral is, don't live in a houseboat.[58]

This dialogue can serve as a compelling illustration of the principle of variability. Trying to determine if a camper van may be searched without a warrant, the judge has the legal representative of California imagine other, similar situations and decide if a warrant would be required in those cases. What the judge is doing, then, is testing various intuitions in an attempt to find a solution that would bring harmony into the mosaic of conflicting intuitions.

The use of an example may sometimes take one of two sophisticated forms, characterized by a certain methodological difference, namely: reasoning by analogy and thought experimentation. The use of analogy has been thoroughly discussed in numerous hefty volumes and weighty tomes.[59] I am not going to review those theoretical studies here; instead, I would like to present arguments in favor of the claim that analogical reasoning is rooted in the human ability of the mental simulation of events, although it goes beyond the use of imagination. In order to get a complete picture of this kind of reasoning, we need to consider the role of language and theory in thinking. However, the fact is that analogy, as a problem-solving technique, cannot work without mental simulation.

Analogy is a special type of thinking with the use of an example. In analogical reasoning we use previous cases in which it was possible to solve problems that were similar to the one at hand. The past situations serve as material that we feed into our imagination and then listen to the voice of intuition triggered by the visualizations. This is an interesting application of the principle of variability. After all, analogical situations may be regarded as variants of the currently considered situation. An advantage of using analogous past cases, in contrast to purely hypothetical ones, is that we know the solutions that were employed to solve them, which might have been preceded by a long reasoning and which are, therefore, well founded and grounded in a given legal tradition.

By way of illustration, let us consider the *Adams* v. *New Jersey Steamboat Co.* case.[60] Adams was a passenger on a steamer belonging to New Jersey Steamboat Co. During the cruise, a certain amount of money was stolen from his cabin in spite of the fact that the door had been locked and the windows fastened. Adams sued New

---

[58]   Ibid.
[59]   See the literature cited in Bartha, 2013.
[60]   Cf. Weinreb, 2005, pp. 41–45.

Jersey Steamboat Co., claiming a compensation. The court had to answer the question whether the defendant company could be held liable for the plaintiff's loss. There had been precedents in the US legal system where similar problems had to be considered (i.e. the service provider's liability for a loss sustained by a client, caused by a third party). For example, in the *Pinkerton* v. *Woodward* case, it had been decided that an innkeeper was liable for the losses incurred by the guests as if he was an insurer, that is despite the fact that there was no evidence of negligence on his part. In another case, that of *Carpenter* v. *N.Y., N.H. H.R.R. Co.*, the question was whether the carrier of a sleeping car was liable for the loss of money stolen from a passenger. In that case, the court decided that the carrier could not be held responsible without a proof of negligence on their part.[61]

Thus, in *Adams* v. *New Jersey Steamboat Co.*, the court was able to draw on the two similar cases as it was easy to recognize the similarities between a passenger boat and an inn, on the one hand, and between a passenger boat and a sleeping car, on the other. Mental simulation of the three situations permits the isolation of the intuitions which were crucial in deciding the *Pinkerton* and *Carpenter* cases. For example, the court could have decided that an instance of theft in an inn evokes a strong intuitive reaction demanding of the innkeeper a higher standard of responsibility since his relations with the guests are based on a special kind of trust; by contrast, a person traveling in a sleeping car will not usually demonstrate that kind of trust. Of course, such considerations do not provide an immediate answer to the question whether the carrier of a passenger boat is liable as an insurer or whether they can only be held responsible for a loss sustained by a passenger if there is evidence of their negligence. There is no doubt, however, that considering such similar cases, or performing proper mental simulations, might brings us closer to reaching a decision, as it helps us organize the initial intuitions and can potentially provide a new insight into Mr Adams's legal situation.

This analysis shows that the use of analogy in legal cases cannot be a purely formal or mechanical procedure. Looking at the *Adams* v. *New Jersey Steamboat Co.* case through the prism of formal logic only brings confusion and does not help explain why analogy is such an effective problem-solving tool. For a logician, every legal case is infinitely characterizable (i.e. it has an infinite number of properties). Which of them should be used to decide on the similarity between two cases? For example, which properties of the *Adams* case should be used to determine its similarity to the *Pinkerton* case? Is it important that Adams had locked his cabin? Or that the cruise was longer than 24 hours? Should we take into account the color of the boat? The quality of food served on the boat? Is it important that Adams was a middle-aged white male? What about the weather conditions? Is it of any significance that it was raining when the money was stolen? A given situation may be characterized in an infinite number of ways, which means that for any two cases, such as those of Adams

---

[61] Ibid., p. 45.

and Pinkerton, there will be an infinite number of common features and an infinite number of differences. Let us, however, assume that we have identified the set of properties that underlie the similarity between two cases;[62] suppose we have concluded that all those features are characteristic of both the *Adams* and the *Pinkerton* cases. What is the consequence? Why should we decide that the solution adopted in the *Pinkerton* case should also be applied in the *Adams* case? After all, there may be situations, as in the *Carpenter* case, that are also similar to the *Adams* case but which suggest a different solution. In such a situation, a logician might say that – if there are two other situations which are analogous to the case under investigation – we should find a way to establish which one of them is "relevantly" or "more" analogous. They might also propose some formal procedure (e.g. "the weighing of legal principles"[63]) that might solve the case.

The problem, however, is that by following this approach, an effective method of reasoning that we use on a daily basis, not only in deciding legal cases, becomes a "theoretical monster," such a complex theoretical structure that it could only be used by the most patient and scrupulous lawyers. It is easier to assume that the ability of analogical thinking emerges from the human ability to imagine alternate states of affairs and to employ such simulations to solve particular problems. I do not mean to say that analogy is a purely heuristic tool, or a smart method for generating hypotheses which then can, but do not need to, prove useful in dealing with a problem. This fundamental, heuristic form of analogy can be given a formal structure (e.g. that of abduction[64]), thanks to which analogical reasoning may not only be used for generating hypotheses but also for justifying claims. This is also an illuminating example of cooperation between imagination and thinking in language, an issue that we will return to in the following chapters.

Another special use of examples in problem-solving is conducting thought experiments. This is a controversial concept and methodologists have not yet reached a consensus as to what mental procedures can be subsumed under it.[65] I do not intend to participate in that debate as it seems to me that it is only a debate about "labels." It goes without saying that we all experiment in our thoughts, imagining nonexistent situations in order to be more successful in real ones. As already argued, this technique is also used by lawyers, especially when they come across a complex case that generates contradictory intuitions. Such nonexistent states of affairs were, for example, imagined by the judges of the US Supreme Court in the *California* v. *Carney* case when they were trying to decide whether the right to privacy extended to a camper van, so that it could not be searched without a warrant. Whether this kind of reasoning can properly be called a "thought experiment" or not is of secondary importance.

[62] Cf. the discussion on this issue in Brożek, 2018.
[63] Cf. ibid; also Alexy, 2005.
[64] Cf. Brewer, 1996.
[65] Cf. Mach, 1973; also Galili, 2009; Sorensen, 1992.

There is no doubt, however, that thought experimentation includes imagining situations that are characterized by a large dose of counterfactuality (i.e. they ignore important psychological facts or even the laws of biology, chemistry, and physics). Imagining such counterfactual situations makes it possible to break away from various thinking habits, thereby increasing the chances of getting an insight and finding a novel conceptualization of the problem under scrutiny. A good example here is the thought experiment at the intersection of law and ethics described by Judith Jarvis Thomson:

> You wake up in the morning and find yourself back to back in bed with an unconscious violinist. A famous unconscious violinist. He has been found to have a fatal kidney ailment, and the Society of Music Lovers has canvassed all the available medical records and found that you alone have the right blood type to help. They have therefore kidnapped you, and last night the violinist's circulatory system was plugged into yours, so that your kidneys can be used to extract poisons from his blood as well as your own. The director of the hospital now tells you, "Look, we're sorry the Society of Music Lovers did this to you – we would never have permitted it if we had known. But still, they did it, and the violinist now is plugged into you. To unplug you would be to kill him. But never mind, it's only for nine months. By then he will have recovered from his ailment, and can safely be unplugged from you." Is it morally incumbent on you to accede to this situation?[66]

This incredible scenario is supposed to represent an argument against the claim that abortion is inadmissible in any circumstances. Although, as Thomson suggests, an unborn child has the right to live – just as the famous violinist does – this is not always a decisive argument. For example, if a woman has been fertilized against her will – as in a case of rape – then her situation is similar to that of the person to whom a dying violinist has been connected without that person's knowledge or will. Thus, Thomson argues that if we agree that we would have the right to demand that the violinist be unplugged (thereby letting him die), then similarly a woman who got pregnant as a result of rape has the right to abortion. In this thought experiment Thomson is also using the principle of variability, wondering how our judgment of the situation might change if the violinist were to be plugged to our circulatory system not for nine months, but for ten years or even forever.[67] All this helps us to break away from the typical context of the question of the permissibility of abortion, to test our intuitions from that new perspective, and perhaps even to achieve some original insight into this difficult problem.

This discussion should have made the heuristic function of imagination fairly clear. By mentally simulating objects and events (such as analogous cases or counter-factual situations) and making use of the principle of variability, we turn our intuition into action. If the intuitions evoked in this way are weak or contradictory

[66] Thomson, 1971, pp. 48–49.
[67] Cf. ibid., p. 48ff.

(i.e. they do not provide a clear clue as to the solution of the problem we are dealing with), mental simulation can still lead to an insight or a certain restructuring of the existing intuitions. Thus, it turns out that imagination, which may give indirect access to unconscious intuitions and insights, is a powerful tool for solving problems and identifying mistakes in existing solutions.

2.4 THE HERMENEUTIC FUNCTION

Mental simulations also have a hermeneutic function: they enable us to understand linguistic utterances and, in the legal context, the articles of laws and other normative acts, the content of court judgments, and the pronouncements of legal doctrine. As already noted, however, this is not that easy because of the fact that legal regulations are expressed in a very abstract language. By way of illustration, let us compare two utterances. The first of them is a casuistic norm from the Code of Hammurabi: "If a man steal ox or sheep, ass or pig, or boat – if it be from a god (temple) or a palace, he shall restore thirtyfold; if it be from a freeman, he shall render tenfold. If the thief have nothing wherewith to pay he shall be put to death."[68] Although this regulation has a rather complex logical structure, the concepts it employs are fairly concrete. It is easy to understand what a mental simulation of such events as stealing a sheep, a pig, or a boat could look like and, therefore, how such a simulation could help to comprehend this legal norm. The situation is different when considering a more abstract regulation, such as Article 278 §1 of the Polish Penal Code: "Whoever, with the purpose of appropriating, wilfully takes someone else's movable property shall be subject to the penalty of deprivation of liberty for a term of between 3 months and 5 years." How can one mentally simulate "appropriating someone else's movable property"?

I have already touched upon this problem, arguing that the nature and processing of abstract concepts represent the greatest challenge for a theory that considers mental simulation a fundamental mechanism of language understanding. Let us remember that a possible way out of the already described dead end is the adoption of a modified dual-coding theory. After all, simulations can be used to process concrete concepts, but it is difficult to explain how they could contribute to the understanding of abstract language. On this approach, mental representations are coded in two ways: they can be multimodal and amodal. The first code is realized by simulations of concrete objects and events (so-called imagens) and it covers different modalities: visual, auditory, haptic, emotional, etc.; the other code, also based on simulation, consists of the representations of linguistic symbols (so-called logogens). What is important is the link between the two systems: understanding concrete words mostly relies on imagens, and relations among logogens are more significant in the case of more abstract concepts. Thus, linguistic meaning is determined by

---

[68] Harper, 1904.

mental simulations of concrete objects and situations and by the formal structure of the relations among logogens. The more concrete a concept, the more strongly it is grounded in multimodal simulations; the more abstract it is, the more its meaning is determined by its place within the network of linguistic relations.[69]

If this picture of the nature of language is correct at least in its outline, then it cannot be ignored by any researcher seeking to develop a theory of interpretation, including legal interpretation. Any attempt to account for language comprehension that ignored the dual nature of the process would be at least incomplete, if not totally incorrect. Let us illustrate this problem, first by considering relatively concrete expressions, for example: "A policeman entered Mr Carney's camper van, where he found drugs, plastic bags, and scales." As already noted, numerous experimental studies clearly suggest that such sentences as this one are understood by performing a mental simulation of the situation described. And it would be difficult to imagine what interpreting this sentence could consist in (unless the context indicates that it was used metaphorically, of course). Such utterances are simply understood, and easily at that, without recourse to any special intellectual procedures. That is because the use of concrete expressions (i.e. ones designating objects and events that we experience on a daily basis) constitutes a kind of constant point of reference for our linguistic practices. This fact is highlighted by Ludwig Wittgenstein, who offers the following observation in his *Remarks on the Foundations of Mathematics*:

> Someone asks me: What is the colour of this flower? I answer: "red." – Are you absolutely sure? Yes, absolutely sure! But may I not have been deceived and called the wrong colour "red"? No. The certainty with which I call the colour "red" is the rigidity of my measuring-rod, it is the rigidity from which I start. When I give descriptions, that is not to be brought into doubt.[70]

The situation changes as we start moving away from the concrete and toward the abstract. The following legal norm from the Code of Hammurabi: "If a man steals the property of a god (temple) or palace, that man shall be put to death; and he who receives from his hand the stolen (property) shall also be put to death" is still a very concrete utterance, but it creates some possibility for interpretation, if only because it employs relatively general expressions, such as "property" or "stolen property." The provision of Article 278 §1 of the Polish Penal Code: "Whoever, with the purpose of appropriating, wilfully takes someone else's movable property shall be subject to the penalty of deprivation of liberty for a term of between 3 months and 5 years" is even more abstract and it cannot be understood solely on the basis of mental simulation; the expressions "taking with the purpose of appropriating" and "someone else's movable property" can be imagined in so many different ways that they are completely different from the color "red" in Wittgenstein's example.

---

[69] Cf. Paivio, 2013.
[70] Wittgenstein, 1978, pt. 6, §28.

How, then, do we cope with abstract expressions, such as those from the Penal Code? When faced with such language, we have three different interpretative procedures at our disposal.[71] The first of them can be called exemplification. It consists in imagining (through conscious mental simulation) a certain event that is (positive exemplification) or is not (negative exemplification) an instance of "taking someone else's movable property with the purpose of appropriating." For example, we can imagine that John, taking advantage of the fact that Peter is looking in another direction, steals his mobile phone; or that Jane – as every year on April Fools' Day – wants to play a trick on a colleague and takes her wallet out of her handbag and then puts it in the pocket of a coat belonging to another colleague of hers. In the first case, we will have no doubts that we are dealing with theft; in the second, we will surely say that the norm described in Article 278 §1 of the Penal Code has not been broken. The problem is that the more abstract a law, the more difficult it is in principle to imagine all kinds of situations that could be covered by it; moreover, the greater the abstraction, the greater the number of borderline cases that are hard to classify as positive or negative exemplifications. Let us suppose that Adam downloads a pirated copy of the latest computer game from the Internet; or that Joseph secretly connects his home electrical system to that of the street light circuit. Are these instances of "taking someone else's movable property with the purpose of appropriating"?

There is no simple answer to this question (at least in abstraction from a broader context, i.e. other legal regulations and legal doctrine; we will return to this problem later in this section). It can be argued that although electrical energy and computer games are not typical instances of movable property, they should be treated as such in law; the opposite strategy can also be adopted. What is important is the fact that courts of law, considering such unclear cases, make decisions that, in the course of time, form "lines of cases" that give rise to an interpretative tradition. If a series of court judgments are based on the decision that computer games should be considered movable property, an experienced lawyer who is familiar with those judgments will have no doubts how to approach a similar case; an intuition will develop in their mind that will automatically suggest a proper judgment.

This observation highlights the important role of examples: they can be used to (re)educate intuition. This is precisely how imagination is used in university classes. In order to understand and be able to apply complex legal regulations on corporate income tax, the student must do something more than just carefully read those regulations. An apt teacher will facilitate the process with the use of multiple, sometimes only slightly different, examples in which the tax regulations are applied in a particular way. In some cases, it will be necessary not only to develop new intuitions but also to get rid of the previous ones, based on folk understanding of the social world. A good case in point is the debate among criminal lawyers in Poland

[71] Cf. Brożek, 2011.

about the status of omission as an act.[72] The claim that omission can be regarded as an act may be difficult to accept for a person who sticks to a common-sense conceptual network. Changing this view requires the "reeducation" of intuition, and a good idea to do this is to perform various mental simulations in which a failure to act in a specified way is considered an act from the point of view of criminal law.

A second procedure that facilitates the understanding of abstract legal regulations is paraphrase. It consists in stating that another utterance is equivalent to the one under consideration. For instance, drawing on previous court judgments and the findings of legal doctrine, it can be argued that the regulation in Article 278 §1: "Whoever, with the purpose of appropriating, wilfully takes someone else's movable property shall be subject to the penalty of deprivation of liberty for a term of between 3 months and 5 years" is equivalent to the following norm: "Whoever, with the purpose of appropriating, unlawfully takes a material object which is detached, can be an independent article of trade, has a monetary value and is not real property, from the control of a person who has controlled it heretofore and brings it under his/her own control, shall be subject to the penalty of deprivation of liberty for a term of between 3 months and 5 years."[73] This paraphrase also includes several abstract concepts, such as "material object," "control," "article of trade," or "monetary value," but it makes it possible to make certain decisions at the level of mental simulations. For example, it will lead to the conclusion that the hypothetical situation in which Adam downloads a pirate copy of a computer game from the Internet does not fulfill the criteria of an act penalized by Article 278 §1 because a computer programme is not a "detached material object." Thus, the paraphrases of legal regulations employed in court judgments and in the study of legal doctrine do not need to be less abstract than the original texts; they are used to facilitate exemplification, whether positive or negative.

Paraphrase constitutes the main tool in the study of legal doctrine, although legal doctrine does not shun other interpretative techniques. However, whereas the judge's or the attorney's task is, ultimately, to decide whether a given case is covered by a particular legal norm, the legal theorist's aim is different, namely: to develop an abstract theory that will facilitate the solution of interpretative problems. For example, according to Article 1 of the Polish Penal Code, "Penal liability shall be incurred only by a person who commits an act prohibited under penalty, by a law in force at the time of its commission." This regulation states that only those instances of behavior are subject to legal evaluation that are acts. What is an act though? Theorists of penal law devote considerable attention to this problem, seeking to make the concept more specific in different ways. For example, they contend that "an act is only such behaviour which is characterised by elements that enable, in accordance with the system of values created in the development of our civilisation,

---

[72]   I will not delve into the details here as it is one of the most controversial issues in the Polish theory of criminal law. Cf. Kulesza, 2007.

[73]   Cf. Wróbel & Zoll, 2016, p. 30ff.

legal liability to be based on the fragment of reality coinciding with human behaviour,"[74] or: "an act is any human behaviour that is characterised by the ability to match one's movements to the needs of the realisation of an imagined goal."[75]

Such statements are undoubtedly very abstract and are themselves subject to interpretation. In order to show how paraphrase contributes to a better understanding of the linguistic utterance under analysis, rather than introducing greater confusion, it is worth adopting the following convention. A meaning bundle will be understood as all the ways in which, prima facie (i.e. outside the context), a given expression can be used. While interpreting legal philosophers' favorite regulation: "Vehicles are not allowed into a public park,"[76] we can ascribe, prima facie, different meanings to it depending on how we understand such expressions as "vehicles," "into," and "public park." "Vehicles" may, but do not have to, include bicycles and scooters; "into" may, but does not have to, refer to entering a park with vehicles participating in a yearly motor show; and "public park" may, but does not have to, denote only those green areas that have been officially recognized as parks in a decision of the municipality or another competent body.

By paraphrasing, we arrive at an expression associated with a different (if only slightly) meaning bundle from that of the original. How can this procedure help in interpreting a text? The answer is simple: the aim of a paraphrase is to narrow down the meaning bundle of the interpreted expression in such a way that the meaning we are looking for belongs to the intersection of two sets: the meaning bundle of the text under interpretation and the meaning bundle of the paraphrase. If the sentence "Vehicles are not allowed into a public park" is paraphrased as "Combustion engine vehicles are prohibited from entering green areas," then the intersection of the meaning bundles of the two sentences includes an interpretation that prohibits cars and motorcycles from entering green areas that are not officially recognized as parks; on this interpretation, however, entering parks with bicycles will not be covered by the regulation.

The situation is similar in the case of the legal understanding of an "act." Its meaning bundle is very broad, encompassing almost any behavior, from fully intentional ones, to those "almost" automatic, based on learned and unconscious reactions. Moreover, it can be argued that the word "act" is simply an equivalent of the word "behavior." However, if we follow the doctrine of the Polish penal law and decide that an act is any human behavior that is characterised by the ability to match one's movements to the needs of the realization of an imagined goal, then certain understandings of "act" will not be allowed. For example, we will not classify as an act such behavior in which the force of inertia during a sudden breaking of a bus makes us fall into an elderly woman, who, as a result, breaks her arm; similarly, my behavior will not be an instance of an act if someone pushes me into another person,

---

[74]   Ibid., p. 30.
[75]   Ibid., p. 30.
[76]   See Hart, 1958, p. 607.

who then falls down and sustains a brain injury. Thus, paraphrase has a special function: it rules out certain positive exemplifications that might otherwise have been included in the coverage of the original text of a legal rule.

A third procedure that facilitates understanding of a legal text consists in embedding the interpreted regulation in a wider context (of the legal system, legal theories, legal tradition, and even more broadly: other non-legal conceptualizations that comprise lawyers' "background knowledge"). The context has a selective role here: it allows certain paraphrases, while disallowing others. For example, Article 115 of the Polish Penal Code includes a legal definition according to which: "A movable item or chattel is also Polish or foreign currency or other means of payment and a document which entitles one to a sum of money or includes the obligation to pay principal, or interest, share in the profits or a declaration of participation in a company [or partnership]." This definition rules out such paraphrases of Article 278 §1 of the Penal Code that do not subsume currency or other means of payment under the concept of movable property. In other words, if we assume that penal regulations should be internally consistent (and this is one of the fundamental assumptions in legal interpretation), then we have to make sure, at least, that our understandings of those regulations are not internally contradictory. That is why it is highly undesirable if a paraphrase of one legal regulation stands in contradiction to another regulation or its previously accepted paraphrase.

It is worth noting that by using the procedure of embedding we remain within the linguistic code. Here, we do not, in principle, resort to imagens (mental simulations of concrete objects or events); instead, we are interested in the logical relations among different linguistic statements, which are formulated in a very abstract language. Thus, embedding represents the "other end" of the spectrum of understanding: it is based on abstract formal relations, rather than multimodal concrete simulations. Of course, even this interpretative procedure is ultimately employed to decide whether a particular state of affairs falls within a given legal norm. But the goal is achieved in an indirect way: by rejecting certain paraphrases as inconsistent with the context, we accept others that restrict the set of possible positive exemplifications.

Taking into consideration the three procedures of legal interpretation, exemplification, paraphrase, and embedding, it is easy to realize that understanding language, and particularly abstract language, has a dual nature. On the one hand, it consists in performing mental simulations of legal regulations, with the caveat that the more abstract the language used in them, the broader and the more indeterminate the range of possible simulations. When trying to understand the meaning of the statement "Whoever has stolen a sheep shall restore thirtyfold," we can obviously imagine various concrete situations, but the simulations will be similar; by contrast, when we interpret the sentence "Whoever, with the purpose of appropriating, wilfully takes someone else's movable property shall be subject to the penalty of deprivation of liberty for a term of between 3 months and 5 years," we may employ numerous, considerably different mental simulations, often with justified doubts as to whether a given simulation really is an instance of "taking someone else's movable property with the purpose of appropriating." What facilitates interpretation of abstract statements is the fact that we regard them as pieces of a large theoretical structure, which we assume, at least, not to be internally contradictory or even to be largely coherent. This can be achieved by finding an adequate paraphrase or by embedding the interpreted expression in a broader context. In this case, a crucial role is played by purely formal relations between a given regulation (or its para-phrase) and other regulations. Such formal procedures aim at restricting the range of possible mental simulations. It can therefore be concluded that legal interpretation – just as interpretation of all abstract statements – is based on a peculiar "game" between mental simulations (exemplification) and formal or quasi-formal opera-tions on sentences (embedding), with paraphrase having an auxiliary function.[77]

These considerations represent a broad outline of a theory of interpretation, one that is far from complete. My intention, however, is not to propose detailed solutions in this regard but to show that the interpretation of legal regulations is crucially based not only on formal and linguistic operations but also on the use of imagina-tion. Imagination constitutes a link between abstract theories and unconscious intuitions; it is the "missing link" in the traditional approach to legal reasoning. However, imagination alone, even if supported by intuition and insight, would be of little use. It is therefore time for a more systematic consideration of the impact of language on legal reasoning.

---

[77] Cf. Brożek, 2016b.

3

Language

Whatever is omnipresent, easily becomes invisible. When asked to describe the features of a printed page, one would pay attention to the composition of the text, the quality of paper, the type of fonts used, or even a small tea stain in the lower right corner; one would probably not mention, however, that the page is white. This is not surprising: we rarely use paper of a different color for printing. In the same way, the fact that lawyers think in language is so obvious that it seems unworthy to mention. We take it for granted that legal argumentation takes advantage of various linguistic constructs, from elaborate conceptual frameworks to the schemes of logically valid inferences. As a consequence, we are unable to fully appreciate the extent of the language's multifaceted influence on legal thinking.

The way out of this conundrum is to take a step back and consider the role and nature of language from a different perspective. This requires us to abandon deeply rooted thinking habits, and such a trick is often achieved by means of a thought experiment. An example is provided by Alf Ross, who, imagining a primitive tribe with a relatively simple system of social rules, masterfully argued that central legal concepts are meaningless. In Section 3.1, I analyze his theoretical position in some detail and come to the conclusion that he is gravely mistaken; but the mistake is an intriguing one, paving the way for a fresh and surprising approach to legal language.

Without language, our experience of the world would be much more subjective, effectively excluding any cooperation on a large scale, such as is necessary for complex social institutions to exist. Without language, we would be condemned to utilizing particular and fragmented conceptualizations of experience. In such a cognitive setting, any social norms (if they were possible at all), would remain highly casuistic. Without language, we would not be able to joint our efforts in constructing theories, and hence no systematic reflection over human behavior would ever be possible. Without language, we would be in no position to engage in any kind of dialogue, and hence be able to contrast different views pertaining to the best organization of social affairs. Of course, one may point out that imagining a social world without language is virtually impossible. But even a partial failure in any attempt to do so may uncover some important aspects of the role of language in legal thinking.

Once we take full advantage of the potential afforded by language, we can develop highly complex and coherent legal systems that provide a unified framework organizing our experience. The legal conceptual scheme, together with the theories we develop to help in creating, interpreting, and applying the law, constitute a support structure for legal decision-making. It is an impressive machinery that is able to take us from the concrete and particular cases to the abstract realm of legal relations, and back. It is no exaggeration to claim that language creates a qualitatively new social world, generating new kinds of problems we have to face, but at the same time providing us with an incredible number of conceptualizations, which make dealing with problems a much simpler task. Language is, indeed, the most powerful tool we have ever discovered. In this chapter, I will try to shed some light on how it shapes the legal mind.

3.1 TÛ-TÛ

In his 1951 article, the Danish philosopher of law Alf Ross takes us to the imaginary Noîsulli Islands in the South Pacific, inhabited by the Noît-cif tribe.[1] The language of the Noît-cif has the word *tû-tû*. Whoever encounters his mother-in-law or kills a totem animal or has eaten the food prepared for the chief becomes *tû-tû*. And whoever is *tû-tû* must be subjected to the ceremony of purification. What is the function of *tû-tû* then? As observed by Ross, *tû-tû* is an intermediary concept only. In fact, instead of using the word *tû-tû* to refer to a person who has perpetrated any of the three acts only to conclude that they must be subjected to the ceremony of purification, one could use the following three conditional statements:

(1) If a person x has encountered their mother-in-law, x must be subjected to the ceremony of purification.
(2) If a person x has killed a totem animal, x must be subjected to the ceremony of purification.
(3) If a person x has eaten of the food prepared for the chief, x must be subjected to the ceremony of purification.

Thus, the concept *tû-tû* could be easily dispensed with without detriment to the communicative potential of the Noît-cif language. As Ross argues, *tû-tû* "is of course nothing at all, a word devoid of any meaning whatever. ... The talk about *tû-tû* is pure nonsense."[2] An anthropologist studying the language and customs of the Noît-cif tribe, when asked about the meaning of the word *tû-tû*, can only say that *tû-tû* refers to someone who has encountered their mother-in-law, has killed a totem

---

[1] Cf. Ross, 1957.
[2] Ibid., p. 812.

animal, or has eaten of the food prepared for the chief of the tribe and that such a person must be subjected to the ceremony of purification – and nothing more!

The thought experiment proposed by Ross is relevant to the reflection on the nature of legal language. Instead of *tû-tû*, let us consider the concept of ownership. In most legal systems, ownership can be obtained in a number of ways: by contract, inheritance, prescription, renunciation, foreclosure, etc. A person who is the legal owner of some property has the right to own it, to use it, to benefit by it, to dispose of it (including the right to transform or destroy it), to encumber it by establishing a limited property right, and to sell it. It can, therefore, be argued that the concept of "ownership" has no meaning, just like *tû-tû*. We could get rid of it and use conditional statements instead, such as:

(4) If a person x acquires a thing by contract, x has the right to use it.
(5) If a person x acquires a thing by inheritance, x has the right to benefit by it.
(6) If a person x acquires a thing by foreclosure, x has the right to destroy it.
     etc.

Still, it is worth noting, following Ross, that such concepts as *tû-tû* or "ownership" can be useful since they enable a more effective presentation of legal norms.[3] After all, if we did not use the concept of ownership, we would have to employ an extremely large number of conditional statements like the ones in (4)–(6), which would combine the different ways in which ownership can be acquired with the various rights enjoyed by the owner. Thus, by incorporating the concept of ownership in legal language we can limit the number of relevant statements to two:

(7) If x has acquired y by contract, inheritance, prescription, renunciation, foreclosure (etc.), then x is the owner of y.
(8) If x is the owner of y, then x has the right to own, use, transform, destroy, encumber, sell (etc.) y.

It can be easily observed that the analysis proposed by Ross can be applied to numerous fundamental concepts of legal language, such as "legal person," "contract," "offence," "marriage," etc. If we accepted this line of reasoning, we would have to concede that a considerable, and very important, share of the language of law is ultimately "devoid of any meaning" and that many of the fundamental legal concepts are just "intermediary" in nature, their sole purpose being to enable "a more effective presentation of legal norms."

Ross's thought-provoking and stimulating discussion is an instance of philosophy at its best: it leads to putting forward a bold hypothesis that takes us off the well-trodden paths of thought and to question views that have so far been considered well justified. As in many other similar cases, the greatest benefit from getting enchanted

---

3   Cf. ibid.

with Ross's thought experiment will be reaped by those who can see that he is wrong; and all that it takes to realize that he is wrong is a bit of common sense.

First of all, it is not true that such concepts as "ownership" and "contract" can only be regarded as elements of legal language and nothing more; we also use them in our everyday language, and it can hardly be argued that they function as intermediary concepts only and that their common meanings have no influence on how we understand them in law. The meaning of the word "ownership" as used in private law is not only determined by the legal regulations pertaining to the different ways of acquiring ownership and the rights of owners but also by all the common connotations of this word, the related concepts, etc. Of course, we perfectly realize that the legal understanding of "ownership" is somewhat different from its meaning in everyday usage. However, legal language is not an isolated system of concepts – it is based on our common conceptualizations of reality. The same is true of other legal concepts. The Latin word *persona* originally referred to a theatrical mask, and it was therefore easy to apply it metaphorically to a "person" (i.e. a bundle of rights and obligations) that an individual has under the law.[4] We no longer remember this etymology when we speak of a legal persons today; at the same time, though, it would be hardly possible to construe "legal personhood" in a totally arbitrary way, for example to bestow it on stones or insects. That is because the legal concept of person is rooted in everyday usage, where a "prototypical" person is an adult human of sound mind.[5] The meanings of words in everyday language and in other registers (e.g. in legal language) are not clearly distinct. There are multiple relations between them – such as the ones established by metaphor, as already noted – and the opposite can only be argued by those who insist on sticking to a model of language based on first-order predicate calculus.

It could be argued, however, that the words "ownership" and "person" may have complex etymologies and that the word *tû-tû*, which has no connotations in English, could in fact be used instead of the word "ownership." Thus, *tû-tû* would only be an intermediary concept, as Ross saw it. This line of thinking would be of no avail though. As I argued in Chapter 2, meaning is a function of two codes: modal imagens and amodal logogens. Our understanding of linguistic expressions is largely determined by the relations among logogens, especially abstract ones, and not only by mental simulations of concrete (prototypical) objects and events. This approach is developed by the advocates of the inferential theory of meaning.[6] In §31 of his *Philosophical Investigations*, Ludwig Wittgenstein is drawing an analogy between language and the game of chess:

> When one [shows] someone the king in chess and says: "This is the king," this does not tell him the use of this piece – unless he already knows the rules of the game up

---

[4] Cf. Brożek, 2017a.
[5] Cf. Brożek & Jakubiec, 2017; also Hage, 2017.
[6] Cf. Brandom, 1994; Sartor, 2008.

to this last point: the shape of the king. You could imagine his having learnt the rules of the game without ever having been [shown] an actual piece. The shape of the chessman corresponds here to the sound or shape of a word. . . . We may say: only someone who already knows how to do something with it can significantly ask a name.[7]

Elsewhere, he makes the following observation:

Well, let's assume the child . . . invents a name for the sensation! – But then, of course, he couldn't make himself understood when he used the word. – So does he understand the name, without being able to explain its meaning to anyone? – But what does it mean to say that he has "named his pain"? – How has he done this naming of pain?! And whatever he did, what was its purpose? – When one says "He gave a name to his sensation" one forgets that a great deal of stage-setting in the language is presupposed if the mere act of naming is to make sense. And when we speak of someone's having given a name to pain, what is presupposed is the existence of the grammar of the word "pain"; it [shows] the post where the new word is stationed.[8]

In this passage, Wittgenstein is considering the possibility of a private language: can a person invent words that for themselves, but not for others, denote particular objects or states of affairs? One immediate answer that springs to mind is: yes, but such a "language" would be completely useless since it could not be used for the purpose of communication. Still, Wittgenstein contends that such a conclusion would be too hasty. In order to "invent a name for a sensation," we first need to have a complex linguistic structure in which there is a "post" for the new word. Members of the Noît-cif tribe were able to "invent" the word *tû-tû* only because their language already had such expressions as "totem animal," "chief," and "ceremony of purification," which were related to each other in various ways. Moreover, there had to be a special linguistic device (i.e. conditional mood) that distinguished different kinds of cause-effect relationships. All of this constituted a structure into which the word *tû-tû* could be inserted, and that structure determined the meaning of the new word.

It is worth asking about the causes of the inadequacy of Ross's line of argumentation. What seems to be at fault here is the methods used by Ross in his analyses of the nature of legal language. Underlying those analyses is the view that first-order predicate calculus provides a good model of language. This has several consequences. First of all, predicate logic is extensional; that is, the meaning of a linguistic expression is thought to be determined only by indicating the set of entities that fall within the range of a given word. The meaning of the expression "totem animal" is the set of all totem animals, while the meaning of a conditional statement (material implication) is based on simple semantic rules according to which a conditional statement is true if its antecedent is false or if its consequent is

---

[7] Wittgenstein, 1958, §31.
[8] Ibid., 1958, §257.

true. Moreover, the first-order predicate logic rests on the assumption that the meanings of linguistic expressions are well delimited. Although there are methods for the formal modeling of such semantic phenomena as polysemy or vagueness, in predicate logic it is impossible to account for more complex issues, such as word etymology or the metaphorical relations between linguistic expressions. According to first-order predicate calculus, the English words "regime," "region," and "regent" have nothing in common despite the fact that they share the same root (*reg*) and partially evoke the same intuitions. In order to determine their meanings, it is enough to indicate the sets of entities or features that are considered as, respectively, regimes, regions, and regents.

In order to illustrate the consequences of such a formal approach to language, we can "reverse the reasoning" proposed by Ross.[9] His argument is based on two assumptions: there is a (partial) semantic postulate for a name T (e.g. If a person x has eaten of the food prepared for the chief, x is a *tû-tû*, where *tû-tû* is T); and there is a norm of conduct that includes T in the antecedent (e.g. If a person x is *tû-tû*, then x must be subjected to a ceremony of purification). If these two conditions are met, we can admit that the name T is devoid of meaning, functioning only as an intermediary concept. The problem is that these conditions can be met by any name, even a proper name if we employed W. V. O. Quine's procedure of replacing a proper name with a predicate.[10] Let us consider the word "book." We can agree that the statement "If x is a novel, x is a book" is true. Now, we need only to introduce the norm "If x is a book, then x should be sold with a reduced VAT rate" to decide that the word "book" is meaningless. In this way, any noun can be *tûtûfied*, which reduces Ross's line of argumentation ad absurdum.

The discussion on *tû-tû* shows, by chance as it were, two important roles of language in law. Ross himself recognizes the first one, though he seems to underestimate its importance, when he states that concepts such as *tû-tû* contribute to "a more effective presentation" of legal norms. For illustration, let us assume that there are only five ways in which property can be acquired: by contract, by inheritance, by prescription, by renunciation, or by foreclosure. Let us also assume that the owner has five rights with respect to property: to own it, to use it, to benefit by it, to destroy it, and to dispose of it. If it were not for the concept "owner," we would have to formulate as many as twenty-five legal norms that established the institutions of ownership. For instance, there would be five regulations for acquisition by inheritance:

(9) If a person x acquires a thing by inheritance, x has the right to own it.

(10) If a person x acquires a thing by inheritance, x has the right to use it.

(11) If a person x acquires a thing by inheritance, x has the right to benefit by it.

(12) If a person x acquires a thing by inheritance, x has the right to destroy it.

(13) If a person x acquires a thing by inheritance, x has the right to dispose of it.

[9] Cf. Brożek, 2015.
[10] Cf. Quine, 1948.

As can easily be calculated, the list can be reduced from twenty-five to ten due to the introduction of the concept "owner." Five of them would specify when a person x becomes the owner of property (e.g. "If a person x acquires a thing by inheritance, x is the owner of it"), while the other five would describe the owner's rights (e.g. "If a person x is the owner of a thing, x has the right to destroy it)."

The introduction of a new concept (such as "owner") really does enable "a more effective presentation of legal norms." However, the obvious "arithmetic" reasons aside, why is that desirable in the first place? The simple answer is that the use of intermediary concepts, such as "owner" or tû-tû, increases the coherence of legal knowledge. Coherence is measured by three criteria: consistency, the number of inferential relations, and unification. A set of statements that includes a contradiction is said to be inconsistent. A set of statements is the more coherent, the greater the number of significant inferential relations that hold among the statements. Finally, the coherence of a set of statements is the greater, the more it is unified (i.e. the more difficult it is to divide it into two or more independent subsets without losing any significant logical consequences of the original set).[11] Because of the inferential relations and unification criteria, the coherence of knowledge is a matter of degree. The set of twenty-five norms, which does not use the concept of "owner," is coherent only to a small extent, particularly because it is not unified: it can be easily divided into subsets (e.g. by putting together the norms concerning the acquisition of property) without losing any significant information. By contrast, removing any norm from the ten-element set with the concept "owner" results in losing significant information (e.g. putting the norm "If a person x acquires a thing by contract, x becomes the owner of it" into a separate set will lead to a situation where it will be impossible to associate any legal consequences with acquiring property by contract). Why is coherence so important? Studies show that it is correlated with important cognitive factors. Knowledge that is highly coherent is easier to learn, remember, understand, and apply.[12] A minimally coherent legal system would be totally dysfunctional.

Increasing the coherence of knowledge, however, is not the only benefit we get from tû-tû and similar concepts. Let us conduct a simple thought experiment. Let us imagine that the Noît-cif council of elders is to decide what to do with a tribesman who has killed a pelican by accident. Pelicans are not totem animals, but in principle they can only be hunted twice a year: on the two days of equinox. Moreover, pelican meat, when properly preserved, is used as the basis of the ceremonial meals prepared for the chief every month. If the Noît-cif legal system did not include the concept tû-tû, the council of elders would have to introduce a completely new rule for all those who have killed a pelican by accident. However,

[11] Cf. Bonjour, 1985.
[12] Cf. McNammara et al., 1996.

considering the crucial role of *tû-tû* in relation to killing a totem animal and eating of the food prepared for the chief, the council has another option: in the interest of the coherence of their legal system, they can extend the meaning of *tû-tû* and decide that a person who has killed a pelican by accident is *tû-tû* and therefore should undergo the ceremony of purification.

Let us consider another situation. According to Ross, as we already know, ownership is a concept whose only function is to link particular states of affairs with their legal consequences. Let us assume that a certain legal system only includes norms concerning movable and real estate property and that the legislator has to consider introducing principles governing that which is called intellectual property. It is obvious that the existing concept of ownership can be very useful in the process. The legislator does not have to introduce a totally new institution; it should suffice to make use of the existing legal framework and adapt it in order to cover the unique features of intellectual property. In other words, incorporating intellectual property norms in the existing legal regulations is different from developing a new institution from scratch. In the first case, we would have to do with an instance of adaptation that takes into account the existing solutions, justifications and the whole knowledge "accompanying" the institution of ownership; in the latter case, intellectual property would be a new legislative solution, one totally independent of the existing conceptual framework. It is easy to see that the quality of the latter solution, and in particular its coherence with other legal institutions, would be far from excellent.

Thus, a close scrutiny of Ross's analysis leads to two crucial observations. Concepts such as *tû-tû* – and, more broadly, language – play a double role in legal thinking, just as mental simulations. On the one hand, abstract linguistic structures have a hermeneutic function, as they facilitate our understanding of the problems we face and the world we live in. This function is mainly indicated by the relationship between cognition and the degree of the coherence of knowledge. On the other hand, language also plays a heuristic role: our ability to employ various linguistic conceptualizations of reality makes it easier for us to cope with new problems. We will consider these two issues in greater detail in Sections 3.3 and 3.4. First, however, it is worth taking a broader look at how language influences the way we think.

3.2 MAN'S GREATEST INVENTION

Karl Popper called language man's greatest invention, arguing that:

> language develops more and more, and is so extremely good at describing reality that there is really very little to be complained of and very much to be wondered at and admired, especially very much to be amazed at that human beings have actually produced this incredibly powerful tool. The power of it is, of course, seen in our moonships and atom bombs. But there are many other things.[13]

[13] Popper, 1996, p. 101.

It would be difficult to disagree with Popper's view in any serious way. Language is indeed unique among the many products of human culture – not because it makes a great impression on us (after all, it is too ordinary and familiar to us to make such an impression), but because without language we could not think and cooperate with each other on such a grand scale. Contrary to Popper's contention that language is a powerful tool for describing reality, its real power resides in the fact that it underlies and shapes our joint cognitive activities.[14] This is manifested in four different dimensions: language objectifies thought, it raises thought to a higher level of abstraction, it allows us to develop theories, and it allows us to conduct a dialogue. It is objectivization, abstraction, theorization, and dialogization that constitute the revolutionary aspects of thinking in language.

In order to understand how language objectifies thought, it is worth following Paul Churchland's insightful observations and taking a bird's-eye view of the functioning of the human brain. The brain receives data from the environment through so-called sensory neurons (e.g. those located on the cone and rod cells of the retina or those in the skin). However, populations of sensory neurons do not form the ultimate representations of the things we perceive; they constitute the first rung in a complex hierarchy of neural structures, where information at one level is processed and transmitted to a higher level.

> And each rung of each of these ladders constitutes a unique cognitive canvas or representational space, a canvas or space with its own structured family of categories, its own set of similarity and difference relations, and its own peculiar take on some enduring aspect of the external world. What happens as sensory information ascends such a ladder is its progressive transformation into a succession of distinct representational formats, formats that embody the brain's background "expectations" concerning the possible ways-in-which the world can be.[15]

In this sense, face recognition, color categorization, and all other cognitive abilities are based on the existence of an adequate neural "ladder." This is because a neural representation of such concepts as "red" cannot be equated with an activation pattern at the level of sensory neurons. "Redness" is part of a whole conceptual system coded in a complex hierarchy of neural networks. In this structure, information from a lower level is processed and transmitted to a higher level, which is why the ability to recognize the red color and to distinguish it from the other colors is determined by the overall configuration of synaptic weights in whole complexes of neural populations.

Importantly, both perception and action are represented in the way just described: "the brain's representations of the world's enduring categorical and causal structure (its 'factual' knowledge), and the brain's representations of its various acquired motor skills and abilities (its 'practical' knowledge), are both

---

[14]   Cf. Brożek, 2016b, p. 85ff.
[15]   Churchland, 2012, p. 35.

embodied in the carefully sculpted metrics of similarities and differences that provide lasting structure to each one of the brain's many activation spaces."[16] Therefore, contrary to various philosophical theories and common views, there is no insurmountable gap between the representations of perception and the representations of action.[17]

Another important aspect of the human mind is that patterns of neural activation emerge in a long-term process of experiencing and learning the world. We are not born with the ability to distinguish between red and orange or between male and female faces. Our brains are designed in such a way that patterns of neural activation emerge over time and form hierarchies of neural networks that underlie categorization and conceptualization of the ways in which we perceive and act in the world. Thus, our mental representations are embodied and action oriented. They emerge from our bodies' interaction with the environment and are shaped by what we do, and not only by what we passively experience.[18]

Let us now consider the situation in which language comes on the scene of our evolution. What impact does it have on our cognitive processes? The answer is simple: it unifies them. When a baby is learning to speak, its conceptual maps acquire a structure that is typical of a given linguistic community. Color categorization provides a good example here. The problem of the relationship between language use and the ability to distinguish colors was already addressed by nineteenth-century researchers. For example, in his classic 1859 study W. E. Gladstone argued that the ancient Greek vocabulary related to color terms was extremely poor and he went so far as to claim that "the organ of colour and its impressions were but partially developed among the Greeks of the heroic age."[19] The influence of language on color perception became the object of insightful empirical research in the second half of the twentieth century. Over 50 years of ongoing debate have given rise to two views: absolutism and relativism. The absolutists argue that the language we use does not have any significant effect on the way we perceive colors; it can only influence the ways in which we communicate the perceptions. By contrast, the relativists, who represent the broad tradition of linguistic relativism pioneered by Benjamin Lee Whorf,[20] claim the opposite: that the linguistic categorization of colors has a fundamental effect on their perception. Today, both views seem to be wrong, with each reflecting only part of the truth. Linguistic categorization of colors is not completely arbitrary or culture-dependent since there are biologically conditioned limits to any "dictionary of colors"; however, staying within those limits, different languages may impose dramatically different categorizations, which can have an impact not only on the way people speak of colors but also on how they

[16] Ibid., p. 49.
[17] Barsalou, 1999, p. 578.
[18] Cf. Brożek, 2016b, p. 9ff.
[19] Gladstone, 2010, p. 488.
[20] Cf. Kay & Kempton, 1984.

perceive them.[21] This is a good illustration of the fact that using the same language unifies cognition. Of course, there may be a certain degree of idiosyncrasy even among members of the same culture, but the variation is much smaller than it would be without language. Individuals who use different languages perceive the world and account for people's behavior in different ways, even though the extent of the differences is debatable.

Let us consider an example connected with the understanding of intentions and mental states. The language of the Ilongot tribe, who inhabit the Philippines, has the word *rinawa*,[22] whose closest English equivalent is the word "mind." The problem is that the word not only refers to thoughts and feelings, but is also used to designate various social contexts, fertility, and health. Moreover, *rinawa* is not unique to human beings; it is also attributed to animals and plants. Accordingly, when the Ilongot people try to understand other people's behavior, they do not focus on their beliefs and desires but rather on social relations and the external causes of actions.[23] However, we do not have to study endemic languages in order to find similar conceptualizations of people's behavior. For example, it has been observed that Asian people explain people's behavior by referring to situational factors, while representatives of Western cultures tend to focus on individual factors.[24] A Chinese newspaper published an article about a mass murder, highlighting the fact that the murderer had recently been made redundant and that his superior was his personal enemy; the article also drew an analogy with a murder committed in Texas a few months before. By contrast, in an article about a similar event, the *New York Times* concentrated on the fact that the murderer manifested violent tendencies and was a martial arts enthusiast, at the same time suggesting that he was mentally unstable.[25]

It is easy to conclude that such dramatic differences in understanding human behavior may be of fundamental importance in law. For an American – and, more broadly, for representatives of Western cultures – the purpose of the law is to regulate behavior, and individual people are seen as mainly, if not solely, responsible for their actions. By contrast, in Chinese culture law is understood in a different way: as an organic and by no means the most important part of social order, which cannot be enclosed in a catalogue of abstract and general rules; one that is largely situational and pragmatic in nature and according to which human behavior must be evaluated in particular social contexts and regarded as an aggregate effect of various "forces" rather than a consequence of an individual's decisions only.[26]

[21]   Cf. Kay & Regier, 2006.
[22]   Cf. Lillard, 1998.
[23]   Ibid., p. 12.
[24]   Cf. Morris & Peng, 1994.
[25]   Cf. ibid.
[26]   Cf. Sheehy, 2006.

Apart from objectifying thought, language also makes it more abstract. However, it must be noted that the concept of abstraction is far from clear-cut and its different understandings can lead to confusion.[27] Contemporary philosophy and linguistics distinguish at least three different, though related, senses of "abstraction."[28] First of all, abstraction can be understood as "mere omission" of certain properties of a given object or situation that are considered irrelevant from the perspective of the problem under consideration. When attempting to teach a person the complex conceptual structures of the penal law, we will disregard that person's height or eye color; however, the person's experience, knowledge of the foundations of law, intelligence, memory, or cognitive style may be regarded as significant factors. Secondly, abstraction can be equated with generalization if it consists in indicating the properties that are common for a given set of entities. I employ abstraction in this sense when I define a square as a plane figure with four equal straight sides and four right angles or when I state that a human being is a rational animal. Thirdly, abstraction can be understood as decontextualization. When we discover the laws of physics (e.g. the second law of thermodynamics: "the total entropy of an isolated system can never decrease over time") or principles of psychology (e.g. according to a law of Gestalt psychology, similar things tend to appear grouped together), we look for such statements which "fit" as many different contexts as possible. The second law of thermodynamics abstracts away from the properties of a physical system (except that it must be isolated) and from the nature of the processes that occur in it, while the Gestalt law of similarity does not say anything about the nature of the things, their number, or the circumstances in which they are perceived.

The three understandings of abstraction – as "mere omission," generalization, and decontextualization – correspond to the classical definition of abstraction formulated by Aristotle. On his approach, the Ancient Greek word αφαιρεσις designated "a specific operation of the intellect consisting in detaching and retaining some property from a thing [or event]."[29] The difference between "mere omission," generalization, and decontextualization boils down to the *goal* of "detaching and retaining some property" – it may be either indicating the properties that are relevant to the problem under consideration, or finding the common features (similarities) in a given set of entities, or else seeking an adequate account of as broad a class of phenomena as possible.

It must also be emphasized that abstraction is not limited to language use.[30] As already mentioned, the human brain creates special conceptual maps: long-term training and interaction with the environment lead to the emergence of durable patterns of neural activity, which underlie the categorization of objects and events. This mechanism ignores some of the stimuli impinging on sensory receptors, while

---

[27] Cf. Angelelli, 2004.
[28] Cf. Williams et al., 2017.
[29] Entry "abstraction" in Maryniarczyk, 2009.
[30] Cf. Barsalou & Wiemer-Hastings, 2005.

at the same time taking others into consideration; hence, it can be concluded that it performs the operation of abstraction. Language not only supports this ability but also significantly contributes to its development.[31] We can surmise that in the prelinguistic phase of human phylogenesis there appeared mental representations of such objects as "tree" or "river." It is unlikely, however, for the human being to have developed such concepts as "plant," "animal," "being," etc. without language. Moreover, the use of language brings to the surface and makes it possible to reflect on the relationships between concepts, thereby enabling us to formulate abstract principles.

Let us consider the following example. It can be assumed that prelinguistic human communities had some social rules: certain ways of behaving were "allowed," while others were "forbidden" (I put these words in inverted commas because the expression of deontic modality, such as permission or command, is impossible without language; therefore, to be more precise, we should say that certain kinds of behavior were typical in those communities and were met with neutral or positive reactions, while others were untypical and triggered negative reactions).[32] In the minds of the members of those communities there emerged conceptual maps that categorized different kinds of behavior, associating them with positive or negative social emotions. There also appeared patterns of reaction to behavior that was regarded as negative. It can be argued that such systems of social rules were very complex, as they were based on numerous categories of behavior and reactions to it; it can also be assumed that there were significant differences among the corresponding conceptual maps in individuals belonging to a given community.

Let us now consider how the appearance of language affects the situation described. In order to be able to address this problem, it is worth examining some of the rules from one of the oldest legal documents, the Code of Hammurabi:

§6. If a man steals the property of a god (temple) or palace, that man shall be put to death; and he who receives from his hand the stolen (property) shall also be put to death.

§7. If a man purchases silver or gold, manservant or maid servant, ox, sheep, or ass, or anything else from a man's son, or from a man's servant without witnesses or contracts, or if he receives (the same) in trust, that man shall be put to death as a thief.

§8. If a man steals ox or sheep, ass or pig, or boat – if it be from a god (temple) or a palace, he shall restore thirtyfold; if it be from a freeman, he shall render tenfold. If the thief has nothing wherewith to pay, he shall be put to death.

§14. If a man steals a man's son, who is a minor, he shall be put to death.

---

[31]   Cf. Dove, 2014.
[32]   Cf. Brożek, 2013b, p. 44ff.

§25. If a fire breaks out in a man's house and a man who goes to extinguish it casts his eye on the furniture of the owner of the house, and takes the furniture of the owner of the house, that man shall be thrown into that fire.[33]

What is striking about this catalogue of offences is the amount of detail in which the different instances of theft are described. Stealing property belonging to a temple or a ruler is clearly regarded as different from stealing the property of fellow citizens; appropriating gold or silver is different from stealing farm animals; and a special category of offence – along with a special type of punishment – is assigned to the stealing of property by a person who is supposed to assist in extinguishing a fire. The regulations contained in the Code of Hammurabi are, then, casuistic in nature since they distinguish between very similar events. However, in comparison with the systems of rules of prelinguistic communities, the legal realm of the times of Hammurabi is considerably different. On the one hand, the existence of linguistically expressed rules of conduct undoubtedly contributes to the objectivization of thinking about people's behavior, thereby unifying the conceptual maps in the minds of Hammurabi's subjects. On the other hand, the Code of Hammurabi shows evidence of linguistic abstraction at work as it makes use of quite general conceptual categories, such as "stealing" or the typical kinds of punishment (death or return of the stolen property or its multiple). In other words, what we have to do with here is a more abstract and coherent pattern of thinking about human behavior.

Let us now compare the provisions of the Code of Hammurabi with the Polish Penal Code, where Article 278 §1 states: "Whoever, with the purpose of appropriating, wilfully takes someone else's movable property shall be subject to the penalty of deprivation of liberty for a term of between 3 months and 5 years." Cultural differences aside (such as the fact that there is no slavery these days), it can be argued that Article 278 §1 of the Penal Code covers all the offences described in the above-mentioned regulations from the Code of Hammurabi (and many others). This is the case because it is much more abstract. It must be noted, however, that it is not the only regulation taken into consideration in making a judgment concerning criminal liability. In order to find a person guilty of an offence, one also has to take into consideration the regulations in the general part of the Polish Penal Code, which specify the conditions of criminal liability in all types of offence. For example, in accordance with Article 1 of the Penal Code, criminal liability "shall be incurred only by a person who commits an act prohibited under penalty, by a law in force at the time of its commission," but "a prohibited act whose social consequences are insignificant does not constitute an offence" and "the perpetrator of a prohibited act does not commit an offence if guilt cannot be attributed to him at the time of its commission." Moreover, there is no offence if the act is committed under any of the circumstances that exclude guilt or unlawfulness, such as: necessary defense (Article 25),

[33] Harper, 1904.

state of emergency (Article 26), cognitive, medical, technical, or economic experiment (Article 27), justifiable mistake (Articles 28–30), and serious mental disease, mental deficiency, or other mental disturbance that precludes the perpetrator from recognizing the significance of the act or controlling their conduct (Article 31). The general part of the Polish Penal Code also specifies the forms of offence: commission, attempt, preparation, incitement, and abetment. The articles that regulate these issues are abstract in the sense that they apply to all types of prohibited acts specified in the special part of the Penal Code. Thus, they delineate the structural elements that are common to all possible offences. There is a similar situation in other branches of law. For example, apart from regulations pertaining to particular types of contract, such as sale, rental, lease, lending for use, or loan, the Civil Code also includes general regulations that describe the structure of any legal contract.

A comparison of how legal regulations were formulated in the times of Hammurabi and today indicates a tendency toward abstraction, resulting in the fact that modern legal regulations cover whole classes of acts, which are broader than the casuistic statements contained in ancient codes of law and, at the same time, "blind" to various particular features of human behavior. The modern penal code speaks of "appropriating someone else's movable property," without mentioning gold, silver, cattle, ox, swine, or boats; it requires that the judge, particularly while deciding on the penalty, should take into consideration the circumstances in which the act was perpetrated but it does so without making particular statements, like demanding a more severe and very particular penalty to be imposed on a person who has robbed a burning house.

What do we get by employing such abstract concepts as "movable property"? It seems that the use of a more abstract conceptual framework simplifies our worldview. "Movable property" is a category that includes many types of entity; it is irrelevant whether they are small or large, man-made, or created by nature. The concept of "movable property" may be "blind" to many features of the situation under consideration but, at the same time, it is relatively easy to use. Let us imagine what would happen if the Penal Code included different regulations for the theft of particular things (e.g. apples produced in the European Union whose weight does not exceed 100 grams and that are not entirely bright red in color; blue bicycles that have been repaired by a certain workshop located on Park Avenue in New York; telephones manufactured in China on January 15–20, 2016; and so on). Such an ultra-casuistic system of legal regulations would be very difficult to apply; the use of abstract concepts introduces order into the system and makes it simple enough to be effectively applied.

This example illustrates the effect of the use of abstract language on our thinking. This effect can be summarized as ignoring the content and appreciating the form. The use of more and more abstract conceptual categories enables us to discern the relationships among them, rather than merely focusing on their embodied meanings. If we used a language in which the key role was played by very concrete expressions, especially proper names ("Aristotle talked with Plato about the *Symposium*"), it would be difficult to imagine the development of logic. Once we start using abstract language ("People are animals," "Animals have material souls"), formal logical considerations become a natural thing. In other words, abstraction creates a space for analysis and the use of formal relations among concepts, thereby allowing us to discern patterns in our thinking.

Another property of thinking in language, which is strictly connected with abstraction, is theorization. Language allows us to build theories, structured sets of statements concerning a particular field of experience. This makes it possible to organize our knowledge of the world into ever larger and more coherent structures, which makes it easier for us to solve problems. Let us imagine that the Penal Code consists of one regulation only: "Whoever, with the purpose of appropriating, wilfully takes someone else's movable property shall be subject to the penalty of deprivation of liberty for a term of between 3 months and 5 years." Let us assume that Adam, passing by the table at which John was sitting, surreptitiously put John's mobile phone in his own pocket and quickly went away. Let us also assume that Adam has blue eyes, suffers from a serious form of schizophrenia, usually wears black clothes, has a very low IQ, and likes ginger ale. What mental operations does a judge have to perform in order to decide whether Adam should be sent to prison?

Let us note that our Penal Code with one rule employs very abstract language. It does not say anything about mobile phones or putting something in one's pocket; instead, it uses such concepts as "movable property" or "taking with the purpose of appropriating." A judge who is to apply such a regulation is faced with a tough challenge. They can resort to their linguistic intuition and decide that a mobile phone is movable property (it is called "mobile" after all!). However, can Adam's behavior be described as taking a thing "with the purpose of appropriating"? Recorded by closed-circuit television, the action may seem totally accidental. Besides, Adam suffers from schizophrenia and, according to psychiatrists, the disease often precludes the patient from deciding on a goal and working toward its realization. The fact that Adam has blue eyes, wears black clothes, and likes ginger ale is surely irrelevant in the evaluation of his behavior, but this conclusion can only follow from the judge's own knowledge of the world, rather than from their knowledge of the law. And what about Adam's intelligence – should the judge take it into account? A person with a low IQ may not be expected to understand a legal regulation, especially one that is not straightforward to an intelligent and educated judge!

The situation becomes clearer if we assume that the Penal Code also includes the general regulations (i.e. the articles pertaining to penal liability and the circumstances that exclude the perpetrator's guilt or unlawfulness of the act). In particular, the judge could decide that Adam is not subject to the penalty of imprisonment if the Penal Code included the provision that "serious mental disease, mental deficiency, or other mental disturbance that precludes the perpetrator from recognizing the significance of the act or controlling his conduct"[34] is a circumstance that excludes guilt.

Of course, a theory that, apart from the rule concerning theft, also includes general regulations pertaining to criminal liability does facilitate deciding particular cases, but it is not free from imperfections. On reading that "penal liability shall be incurred only by a person who commits an act prohibited under penalty, by a law in force at the time of its commission,"[35] but "a prohibited act whose social consequences are insignificant does not constitute an offence"[36] and "the perpetrator of a prohibited act does not commit an offence if guilt cannot be attributed to him at the time of its commission,"[37] we can sometimes have reasonable doubts as to the proper understanding of the abstract concepts used in these statements, such as "act," "insignificant social consequences," or "guilt." This problem can be addressed by elaborating and clarifying the theory, which – at least in the context of the continental legal systems – is done by legal doctrine. For example, it can be assumed that "an act is only such behavior which is characterized by elements that enable, in accordance with the system of values created in the development of our civilization, criminal liability to be based on the fragment of reality coinciding with human behavior";[38] that the significance of social consequences is determined based on the analysis of the kind and nature of the good that has been violated, the extent of the caused or pending damage, the manner and circumstances in which the act was perpetrated, the importance of the duties neglected by the perpetrator, the form of the intent, the perpetrator's motivation, the kind of the rules of caution that have been violated, and the extent of their violation;[39] while "the perpetrator's guilt is determined when they can be accused of not taking heed of a legal norm while committing a penal and criminal act despite the fact that they could have been expected to obey the legal norm. ... Therefore, guilt is an unjustified fault in the decision-making process, assessed from the point of view of social and ethical criteria."[40]

These types of dogmatic theories still employ abstract language: they embed legal regulations in a broader context and paraphrase them (these two procedures were discussed in Chapter 2). Embedding the regulation concerning theft in the theory of general principles of criminal liability or accepting that the significance of social consequences is assessed according to particular criteria makes the relevant legal regulations – those penalizing theft and those excluding criminal responsibility on account of minor significance of social consequences – part of a larger conceptual structure. Paraphrasing such concepts as "act" or "guilt" also enables their

---

[34] Article 31 §1 of the Polish Penal Code.
[35] Article 1 §1 of the Polish Penal Code.
[36] Article 1 §2 of the Polish Penal Code.
[37] Article 1 §3 of the Polish Penal Code.
[38] Wróbel & Zoll, 2004, p. 30.
[39] Ibid., pp. 37–38.
[40] Ibid., pp. 40, 41.

integration into the existing theoretical constructs (e.g. the system of values developed by our civilization). This, in turn, facilitates positive and negative exemplification, thereby making it easier to decide whether a particular event falls within the application scope of a given legal regulation. The judge does not have to rely exclusively on an abstract regulation because they have a much broader cognitive structure at their disposal, one offering a relatively coherent view of the world.

This discussion shows that theorization helps to unify our knowledge of the world, such as the knowledge required to decide criminal or contractual liability. In order to understand what unification is about, let us take a look at a totally different field of knowledge, namely physics. Before James Clerk Maxwell's 1861 discoveries, electricity and magnetism were accounted for with the use of two different and unrelated theories. However, Maxwell discovered, and expressed in the exact language of mathematics, that electricity and magnetism are in fact two manifestations of the same phenomenon – electromagnetism. The development of quantum mechanics and later discoveries allowed another unification, that of electromagnetism with weak interactions, in the form of the so-called quantum field theory. Contemporary physicists strive to make further steps on the path to the unification of all basic physical interactions into one theory: they want to integrate the theory of electroweak interaction with quantum chromodynamics into a grand unified theory and the latter one, along with general relativity, into a theory of everything.[41] Such a course of action may afford a better understanding of the world, but:

> the kind of understanding provided by science is global rather than local. Scientific explanations do not confer intelligibility on individual phenomena by showing them to be somehow natural, necessary, familiar, or inevitable. However, our overall understanding of the world is increased; our total picture of nature is simplified via a reduction in the number of independent phenomena that we have to accept as ultimate.[42]

We can look at unification in any field of knowledge in a similar way. If the Penal Code did not contain the general part with the principles of criminal liability unified for the whole legal order and if there were no legal-dogmatic theories at our disposal, we could only engage in unrelated casuistic considerations of many different types of offence. Our view of the penal law would then be more fragmentary, thereby making our understanding of its institutions much less coherent. Just as abstraction allows us to ignore various aspects of reality that are irrelevant from the perspective of the goals of law, theorization brings order into the legal conceptual framework. Of course, striving for unification at all costs may lead to undesirable consequences. Thus, we could wonder whether implementing the same standards for the assessment of behavior in penal law and in legal regulations pertaining to civil liability (e.g. the

---

[41] See e.g. Barrow, 1991.
[42] Friedman, 1974, p. 18.

same understanding of perpetration, its forms, guilt, etc.) would have an advantageous or detrimental effect. For example, removing strict liability from civil law, which would be a consequence of such a unification, does not seem to be a reasonable idea.

Finally, let us consider the fourth way in which language shapes legal thinking: dialogization. The possibility of formulating more or less elaborate theories in language enables the development of alternative solutions to problems, their comparison and criticism. It must be noted, though, that the ability to adopt alternative points of view is not contingent on the use of language. On the contrary: cognitive and evolutionary scientists agree that the human ability to ascribe mental states to other people (i.e. to understand that they have their own views, adopt their own goals, and aim at their realization) is, besides learning by imitation, one of the "driving wheels" of cultural evolution.[43] As stated by Michael Tomasello,[44] from the phylogenetic point of view, "modern human beings evolved the ability to 'identify' with conspecifics, which led to an understanding of them as intentional and mental beings like the self." In historical (as opposed to evolutionary) time, "this enabled new forms of cultural learning and sociogenesis, which led to cultural artifacts and behavioral traditions." Finally, from the ontogenetic point of view,

> human children grow up in the midst of these socially and historically constituted artifacts and traditions, which enables them to (a) benefit from the accumulated knowledge and skills of their social groups; (b) acquire and use perspectively based cognitive representations in the form of linguistic symbols ... and (c) internalize certain types of discourse interactions into skills of metacognition, representational redescription, and dialogic thinking.[45]

Let us take a closer look at these statements as their import is of crucial significance, although not necessarily clear. When we say that language developed in a social context, as a form of joint action, we put forth a hypothesis that may seem trite; yet, when we examine the claim more closely, we can reach conclusions that are far from obvious. Textbooks on logic, philosophy of language, and grammar tend to characterize language as a system of symbols that can be used to describe reality. If evolutionary scientists are right, however, the basic function of language is different: it allows us to influence one another, to understand other people's situations and to coordinate joint efforts. In other words, the "natural environment" of language is dialogue rather than monologue. The fact that we can describe an object in detail, formulate general laws of nature, or tell fascinating stories is secondary to the dialogic dimension of language. Representing a philosophical tradition that looks at the findings of the natural sciences with a deal of mistrust, Hans Georg Gadamer has aptly expressed this idea:

---

[43] Cf. Tomasello, 1999; Brożek, 2013b.
[44] Tomasello, 1999, p. 10.
[45] Ibid., p. 10.

"text" must be understood as a hermeneutical concept. This means that the text will not be approached from the perspective of grammar and linguistics, divorced from any content that it might have. That is to say, it is not going to be viewed as an end product whose production is the object of an analysis whose intent is to explain the mechanism that allows language as such to function. In contrast, from the hermeneutical standpoint – which is the standpoint of every reader – the text is a mere intermediate product [*Zwischenprodukt*], a phase in the event of understanding that, as such, certainly includes a certain amount of abstraction, namely, the isolation and reification that is involved in this very phase.[46]

It therefore transpires that the dialogical dimension of thinking in language is a manifestation of a more fundamental phenomenon: the human mind is a dialogue device rather than a vehicle for lonely expeditions in search of the truth. It enables us to justify our beliefs and actions to others, persuade them to share our views, and analyze their arguments.[47] Intuition is insufficient to realize these goals; it may help us to make a quick assessment of a given situation and suggest a course of action, but it will prove useless if we face completely new circumstances or if the problem we face needs to be examined from a different point of view. Imagination will fare better in this respect; we can perform mental simulations of various situations or even try to imagine what the world looks like from another person's point of view. However, imagination has serious limitations: it can only deal with concrete situations and, more importantly, is not a means of communication. Only language – even in its simplest form, based on gestures and deprived of the symbolic character – can function as a means of dialogic thinking.

Let us take an example to illustrate the dialogic dimension of thinking in language. In the previous chapter, we considered the *Adams v. New Jersey Steamboat Co.* case. It concerned a situation in which a certain amount of money was stolen from Mr Adams's cabin on a steamer belonging to New Jersey Steamboat Co. despite the fact that the door to the cabin had been locked. The passenger claimed a compensation from New Jersey Steamboat Co., but the problem was that there had been no precedent in the US legal system that could be directly applied to Mr Adams's case. However, certain similar cases had been previously decided. On the one hand, US courts of law had decided that an innkeeper could be held responsible for the loss incurred by the guests even if there was no evidence of negligence on the innkeeper's part (an instance of strict liability); on the other hand, a carrier of sleeping cars could be held responsible for the losses incurred by the passengers only when found guilty (i.e. if negligence on the carrier's part could be demonstrated).[48]

In Chapter 2, I argued that imagination must have played a crucial role in deciding the *Adams* case. The judge may have mentally simulated Adams's situation

---

[46] Gadamer, 2007, p. 169.
[47] Cf. Mercier & Sperber, 2017.
[48] Cf. Weinreb, 2005, pp. 41–45.

and registered the arising intuitions; the judge may also have compared those intuitions with the ones triggered by imagining a situation in which the theft took place in an inn or a sleeping car; finally, the judge may have applied the principle of variability to see if the intuitive reaction would change if Adams had behaved in a different way (e.g. if he had not locked the cabin). All this may have proved useful, but something else was of crucial importance in the case in question. The judge's task was not to answer the question whether the *Adams* case was more similar to that of *Pinkerton* (theft in an inn) or to that of *Carpenter* (theft in a sleeping car), but to decide whether New Jersey Steamboat Co. was strictly liable or their negligence had to be established. It is only in this way that the decision on the *Adams* case could have been incorporated in the "bloodstream" of US law. Let us also observe that the problem itself – strict liability or negligence – could not have been addressed if there had been no previous court decisions and abstract conceptualizations of similar cases associated with them. Thus, the most important feature of the *Adams* case was its dialogical character.

Let us now consider what would happen if the case at hand had been deprived of its dialogical dimension. For example, let us suppose that US courts of law had never considered the liability of innkeepers before or that they had decided that, just as carriers of sleeping cars, they could be held responsible only if found negligent. In such a situation, the *Adams* case would have been similar only to those precedents in which the service provider was held responsible for a loss incurred by the customer only if there was evidence of particular negligence on the service provider's part. This would considerably impoverish the ways in which we think of the case in question.

First of all, the theories and conceptualizations of the world that we accept come with numerous implicit assumptions which we cannot become aware of only by analyzing the accepted statements.[49] If I see a table in full light, I can state with high certainty that its color is brown. If I see another table in semidarkness and if that table evokes similar color sensations, I will probably say that "it seems" brown. This is a very natural way to express things, but it heavily depends on certain unconsciously made assumptions. In particular, it is assumed here that perceiving an object under "optimal" conditions (for instance, in adequate light) allows us to discover its "real" properties. Nevertheless, this is merely an illusion caused by the fact that the mind usually operates in a particular type of environment. If we mostly lived in semidarkness, a table seen in such conditions would be brown, while it would only "seem" brown in bright light.[50] In order to understand this, though, we need to question something that we tacitly accept. As Paul Feyerabend put it, "how can we possibly examine something we are using all the time? ... How can we discover the kind of world we presuppose when proceeding as we do?"[51] He answers: "we need

[49]   Cf. Feyerabend, 1993.
[50]   Ibid., p. 22.
[51]   Ibid., p. 22.

a dream-world in order to discover the features of the real world we think we inhabit."[52] In other words, a full understanding of the accepted theories, along with all the implicit assumptions, is impossible without contrasting them with alternative theories, even if the latter are obviously false. This is also true in legal cognition. If liability based on negligence was the only option that could be taken into consideration in the *Adams* case, it would be difficult to discern all the assumptions that are tacitly made (e.g. that there is no need to identify the special features of certain types of services if all of them are subject to the same regime of contractual or tort liability). In other words, because of dialogization, it is easier to understand the problem considered by the court in the *Adams* v. *New Jersey Steamboat Co.* case.

Secondly, identifying the contrasts between two alternative solutions to a given problem allows us to find ways to improve them. A comparison of an innkeeper's liability with the situation of sleeping car carriers makes it possible to "expose" the conditions that have to be met in the relation between a service provider and a customer in order for the first of them to be held strictly liable. One such condition is, in particular, the trust that the guests place in the innkeeper. If the principle of negligence was not an alternative option in this case, we would not need to specify the conditions for strict liability and, as a result, we would have a much less useful and more cumbersome conceptual apparatus.

Thirdly, the dialogical dimension of thinking in language opens the way for justifying the claims we put forth. If the judge had only considered the analogy with the *Pinkerton* case (theft in an inn) in the *Adams* case, and decided that New Jersey Steamboat Co. could be held liable on the no-fault basis, such a decision would have been justified to a certain extent; however, the decision is much more convincing if it follows from the comparison of alternative points of view! A court decision that results from the comparison of alternative solutions has greater legitimacy than a decision reached in a "dialogical vacuum." This is particularly significant in law, where it is impossible to apply other criteria for justification, such as verification or falsification.[53]

In view of this analysis, there can be no doubt that language has a considerable influence on the way we think: it objectifies thought, elevates it to a higher level of abstraction, enables the use of theories, and finally encourages and strengthens the dialogical aspect of thinking. Because of all this, thinking in language – although it is impossible to fully separate it from other cognitive abilities – goes far beyond that which can be offered by intuition and imagination. Of course, it must be borne in mind that thinking is never limited to language, even if introspection suggests it is. The use of abstract language, complex theory construction, and comparison of arguments are not ends in themselves; they rather help us to create a framework

---

[52] Ibid., p. 22.
[53] Cf. Rescher, 1977.

for our intuitions and mental simulations. Language provides us with a common formal structure that has to be filled with (conscious or unconscious) conceptual content. In this way, however, language allows us to think about things that we could not otherwise think about. "Language, like the beaver's dam, is a collectively constructed trans-generational phenomenon. But human language, unlike the beaver's dam, provides our species with a distinctive, general purpose cognitive niche: a persisting, though never stationary, symbolic edifice whose critical role in promoting thought and reason remains surprisingly ill-understood."[54]

3.3 LIMITS OF UNDERSTANDING

Many different philosophical schools, from the Oxford School of Ordinary Language to Gadamer's hermeneutics, stress that understanding is impossible without language.[55] Although this claim may be somewhat exaggerated,[56] there can be no doubt that language enables us to understand reality in a particular, extremely complex way. A question arises then: how do the mechanisms of objectivization, abstraction, theorization, and dialogization shape our understanding of the world? In order to address this question in the context of legal cognition, it is worth analyzing two episodes from the history of law: the development of the institution of *regulae iuris* and the debate on the idea of codification.

The *regulae* were one of the most interesting conceptual tools of Roman law, with some of them, such as *ignorantia iuris nocet* or *nemo plus iuris ad alium transferre potest quam ipse habet*, being still in legal use. On Paulus's definition, formulated at the turn of the third century AD,

> A rule is something which briefly describes how a thing is. The law may not derive from a rule, but a rule must arise from the law as it is. By means of a rule, therefore, a brief description of things is handed down and, as Sabinus says, is, as it were, the element of a case, which loses its force as soon as it becomes in any way defective.[57]

It is worth taking a closer look at this statement. Let us first note that Paulus characterizes a rule as "a brief description of things": rules should be brief and only refer to the essence of a given legal institution. In order to explain the purpose of the brevity, it must be remembered that Roman law – even when it was implemented in the form of laws, or *leges* – was to a large extent casuistic in nature. When we examine the Law of the Twelve Tables, we find not only general but also very specific regulations, such as "If a father thrice surrender a son for sale, the son shall be free from the father" or "If a person has broken or has bruised a bone with hand club, he shall undergo a penalty of 300 copper coins, if to an injured freeman, of 150

---

54   Clark, 2005, p. 257.
55   Cf. Gadamer, 2007; Clarke, 1997; Hacking, 1975.
56   Cf. Brożek, 2013b.
57   Paulus quoted after Atria, 2001, p. 151.

copper coins, if to an injured slave. If a person shall have done simple harm to another, penalties shall be 25 copper coins."[58] *Regulae* constituted a remedy against this casuistry, as they were expressed in a more concise form and in more abstract language. And it may be supposed that the use of rules was quite a natural cognitive procedure; as already mentioned, it is easier to remember, understand, and apply formulations that embody a synthetic look at a fragment of reality without superfluous detail. Thus, simplicity and generality represent a significant cognitive advantage. A similar role was played by the so-called *causae coniectio* in the very formalized Roman legal procedure; Paulus himself mentions it in the third sentence of his characterization of rules, pointing out that a rule "is, as it were, the element of a case" (i.e. a *causae coniectio*). In the *legis actio* procedure in the times of the decemvirs, court hearings took place before a private judge nominated by a *magistratus*. The hearing began with "an outline of the essence [of the case], . . . briefly familiarizing the judge with the merits in the form of a list (*per indicem*). This brief introduction was called *causae coniectio*."[59]

Secondly, Paulus emphasizes that rules do not constitute the source of law, but an elegant and useful way of presenting it. The *regulae* were a means of systematizing the complex legal substance; they captured the similarities between multiple legal cases, thereby helping to navigate through the labyrinth of the *leges*, praetorian edicts, or the Caesarean constitutions. That is why a rule, which is a "summary of a law" rather than the law itself, "loses its force as soon as it becomes in any way defective." In other words, rules did not have a normative character for a Roman lawyer. The problem is that it is difficult to distinguish a normative statement from a simple synthetic description, and doing this requires extraordinary methodological discipline. What might have been natural and easy for a lawyer of the late Republic or early Empire would not be that obvious in later periods, especially in the Middle Ages, when *ius commune* began to develop, partly under the influence of canon law.[60] Over time, the *regulae* became something more than just a "brief description of things": they acquired normative power.

It must also be noted that, although the theoretical reflection on *regulae iuris* emerged only in a later period, rules were familiar to Roman law from the very beginning. It is often pointed out that many of the regulations in the Twelve Tables are succinct statements; for example, *Si in ius vocat, ito. Ni it, antestamino* – "If the plaintiff summons the defendant to court, the defendant shall go. If the defendant does not go, the plaintiff shall call a witness thereto"; or *Si membrum rupserit, ni cum eo pacit, talio esto* – "If a person has broken another's limb, unless he makes agreement for compensation with him, there shall be retaliation in kind." Henryk Kupiszewski argues that

---

[58] Johnson et al., 1961, p. 10.
[59] Kupiszewski, 2013, p. 200.
[60] Cf. Cairns & Plessis, 2010.

the simplicity and matter-of-factness in the treatment of the regulated issues, the brevity and clarity of the expressions and the certainty and beauty of the statements suggest that these dicta were not developed by the *decemviri legibus scribundis* but excerpted by them from the vernacular language. What is impressive here is their rough determinism: *ita ius esto* – "so shall be the law." Behind such expressions one can sense ... men of action, warriors who frame their thoughts clearly and succinctly, people accustomed to orders and discipline.[61]

This historical trajectory of *regulae iuris* – from folk wisdom, expressing a common legal awareness, through a methodologically conceived tool for understanding and teaching law, to normative statements – is quite illuminating. It points to a natural drift toward abstraction as well as the need to break away from casuistic court decisions and to search for patterns in the complex labyrinth of Roman law. And this tendency is hardly surprising: our minds find it easier to solve problems on the basis of a relatively small set of comparatively abstract rules than to apply very concrete and very similar normative rules. It must be borne in mind, though, that the drift toward abstraction was only a tendency that allowed numerous exceptions, rather than a strict rule in legal thinking. A more systematic and conscious attempt to develop an abstract and theory-informed legal order came only with the emergence of a modern approach to legal codification (i.e. in the early modern period).

Historians of law agree that the codification of law is a relatively new idea, despite the fact that various, more or less systematic legal compilations appeared very early in history, the best example of which is the Sumerian Code of Ur-Nammu from the beginning of the twenty-first century BC. The idea of codification emerged and gradually developed in the early modern period. One of its advocates was G. W. Leibniz, who proposed the creation of a new code of laws for the whole of Germany that was to be *brevis, clarus* et *sufficiens* (brief, clear, and sufficient).[62] His proposal embodied the spirit of a period in which René Descartes, through his methodological skepticism, sought to destroy the whole edifice of human knowledge and to build it anew on more durable foundations; Leibniz's own dream was to create a *Demonstrationes Catholicae*, a great system that would expound all the tenets of the faith in a manner that would raise no doubts;[63] and Baruch Spinoza strived to deduct ethical principles *more geometrico* from simple and obvious statements. Those ideas were undoubtedly inspired by mathematics, which offered certainty, clarity, and accuracy, and which could be captured in a coherent system of theorems, and by the progress in the natural sciences, especially physics.

The most famous supporter of the idea of legal codification and its first theorist was Jeremy Bentham. As a sixteen-year-old boy, he attended William Blackstone's Oxford lectures on English law. To say that he did not like those lectures would be

---

[61] Kupiszewski, 2013, p. 208.
[62] Quoted after Sójka-Zielińska, 2010, p. 10.
[63] Cf. Antognazza, 2009, p. 92ff.

a gross understatement. The epithets that he used to criticize Blackstone included such expressions as "the treasury of vulgar errors," "infected with the foul stench of intolerance," "the dupe of every prejudice," and "the abettor of every abuse."[64] What was the source of his overt dislike of Blackstone?

In his monumental, four-volume *Commentaries on the Laws of England* (1765–1769), Blackstone made an attempt to systematize English common law, repeatedly contending that, although it had its flaws, English law was a well-designed normative system; at any rate, it would be difficult to imagine any reasonable alternative. He argued that

> when laws are to be framed by popular assemblies, even of the representative kind, it is too Herculean a task to begin the work of legislation afresh . . . . A single legislator or an enterprising sovereign, a Solon or Lycurgus, a Justinian or a Frederick, may at any time form a concise, and perhaps an uniform, plan of justice . . . . But who, that is acquainted with the difficulty of new-modelling any branch of our statue laws (though relating but to roads or to parish settlements), will conceive it ever feasible to alter any fundamental point of the common law, with all its appendages and consequents, and set up another rule in its stead?[65]

Thus, Blackstone argues for evolutionary progress in law rather than revolutionary; he claims that it is impossible to reject all the existing laws and replace them with new laws at one go. He considered that impracticable if only because of the complexity of the matter and the impossibility of predicting all the circumstances that the law must regulate and because of the fact that it would be extremely difficult to break away from the centuries-old tradition and habits of thinking.

Bentham, one of the most radical reformers of his time, had no such scruples. He thought that English law, based as it was on judicial precedents, is a source of considerable uncertainty, which makes it impossible to take reasonable decisions. And "[t]he grand utility of the law is certainty: unwritten law does not – it cannot – possess this quality; the citizen . . . cannot take it for his guide."[66] Bentham's answer to this problem was codification, or creating a code of laws that "would not require schools for its explanation . . . . It would speak a language familiar to everybody . . . . It would be distinguished from all other books by its greater simplicity and clearness. The father of a family, without assistance, might take it in his hand and teach it to his children."[67] Bentham imagined that such a perfect code of laws would be complete (i.e. it would be characterized by exclusivity: "Whatever is not in the code of laws, ought not to be law"[68]), would have no gaps, and would cover all the issues that should be the focus of law. Such a code of laws would also be adequately

[64] Quoted after Posner, 1976, p. 590.
[65] Blackstone, 1830, vol. 3, p. 267.
[66] Bentham, 1843, vol. 3, p. 206.
[67] Ibid., p. 209.
[68] Ibid., p. 205.

systematized (in many of his papers, Bentham sought to create new taxonomies of law[69]) and comprehensible.[70]

The dispute between Blackstone and Bentham is usually regarded as a clash between a radical reformer and a conservative legal theorist. These are, however, linguistic labels only, and what is really important is the underlying epistemological dimension of the dispute. It can be argued that Blackstone and Bentham disagreed on the nature of legal thinking. Blackstone contended that legal rules could not be too abstract because reality is too complex to be regulated by a simple and coherent normative system. According to him, the legal conceptual apparatus is the result of a time-honored history, and it could not be replaced overnight with something completely new. Such a revolution would surely end in a cognitive disaster: instead of a better understanding of the law, there would be confusion and a decision-making impasse. Bentham ignored the latter problem, but he appreciated the former, claiming that it could be resolved. He wrote: "It is objected to the forming a code of laws, that it is not possible to foresee every case which can happen. I acknowledge that it is not possible to foresee them individually, but they may be foreseen in their species ... With a good method, we go before events, instead of following them."[71]

Thus, Blackstone and Bentham differ in their assessment of the role and significance of abstract theories in legal thinking. Blackstone seeks to construct "local" theories (i.e. small-scale generalizations that would be close to particular legal cases and that would introduce a bit of taxonomic neatness into the complex corpus of common law). He, therefore, follows a strategy that the Roman *regulae iuris* were based on: legal understanding is always rooted in particulars, while the purpose of abstraction, used in moderation, is to maintain order. By contrast, Bentham, influenced by the spirit of an age fascinated by the great success of Newton's physics, believed that the construction of abstract and unified theories was the best way to create just and effective law. Progress can only result from a great theoretical enterprise rather than careful reflection, which cannot do away with legal particulars.

The two opposing viewpoints resemble a debate that has centered for several decades around the nature and limits of scientific explanation. The question is whether scientific explanation is about discovering the mechanism of nature or formulating abstract laws that cover the broadest possible classes of phenomena. One of the advocates of the first approach is Michael Scriven, who has the reader reflect upon the following situation:

> As you reach for the dictionary, your knee catches the edge of the table and thus turns over the ink-bottle, the contents of which proceed to run over the table's edge

[69] Cf. Weiss, 2000, p. 479.
[70] Cf. ibid.
[71] Bentham, 1843, vol. 3, p. 205.

and ruin the carpet. If you are subsequently asked to explain how the carpet was damaged you have a complete explanation. You did it, by knocking over the ink. The certainty of this explanation is primeval. It has absolutely nothing to do with your knowledge of the relevant laws of physics; a cave-man could supply the same account and be quite as certain of it.[72]

What Scriven is suggesting here is that a sophisticated explanatory model based on general laws and deduction is a far cry from our everyday experience. We normally explain facts by referring to other facts; for example, a stain on the carpet is a result of spilling a bottle of ink. We perfectly understand what has happened and why, without recourse to a general law. What is more, such a law (e.g. "Every time a knee knocks against a table with a bottle of ink on it and additional conditions K are met, where K stands for the strength of the knock, etc., the bottle of ink will fall down on the floor") would not help us to explain the event better. Wesley C. Salmon shares Scriven's view, arguing that the goal of science is to discover the mechanisms of nature rather than to formulate explanations that meet particular formal criteria:

there is a different fundamental notion of scientific understanding that is essentially mechanical in nature. It involves achieving a knowledge of how things work. One can look at the world, and the things in it, as black boxes whose internal workings we cannot directly observe. What we want to do is open the black box and expose its inner mechanisms.[73]

Michael Friedman argues for the opposite approach. On his view, the goal of science is to search for ever more fundamental laws, as it was done by Newton, who reduced Kepler's laws of planetary motion to three laws of motion. Friedman contends that scientific explanation must lead to increasing unification: our goal is to describe all reality with as few general laws as possible. At the same time, he observes that this approach contributes to a better understanding of the world, although, as he emphasizes in an already quoted passage,

the kind of understanding provided by science is global rather than local. Scientific explanations do not confer intelligibility on individual phenomena by showing them to be somehow natural, necessary, familiar, or inevitable. However, our over-all understanding of the world is increased; our total picture of nature is simplified via a reduction in the number of independent phenomena that we have to accept as ultimate.[74]

However, Salmon notes that the two kinds of explanation are complementary as they make use of two different kinds of understanding. Unification contributes to increasing "global understanding; in order to understand a situation, we need to

[72] Scriven, 1959, p. 464.
[73] Salmon, 1990, p. 18.
[74] Friedman, 1974, p. 18.

locate its place within a broader picture of the world."[75] On the other hand, though, causal-mechanistic explanations contribute to the "local understanding" of how particular things work. Yet, instead of saying that the two approaches are complementary, it seems better to talk of a continuum of different types of theories and the explanations they offer. At one end, there are concrete theories, which relate to individual events without the use of general laws. When I say that I soiled the carpet because I knocked my knee against the table, which made a bottle of ink fall on the floor, I am not explicitly referring to any law. Instead, I use my knowledge of causal connections, which is implicitly embodied in my brain. Further away from that end of the continuum, there are only slightly more abstract theories, which make use of explicitly stated regularities. The closer we get to the other end of the scale, the more abstract the theories, with the understanding they afford becoming less "local" and "embodied" and more global. Finally, at the other end of the continuum (or close to it), there are theories in the form of axiomatic systems.[76] What is important here is the fact that we could not construct and employ abstract theories without experience in constructing and employing more concrete ones. That is why it may be better to imagine the continuum as a vertical line, with concrete theories at the bottom, offering local understanding, and axiomatic systems at the top; the whole thing shows that abstraction must be rooted in the concrete.

Let us now return to the dispute between Blackstone and Bentham. Blackstone turns out to be an advocate of local understanding and of legal reflection strongly anchored to the concrete. This strategy allows easy application of intuition and imagination, but it does not make full use of the potential offered by language. By contrast, Bentham prefers abstraction and theorization; he believes that this approach will let us achieve a more coherent view of the legal world. It must be noted that each of these two strategies has its disadvantages. Blackstone's approach, strongly based on particular cases, can lead to excessive fragmentation of law, while Bentham and his followers, who strive for the highest degree of the unification of legal knowledge, run the risk of "losing touch with reality." Although unification is a natural tendency in constructing any theory (who would not like to have a simple and universal recipe for solutions to all problems!), in practice we have to seek balance between that which is maximally abstract and that which is concrete and easy to understand. Unification may be highly attractive, but if we succumb to it too much, at best we end up with contentless theories.

This is how thinking in language fulfills its hermeneutic function: not only does it enable local understanding, it also takes us to the level of global understanding. It provides a lawyer with a relatively coherent view of the world, so that they are not limited to a disorderly set of cases. However, abstraction and theorization have their limitations. Even the most sophisticated theories will prove totally useless if we cut

---

[75] Cf. Salmon, 1990, p. 17.
[76] Cf. Brożek, 2016a.

them off from particular experience. The need to find a balance between the abstract and the concrete, between global and local understanding, between thinking in language and the use of intuition and imagination, is a great challenge for the legal mind.

3.4 A NEW COGNITIVE NICHE

Language and thinking with the use of linguistic structures are typically human. Theorists agree that the development of language (along with the other abilities) brought us into a so-called cognitive niche:[77] we can acquire information and reason in order to get resources from the environment. It is because of these unique abilities that humans were able to invent tools and engage in coordinated activities on a grand scale,[78] thereby creating complex social structures and normative systems. Language is more than an effective means of communication or a tool for understanding the world: it is a substance that allows us to construe the world we live in. As Michael Tomasello puts it, "linguistic symbols embody the myriad ways of construing the world intersubjectively that have accumulated in a culture over historical time, and the process of acquiring the conventional use of these symbolic artefacts, and so internalizing these construals, fundamentally transforms the nature of children's cognitive representations."[79]

This creative function of language can be considered from several perspectives. The kinds of problems that biological organisms grapple with are practical in character: get nourishment, find a mate, and avoid danger (e.g. predators). By contrast, apart from these, man also faces other types of problems, which appeared in history only with the development of language. They can be collectively called metaproblems since ultimately they concern the ways in which we approach our theories: their understanding, construction, and assessment. First of all, they include interpretative (meta)problems: when we hear a sentence directed at us or read a text, we seek to understand its meaning. This can be a complex task, especially when we deal with a very abstract text. A second type of (meta)problems connected with the use of language can be characterized as theoretical. Constructing and applying theories is associated with numerous issues: What properties should a good theory have? When should a theory be rejected altogether, and when can we try to modify it? How can we compare alternative accounts of a given phenomenon? Thirdly, thinking in language leads to reflecting on the (meta)problems of persuasion. It is only in the cognitive niche that we can think of the effective ways of persuading others or of the criteria for justifying our beliefs.

Whenever there are problems, there are various ways of solving them. Language allows us to create theories and metatheories whose purpose is to support us in

[77] Cf. Pinker, 2010.
[78] Ibid., p. 8994.
[79] Tomasello, 1999, pp. 95–96.

finding answers to practical, interpretative, and theoretical questions, as well as solutions to problems of persuasion. It must be remembered that problems, just like solutions, do not arise in a vacuum; they have their histories. As noted by Michał Heller, "This must be similar to the Greek drama: there is a situation which gives rise to the plot and the development of various threads that compete with one another and intertwine to create a problem."[80] Reflection in every field of study, including law, involves a series of questions and answers, or problems and theories that constitute more or less successful attempts to solve them.[81] In other words, solutions to problems, at least the more complex ones, tend to form chains of successive theories. Thunder was initially regarded as the expression of the anger of gods, but Aristotle considered lightning to be an effect of a collision between clouds, with the resulting thunder produced when a blow triggered by the lightning hits a mass of dense clouds.[82] Today, we know that thunder is the effect of the rapid expansion of air, whose temperature and pressure had suddenly increased due to lightning. What is important is the fact that the historical theories of thunder, though false, contributed to our current understanding of the problem. Incorrect theories are not discarded for good; they constitute the background for current theoretical pursuits. Moreover, solving a problem often causes the emergence of other problems that have not been considered so far. For example, the discovery of the electrical nature of lightning made Benjamin Franklin pose the question of how houses can be protected against it, which in turn led to the invention of the lightning rod.

Apart from problems and theories, the cognitive niche is also equipped with forms of reasoning; that is, generally speaking, a set of procedures that tell us what to do with theories. A good example is logic, which indicates the correct inferential patterns (i.e. ones in which the truth of the premises guarantees the truth of the conclusions). There are also other, similar modes of thinking, such as rules of reasoning and argumentation, principles of question formation and definition building, rules of induction, probability theory, etc. Thus, forms of reasoning provide us with tools that guide us in thinking of all types of problems: practical, theoretical, and interpretative ones, as well as those connected with persuasion.

The cognitive niche of law includes all these elements. The lawyer's most fundamental task is, undoubtedly, to look for solutions to practical problems; after all, an advocate has to find the best line of defense for their client, a judge has to reach a decision, and the legislator has to formulate legal regulations in such a way as to achieve the desired effect. However, all of this takes place in a very complex world that is full of various conceptions, which is why we constantly come across interpretative, theoretical, and persuasion-related (meta)problems. Judges engage in text interpretation every day to such an extent that their work may be compared, as it was

---

[80] Heller, 2008, p. 99.
[81] Cf. Brożek, 2016b, pp. 118–123.
[82] Cf. Aristotle, 2006, bk. 1, pt. 9.

done by Ronald Dworkin, to writing new passages in a great book called "Law."[83] It would be impossible to write those new passages (i.e. new court decisions) without understanding the contents of the previous chapters; otherwise, we would only have to deal with a set of incoherent and unrelated fragments of text. It is not only judges, though, who face the problem of interpretation: a lawyer must understand the regulations contained in legal codes, statements of legal doctrine, and judicial opinions, as well as the documents and statements produced by those involved in legislation. Law also generates a number of theoretical problems, which can best be seen in theoretical and dogmatic studies. The authors of such studies reflect on how to describe the law, how to create an effective and relatively simple conceptual framework for different branches of law, how to avoid contradiction while reconstructing the complex institutions of tax law, etc. Finally, legal thinking is concerned with persuasion: the lawyer's task is not only to look for solutions to practical problems, those solutions must also be convincing. The history of legal philosophy is full of discussions concerning this issue: Can the reasons given for a court judgment consist in a simple legal syllogism? Is coherence a good measure of the quality of the reasons provided for a court decision? Can a lawyer take the *per fas et nefas* approach or are they bound by some moral standards in this respect?

In view of all these problems, legal thinking is grounded in a very broad and complex theoretical context. We have theories that tell us how to cope with practical problems developed in judicial opinions and legal doctrine. The methodology and philosophy of law mostly deal with the construction of metatheories, which make it easier to cope with problems of interpretation, theory, and persuasion. Examples of such metatheories can be found in the disputes between the advocates of static vs. dynamic approaches to legal interpretation,[84] between the supporters of positivist vs. natural law theories,[85] and between the defenders of argumentative vs. topical nature of legal discourse.[86] I am not going to discuss them in detail here as it would make no sense to repeat discussions that can be easily found in numerous volumes on the philosophy of law. Nevertheless, I would like to point out three issues connected with the nature of theoretical constructions in law. First of all, there are different kinds of theories used in legal thinking. The simplest examples are legal topoi, and among them numerous Roman *regulae iuris* (i.e. concise generalizations of different aspects of Western European "legal consciousness"), such as: *lex retro non agit, ignorantia iuris nocet, lex iniustissima non est lex, impossibilium nulla obligatio est*, etc. They constitute special mini theories that can be invoked to solve particular problems. There are also more complex legal theories covering whole institutions or even branches of law (e.g. theory of criminal liability). It is worth noting that they usually incorporate not only legal regulations but also doctrinal

---

[83]   Cf. Dworkin, 1986.
[84]   Cf. Eskridge, 1987.
[85]   Cf. Finnis, 1980.
[86]   Cf. Stelmach & Brożek, 2006.

theories and judicial opinions. All this constitutes legal knowledge – a broad theoretical background that includes multiple, often mutually contradictory theories.
Secondly, as in other disciplines, the theoretical background in law is pluralist in
nature, with competing theories recommending different approaches to certain
types of problems. It must be emphasized that there is nothing strange about this
situation: the law is constituted jointly by the theories developed as part of it; thus,
being dependent on the theoretical constructs, it does not represent a separate entity
that can be described objectively. Lawyers may have different opinions on how
practical, interpretative, theoretical, or persuasion-related problems should be
solved, and they express them in their theories. And this plurality is a strength rather
than a weakness of law. As already mentioned, the principle of contrast, according to
which alternative theories must be compared, is a very useful problem-solving tool.
Thirdly, different legal traditions prefer particular theoretical constructs and ignore
others. For instance, continental positivism considers law to be independent of
morality and emphasizes the special role of man-made laws along with the logical
and linguistic methods of their interpretation. This means that there can be – and
there are – approaches to legal philosophy that regard certain theories as uncontroversial, thereby rejecting other theoretical solutions.

Lawyers also have a range of argumentative devices, from the basic forms of
reasoning such as the legal syllogism, through various types of argument (*a simile*,
a contrario, a fortiori, *ab exemplo, a loco communi, a loco specifici, a cohaerentia*,
etc.),[87] to canons of legal interpretation (textual, substantive, and deference).[88] It
must be immediately noted, however, that there is nothing like one coherent
"lawyer's toolkit." Different methods of reasoning can lead to differing conclusions;
moreover, depending on the legal tradition, those methods may be differently
structured and employed in different ways. Analogical reasoning serves as
a particularly illuminating example here. In continental positivism, for instance in
various strands of the German *juristische Methodenlehre*, the use of analogy is
regarded as an interpretative device.[89] The existence of a loophole in the law (i.e.
a situation in which one cannot indicate a legal norm that would regulate a given
state of fact) makes it necessary to adopt an interpretation in which the case in
question is treated in the same way as similar cases. By contrast, in non-positivist
approaches, according to which there are both rules and principles in a legal system,
analogy is a method of the application of law: first, one looks for a previously decided
case (or cases) that is similar to the one under consideration; then it is determined
what legal principles underlay the previous decision(s); and finally, the competing
principles are weighed against each other in order to reach a decision.[90] In the
common law tradition, analogy can be regarded as a basic mental operation that

[87]   Cf. ibid., 2006.
[88]   Cf. Wróblewski, 1992.
[89]   Cf. Larenz, 1991; Wróblewski, 1992.
[90]   Cf. Alexy, 2005; Brożek, 2018.

helps to relate a given case to a previous precedent. This can be illustrated as follows: when we are considering a case, for example that of *Adams* v. *New Jersey Steamboat Co.*, we find out that there are similar precedents in US law, such as the *Pinkerton* case. Then, applying what logicians call abductive reasoning, we move on to ask what would a legal rule that covered both the *Adams* and *Pinkerton* cases look like. Such a rule would state that any time the service provider and the customer are bound by a special level of trust, the service provider is strictly liable for any loss incurred by the customer.[91]

It would be a mistake to ask which of these approaches to analogy is correct. There is simply no one correct pattern of analogical reasoning. What we find in textbooks on legal methodology is different (sometimes very different!) understandings of this mental operation. Some of them are closer to the tradition of continental positivism, while others are in line with the fundamental assumptions of common law. It is important to note that we employ the same mental mechanisms in each situation: not only thinking in language, but also intuition and imagination. We use them to place the case in question within a broader context of legal knowledge, and we do that by comparing it with similar, previously decided cases. The comparison is impossible to carry out without resorting to imagination and the intuitions produced by it. On the theoretical level, this procedure can be described and structured in different ways: as a special approach to legal interpretation, as a procedure of weighing the legal principles, or as searching for a ratio decidendi that a given case has in common with some established precedents. This clearly shows that the lawyer's toolkit of mental operations, just like the legal theories at their disposal, are characterized by a certain pluralism, with different legal traditions and paradigms preferring some of the tools and rejecting others.

We can now answer the question of how language fulfills its heuristic function (i.e. how it helps the lawyer to find solutions to problems). Legal knowledge constitutes a reservoir of different theories and forms of reasoning that can be employed to address a new legal problem. Of course, our choice is never arbitrary: the use of some theories rules out the application of others, and different methods of reasoning can lead to totally different conclusions. We are also restricted by our understanding of the "valid law" and, at least to some extent, by our legal tradition, which prefers certain theories and forms of reasoning, while rejecting others. Still, the fact is that the theoretical apparatus we have created with language is an outstanding achievement that enables much faster, much more accurate, and more effective solution of legal problems. If we only had intuition and imagination at our disposal, legal thinking would be much more limited, which can be illustrated with particular examples.

---

[91] Cf. Brewer, 1996, which presents the complex conceptual apparatus that describes this type of reasoning.

Let us first return to the *Van Gend en Loos* case, already analyzed in Chapter 1 and Chapter 2. The Dutch company Van Gend en Loos was charged a higher customs duty as a result of a changed classification of a substance it imported from Germany. The company appealed from that decision to the ECJ, arguing that the imposition of a higher duty was contrary to Article 12 of the Treaty of Rome, which states: "Member States shall refrain from introducing between themselves any new customs duties on imports or exports or any charges having equivalent effect, and from increasing those which they already apply in their trade with each other." In that case, the problem was that Article 12 of the Treaty of Rome explicitly refers to the relations between EEC member states, without mentioning their citizens. What is more, one of the fundamental principles of international law states that international treaties are binding for states and have no direct application to the citizens of the states. Yet, the ECJ decided that Article 12 must be interpreted as directly applicable and as a source of individual rights that shall be protected by national courts, thereby upholding Van Gend en Loos's appeal.

In the previous chapters, I argued that deciding that case must have required intuition, insight, and imagination. The judges must have experienced two conflicting intuitions: a legal one, which told them to regard international treaties as binding for states, rather than citizens; and a moral one, which told them to decide that the Dutch authorities had treated the plaintiff company unfairly. In order to break the deadlock, the judges needed an insight that would allow them to view the problem in a novel way, and imagination must have been helpful in achieving that insight. For example, the Court may have imagined what the situation would look like if there was no Article 12 in the Treaty of Rome; what would happen if the Treaty was only binding for the Netherlands and Germany and if it only concerned customs law; and so on. However, it seems highly unlikely for the Court to have reached its decision by employing intuition and imagination only.

First of all, it must be pointed out that the problem with the *Van Gend en Loos* case would not have arisen if it had not been for language: it is the abstract statements in the Treaty of Rome and other EEC laws that had set the stage for considering such cases. It should also be noted that the Court had various theories to choose from, in particular the classical doctrine of international law that sees treaties as binding for states only. However, the judges decided to reject this theory and construct a new one; but rather than doing that ex nihilo, they used the existing conceptual apparatus. For example, they may have argued that in some cases international law could be a source of obligations and rights for individuals; that such rights do not have to be stated directly as they can be a result of obligations explicitly imposed on other legal entities; or that one legal entity's obligation to refrain from action can be used to infer another legal entity's rights.[92] The Court also

---

[92] ECJ February 5, 1963, Case 26/62 *Van Gend en Loos* v. *Nederlandse Administratie der Belastingen* [1963] ECR 1.

used various forms of reasoning, especially the canons of interpretation pertaining to the structure of the legal system or the values protected by the law. For example, it concluded that the "objective of the EEC Treaty . . . implies that this Treaty is more than an agreement which merely creates mutual obligations between contracting states."[93] It also decided that a "restriction of the guarantees against an infringement of Article 12 by Member States to the procedures under Articles 169 and 170 [which enable the Commission and the Member States to bring before the Court a State which has not fulfilled its obligations] would remove all direct legal protection of the individual rights of their nationals."[94] This clearly shows the significant role of linguistic structures in legal thinking. Admittedly, the judges of the Court must have resorted to intuition and imagination, but it is theories and patterns of reasoning that provided a structure that could be filled with the intuitive or imaginative material.

Let us consider another example. One of the most heated legal debates in recent years concerns the granting of the status of a legal person to autonomous robots – artificial systems that are reactive (they react to changes in the environment), self-controlling (their activity is not directly controlled by other subjects), and goal-oriented (their action is not limited to reacting to changes in the environment).[95] Because technological progress has led to the development of robots that meet these criteria, or will most probably meet them in the near future (e.g. autonomous cars and autonomous weapons systems), the lawyer cannot avoid the question of how to treat them, and in particular if they should be granted the status of a legal person.

Many competing views on this problem have emerged. According to one of them, which can be described as extreme restrictionism, machines – no matter how intelligent or autonomous – may never be granted legal personhood and be held responsible for their actions. This view is usually supported by the argument that human beings have certain unique features, such as intentionality, free will, or consciousness, which seem to represent the most fundamental criteria for legal and moral responsibility and which are lacking in even the most sophisticated robots.[96] On the other end of the spectrum, there is extreme permissivism, according to which law is a flexible tool of social engineering and it can be used to grant the status of a legal person to anyone and anything. On this view, autonomous robots can have legal rights and obligations, just as any other thing: a stone, a river, or a comet. The history of law proves that this is not impossible: legal systems in the past often outlawed human beings (slaves, children, etc.) or gave the status of a legal person to entities with no free will, intentionality, or consciousness (e.g. the Whanganui River in New Zealand).[97]

93   Ibid.
94   Ibid.
95   Cf. Franklin & Graesser, 1997.
96   Cf. Fischer & Ravizza, 2000.
97   Cf. Hutchison, 2014.

There are also less extreme approaches. For example, it is argued that although from a theoretical point of view autonomous robots could be granted legal personhood, that would probably lead to unacceptable consequences and possibility of abuse. Given the experience with legal persons, such as companies or international organizations, the danger is real, not only theoretical.[98] According to yet another view, there are more fundamental arguments against granting artificial systems the status of a legal person. The concept of legal responsibility is deeply rooted in the so-called folk psychology (i.e. in the ways in which we understand and predict our and other people's behavior).[99] We believe that participants in social relations must be characterized by consciousness, intentionality, and free will; this is our "default programme" for interpreting the world. It can be argued, then, that giving the status of a legal person to robots and treating them and human beings on equal terms would be incomprehensible for us and would ultimately fail. This can be illustrated with the notion of legal person: although we accept that a legal person can have rights and obligations, and can even be subject to criminal law, there is a human being behind every legal person and it is their actions that we evaluate, even if it is the legal person that is "credited with" those actions.[100]

In order to solve the problem of the legal status of autonomous robots, and decide whether and to what extent they can or should be regarded as subjects of rights and obligations, we can use different cognitive abilities, including intuition and imagination. Our first intuitive reaction to this problem depends on our legal knowledge and our experience with artificial intelligence, although it may be assumed that the intuitive response will be negative in most of us: autonomous robots should not be granted legal personhood because they are artificial, man-made machines. We can also employ the ability of mental simulation and imagine that the problem does not concern specialized robots (autonomous cars or weapons) but "general-purpose" androids capable of doing anything that a human being can do. Is now our intuitive assessment different? And what if the androids could imitate human behavior so well that we could not tell if we were dealing with a human being or an android? Will it change anything if we assume that half of our society are humans and the other half androids?

Intuition and imagination, however, are not the only tools at our disposal in considering the problem of the legal status of autonomous machines. They enable us to mentally simulate various, even highly counterfactual situations (such as androids whose capabilities far exceed the current technological state of the art) and to register the intuitive reactions that those situations trigger. However, our analysis will be much more comprehensive if we also employ language. First of all, we will then be able to use the existing theories – the notion of a legal personhood, the idea of a technical (instrumental) character of law, the construct of the legal

---

[98]   Cf. Brożek & Jakubiec, 2017.

[99]   Cf. Brożek & Kurek, 2018.

[100] Cf. Brożek & Jakubiec, 2017.

responsibility of legal persons – or historical solutions (e.g. the one that gave an inanimate entity legal rights and obligations). What is important is the fact that we will no longer analyze our problem in a theoretical vacuum; instead, we will consider it against the backdrop of the long history of theoretical reflection on the notion of legal person. It is impossible to look for solutions beyond this framework: we cannot simply create a totally new concept of a legal person that would be completely unrelated to the existing ways of thinking. This fact is a blessing though: a dramatically different conceptual construct would simply be incomprehensible, and it would be impossible to integrate it into our current worldview.

The discussion on the legal status of autonomous robots also illustrates the dialogical dimension of thinking in language. In our attempts to address this peculiar problem, we draw on a broad range of theories in order to propose alternative solutions. Then we compare the theories by employing intuition and imagination. For example, we imagine what would happen if this, rather than that, legislative solution was adopted (Would it not lead to the possibility of abuse? Would it be comprehensible for those to whom the law is addressed?). This helps us to understand the theoretical constructs that we propose (e.g. to discern the strong metaphysical assumptions underlying the restrictionist view), to modify them, and finally to adopt the one that fares best in the scenarios imagined and that best coheres with the broad context of legal knowledge.

This is yet another example that shows that legal thinking must be seen as a constant interplay between intuition, imagination, and language. The architecture of the legal mind is based on these three mechanisms: intuitive reactions shaped by years of experience, mental simulations, and theoretical constructs. They determine the space in which we attempt to solve the problems we have encountered, but they do not indicate a particular procedure or pattern of reasoning that would lead to the best decision. In other words, the aim of this discussion was to characterize the mental toolkit that the lawyer has at their disposal. Now we can ask ourselves yet another question: how can this mental architecture be put to its best use? This question will be considered in the following chapters.

4

Structure

Having described the architecture of the legal mind, identifying in the process the three mechanisms that work in concert to solve legal problems, I would like to shift the focus in this chapter somewhat to consider the structure of legal thinking. The main thesis defended in this chapter is that the structure in question is a product of the combination of two approaches to problem-solving: top-down and bottom-up. The top-down approach is based on the idea that legal reasoning proceeds from abstract rules and ends with concrete decisions; the bottom-up strategy takes previously decided concrete cases, and nothing more, as the point of departure of legal thinking. I will argue in this chapter that neither of the two approaches is sufficient. For very fundamental and general reasons, they fail to deliver their promise of solving legal problems. Thus, I will conclude that legal thinking is non-foundational, necessarily combining the top-down and bottom-up strategies.

Against this background, I will try to identify some principles that may be applied to increase the likelihood of finding an acceptable solution to a legal problem. These will include the principles of experience, caution, exemplification, variability, unification, and contrast. My claim is that while they do not form a unique procedure of solving legal problems, they constitute a very useful "thinking manual" for lawyers to have at their disposal. Mastering these precepts means becoming better in dealing with legal issues.

The thinking manual is a set of instructions for generating hypotheses, yet it is not designed to justify legal decisions. Therefore, at the end of this chapter I will delve into the controversies surrounding the concept of justification in the law. I defend the thesis that there exists no unique standard of legal justification. Instead, I claim that the legal "justification space" is determined by two different but interconnected conceptions: the pragmatic or dialogue-based, and the formal or theory-based. According to the former, a justified legal decision is the one that prevails in a comparison of competing solutions; the latter, in turn, considers a decision (or a belief) justified when it is a part of a theory exhibiting certain formal features.

Before addressing these theoretical issues in detail, I will make a brief digression in order to consider an important debate in US jurisprudence. The protagonists of this discussion included both famous lawyers and philosophers: Oliver Wendell Holmes, Roscoe Pound, John Dewey, and Karl Llewellyn. Their goal was, among other things, to question the central role afforded to logic in legal thinking. Irrespective of whether and to what extent one agrees with them, their insightful observations and somewhat controversial conceptions constitute a perfect point of reference for the considerations that follow.

4.1 AGAINST LOGIC

One of the most famous texts in the history of US jurisprudence was first presented in the form of a lecture delivered by the Massachusetts Supreme Court judge Oliver Wendell Holmes at the beginning of 1897. The audience comprised students and lecturers of the Boston University School of Law. The lecture, entitled "The Path of the Law," was immediately published in *Boston Law School Magazine* of February 1897, and later the same year in *Harvard Law Review*.[1] It is a masterful characterization of law, filled with deep insights and far-reaching ideas. It is usually claimed that in "The Path of the Law" Holmes presents his predictive theory of law as "the prophecies of what the courts will do in fact."[2] This is undoubtedly true, yet the lecture includes so much more: the rejection of the quest for the "nature of law," the idea of utilizing the tools of economics in legal thinking, the critique of law as a set of normative standards, and finally some questions concerning the use of logic in legal reasoning.

Indeed, this was somewhat stronger than mere "questioning" since Holmes speaks of "the fallacy of logical form," which amounts to the claim that logic is "the only force at work in the development of the law."[3] That we tend to commit this fallacy is hardly surprising, since we are accustomed to a certain way of thinking about the world. It consists of identifying and using causal connections, which capture the encountered phenomena in a network of logical relations. "If there is such a thing as a phenomenon without . . . fixed quantitative relations, it is a miracle. It is outside the law of cause and effect, and as such transcends our power of thought, or at least is something to or from which we cannot reason."[4] It is hardly surprising, therefore, that we try to account for the law in the same way: we strive to turn it into a well-determined network of logical connections. This approach is reinforced by legal education. "The training of lawyers is a training in logic. The processes of analogy, discrimination, and deduction are those in which they are most at home. The language of judicial decision is mainly the language of logic. And the logical method

[1] Holmes, 1897.
[2] Ibid., p. 458.
[3] Ibid., p. 465.
[4] Ibid., p. 465.

and form flatter that longing for certainty and for repose which is in every human mind."[5]

Our faith in the means and methods of logic constitutes, according to Holmes, a grave misunderstanding that leads to various dangers and perils. The problem is not that logic has nothing to do with the law but rather that one needs to understand that the legal order cannot be modeled like a branch of mathematics and captured in a coherent system of abstract axioms. "Behind the logical form lies a judgment as to the relative worth and importance of competing legislative grounds, often an inarticulate and unconscious judgment, it is true, and yet the very root and nerve of the whole proceeding."[6] Logical form is of secondary importance; ultimately, every conclusion can be inserted into some logically valid scheme of reasoning. What is of essence in legal thinking is the content, not the form. One should also bear in mind that the opinions that serve to justify legal decisions rarely take the shape of precise, verifiable statements. "Such matters really are battle grounds where the means do not exist for the determinations that shall be good for all time, and where the decision can do no more than embody the preference of a given body in a given time and place. We do not realize how large a part of our law is open to reconsideration upon a slight change in the habit of the public mind."[7] If so, then it is impossible to develop a coherent, ordered, and precise legal system, which would serve as the basis for issuing legal rulings with any kind of "logical certainty." As Holmes puts it in his lectures on the common law:

> The life of the law has not been logic: it has been experience. The felt necessities of the time, the prevalent moral and political theories, intuitions of public policy, avowed or unconscious, even the prejudices which judges share with their fellow-men, have had a good deal more to do than the syllogism in determining the rules by which men should be governed.[8]

Eleven years after Holmes's lecture, on September 25, 1908, another leading light of US jurisprudence, Roscoe Pound, delivered a talk for the members of the Bar Association of North Dakota. Its title was "Mechanical Jurisprudence," and it was published that same year in *Columbia Law Review*.[9] Pound's point of departure was the question about the putative scientific character of jurisprudence, and more importantly an obsession of many of his fellow lawyers to be "scientific." But what does "scientific" mean? According to Pound it effectively amounts to three slogans: conformity to reason, uniformity, and certainty. In 1908, it must have seemed that these were genuine scientific features that had enjoyed enormous success. The Darwinian theory of evolution was still a subject of heated debate, merely 30 years

[5]   Ibid., p. 466.
[6]   Ibid., p. 466.
[7]   Ibid., p. 466.
[8]   Holmes, 1881, p. 1.
[9]   Pound, 1908.

had passed since the groundbreaking works of Pasteur, and ten since the discovery of Roentgen radiation. The beginning of the twentieth century witnessed the first successful powered flights of the Wright brothers, and 1905 was Einstein's annus mirabilis, when he published three articles devoted to the photoelectric effect, Brown's motions, and the special theory of relativity. What was the driving force behind all those spectacular successes? They were the triumph of reason equipped with logic, driven by the dream of a unified, scientific view of the world, and characterized by an unparalleled level of certainty.

The problem is, Pound observes, that the enthusiasts of "scientific jurisprudence" do not really understand the nature of the empirical sciences. They imagine that the "scientific character" of a discipline – be it physics, biology, or jurisprudence – is secured when the theories of that discipline are embodied in a grand, static system of logical connections, which constitutes the basis for producing theorems and solve problems in a purely mechanical way. "But in truth it is not science at all. We no longer hold anything scientific merely because it exhibits a rigid scheme of deductions from a priori conceptions."[10] To the contrary: "The idea of science as a system of deductions has become obsolete, and the revolution which has taken place in other sciences in this regard must take place and is taking place in jurisprudence also."[11]

The need to reject the idea of "mechanical jurisprudence" results from the fact that it brings more trouble and confusion than benefits; in particular, it endorses a view of a static legal order, which is unable to adjust to the changing social reality. In the history of law one can identify periods of the domination of mature and complex yet inflexible theories, where legal reasoning boils down to simple deduction. In such contexts, legal decisions are filled with magic or "decisive" words: "estoppel, malice, privity, implied, intention of the testator, vested and contingent – when we arrive at these we are assumed to be at the end of our juristic search. Like Habib in the Arabian Nights, we wave aloft our scimitar and pronounce the talismanic word."[12] Meanwhile, "the task of a judge is to make a principle living, not by deducing from it rules, ... but by achieving thoroughly the less ambitious but more useful labor of giving a fresh illustration of the intelligent application of the principle to a concrete cause, producing a workable and a just result."[13]

The next step in the discussion pertaining to the role of logic in law was taken by one of the most important figures in US philosophy, John Dewey. In his article "Logical Method and the Law" of 1924 he endorsed the severe assessment of legal syllogism first expressed by Holmes and Pound:

[10] Ibid., p. 608.
[11] Ibid., p. 608.
[12] Ibid., p. 621.
[13] Ibid., p. 622.

According to this model every demonstrative or strictly logical conclusion "subsumes" a particular under an appropriate universal. It implies the prior and given existence of particulars and universals. … It thus tends, when it is accepted, to produce and confirm what Professor Pound has called mechanical jurisprudence; it flatters that longing for certainty of which Justice Holmes speaks; it reinforces those inert factors in human nature which make men hug as long as possible any idea which has once gained lodgment in the mind.[14]

In addition, Dewey suggests that the development of formal logic had little to do with actually occurring mental operation; rather, it was needed to provide justifications for one's decisions to convince others about their merit.[15]

It is quite conceivable that if no one had ever had to account to others for his decisions, logical operations would never have developed, but men would use exclusively methods of inarticulate intuition and impression, feeling; so that only after considerable experience in accounting for their decisions to others who demanded a reason, or exculpation, and were not satisfied till they got it, did men begin to give an account to themselves of the process of reaching a conclusion in a justified way. … It is at this point that the chief stimulus and temptation to mechanical logic and abstract use of formal concepts come in.[16]

We need to constantly remind ourselves, claims Dewey, that thinking has nothing to do with formal schemes of logic. People do not solve problems by beginning with general premises. Confronted with a complex case, a lawyer will consider various courses of action and a number of different solutions. A general legal rule and a correct description of facts are the goal of their cognitive process, and not its point of departure. The implications of this observation "are more revolutionary than they might at first seem to be. They indicate either that logic must be abandoned or that it must be a logic relative to consequences rather than to antecedents, a logic of prediction of probabilities rather than one of deduction of certainties."[17] Dewey postulates here the utilization of the logic of discovery instead of the logic of justification. The former may be used in dynamic and creative decision-making processes; the latter is only able to operate within the framework of a static, inflexible legal order, whose beautiful façade crumbles in contact with social change.

In 1929 Karl Llewellyn delivered a series of lectures on law for the students of the Columbia Law School. He envisaged it as an introductory course for the aspiring lawyers, which explains why the language of the lectures is plain rather than technical; and why the problems he deals with, in addition to key issues such as the nature of law, include a number of less important if not trivial questions. All

---

[14]   Dewey, 1924, p. 22.
[15]   Cf. ibid., p. 24. It is a farsighted remark, one that resembles the theses endorsed by Hugo Mercier and
       Dan Sperber in Mercier & Sperber, 2017.
[16]   Dewey, 1924, p. 24.
[17]   Ibid., p. 26.

these features are also visible in the published version of the lectures, which Llewellyn titled *The Bramble Bush*.[18]

The Bramble Bush is a book filled with the realist understanding of the law. Llewellyn repeats, after his great predecessors, that judges are not guided by legal rules and that the justifications they supply for their decisions are often no more than a rhetorical or eristic device; that there exists no such thing as a "naked fact," since we look at facts through the glasses colored with our legal education, the nature of the case at hand, as well as prejudices; that the judge is not a machine automatically producing just and fair verdicts, but a human being, with all the attached flaws and limitations; and that we will find no truth in the thick volumes devoted to the law, which is not to say that we should not read them.[19]

Llewellyn agrees with Holmes, Pound, and Dewey that the law is not made up of principles and rules; there is no "master craftsman . . . able to arrange them in one great hierarchical scheme."[20] A legal order, whatever it is, is not a logically structured set of statements. When one looks at "the law in action," it turns out that reality is too complex and variable to be captured in a perfect conceptual scheme. For that reason, the judge is not and cannot be a "logical engine," carrying out infallible deductions on the basis of a coherent and complete legal system.

At the same time Llewellyn admits, somewhat surprisingly given the positions of Holmes, Pound, and Dewey, that the lawyer has a peculiar duty: to keep trying to turn the law into a logically perfect structure.[21] Such a structure constitutes a "technical ladder," which is a useful tool in legal problem-solving. The weak judges and attorneys are "penned" within the wall of the formal stronghold built by their predecessors; strong lawyers can use the logical ladder and add another brick to the wall.[22] In both cases, "the logical ladder, or the several logical ladders, are ways of keeping . . . in touch with the decisions of the past."[23]

Llewellyn underscores the fact that logic is not dedicated to the "global task" (i.e. to reconstruct an entire legal order); to the contrary: more often than not one uses it "locally," to construct a "mini legal system" around a set of precedents (e.g. pertaining to car accidents or the liability of innkeepers). This "*ad hoc* approach to logic, this building of major premises out of a group of cases not so much to find what is in them as to decide a case in hand – this is of the essence of . . . case-law system."[24] Further, one needs to remember that the same legal material, the same set of cases, may usually be presented with the use of a number of different, competing logical constructions; there will be alternative ways of ordering these cases. This is yet another typical and important feature of the common law.

---

[18] Llewellyn, 2012.
[19] Cf. Gilmore, 1951, p. 1252.
[20] Llewellyn, 2012.
[21] Cf. ibid.
[22] Cf. ibid.
[23] Ibid.
[24] Ibid.

The views expressed by Holmes, Pound, Dewey, and Llewellyn amount to a forceful attack on a certain form of rationality – one that requires to make decisions on the basis of a coherent system of abstract rules with the use of the infallible method of deduction. Therefore, it was, first and foremost, an assault on the theory that the law consists exclusively of general rules. This cannot be the case, since on the one hand the world is too complex to be captured within any abstract conceptual scheme, and on the other hand social reality changes so quickly that such rules would be unstable; once introduced, they would immediately require modifications. Secondly, Holmes and Co. are against the systematic nature of law. The legal order is nothing like a mathematical axiomatization. There will never be a legal Euclid, who, by identifying a few postulates and inference rules, would leave sentencing to machines. The law is not a coherent story, although sometimes we treat it as such; it is full of contradictions, competing points of view, and alternative solutions to the same problem. It is a Jackson Pollock painting rather than a still life by Rembrandt. Thirdly, the realists' attack was also directed at deduction as a method of decision-making. Although lawyers sometimes take advantage of infallible logical schemes, it is an outcome rather than the essence of the mental processes they employ. Deduction would be useful if there were but one way from the point of departure (an abstract rule) to the destination (the decision in the given case). Meanwhile, a lawyer's daily routine demands – as Llewellyn puts it – to consider alternative ways of solving a problem. It is also a world where – to use Dewey's words – we need a logic relativized to consequences, not premises. To put it differently: a lawyer must reject those deductive arguments that lead to unacceptable conclusions, and this obviously is no longer deduction.

However, one can ask whether anyone has ever believed in the form of rationality so forcefully rejected by Holmes, Pound, Dewey, and Llewellyn. As Ronald Dworkin observes:

> Of course, the [legal realists] think they know how the rest of us use these concepts. They think that when we speak of "the law," we mean a set of timeless rules stocked in some conceptual warehouse awaiting discovery by judges, and that when we speak of legal obligation we mean the invisible chains these mysterious rules somehow drape around us. The theory that there are such rules and chains they call "mechanical jurisprudence," and they are right in ridiculing its practitioners. Their difficulty, however, lies in finding practitioners to ridicule. So far they have had little luck in caging and exhibiting mechanical jurisprudents.[25]

Naturally, Dworkin is right; perhaps no legal philosopher has ever in all seriousness claimed that the law is an unchangeable system of rules that are to be applied "mechanically," without reflection on their content and the values they embody. It does not mean, however, that some essential aspects of this way of thinking – let us term it "naïve deductivism" – have been absent from the legal-philosophical

---

[25]　Dworkin, 1968, p. 27.

mainstream. It suffices to recall Leibniz, who wanted to shape the law along mathematical lines;[26] the views of codifiers, and Bentham in particular, who postulated the development of a perfect legal code, one that needs modifications only once in a century;[27] or some threads in the theories of continental positivists, in order to see something more than a distant resemblance with naïve deductivism. From this perspective, Dworkin's spiteful comments seem somewhat exaggerated. Granted, mechanical jurisprudence may well be merely a product of the imagination of a few American legal realists, who strived to create "a whipping boy" to further their cause and possibly also to let their frustrations out. However, this picture had some foundation in reality. In the reflection over the law, both in refined theory and crude practice, the tendency to see the law as a perfect system of rules has always been present, and warning against its dangers had its merits.

Let us further observe that legal realists, and Dewey and Llewellyn in particular, were far from saying that the law has nothing to do with logic or that legal syllogism is the source of all evil. Legal thinking may and should take advantage of logically valid schemes, but their function is different than assumed by naïve deductivism. Logic is not the ultimate foundation for justifying legal decisions, since in face of the complexity of the social life, the dynamics of the social change, and the nature of human cognitive processes, logic is simply unable to do the job. At the same time, it is difficult to imagine legal thinking without a logical structure. If legal reasoning had no structure whatsoever, the judge would indeed be replaceable by a machine; not a logical one, though, but such that decides legal cases by drawing lots. Logic imposes structure on legal reasoning; it serves as a "technical ladder," which is a support frame for our cognitive processes. The point is that the ladder cannot hang in the air; it must be put on the ground and lean against something. Abstract legal constructs are useless if not firmly set in the concrete. It is for that reason that naïve deductivism remains a pipe dream: legal thinking is a constant interplay between the abstract and the concrete, not a process powered by an "inferential engine."

4.2 TOP-DOWN AND BOTTOM-UP

Certainty has always been one of the biggest dreams of philosophers. It was perhaps best expressed by Descartes, who set forth to eliminate uncertainty and falsehood from philosophy by applying a strategy of methodic doubt to everything, as described in *Meditations on First Philosophy, Discourse on Method*, and other works. His strategy was modeled on the example of mathematics and can be encapsulated in two words: foundation and method. First, one needs to establish what cannot be doubted, a firm foundation for our theoretical constructs. These constructs, in turn, must have the same level of certainty as the foundation; thus, they are not developed

---

[26] Cf. Leibniz, 1989, p. 84.
[27] Bentham, 1843, vol. 3, p. 210.

in a capricious way, but with the use of an infallible method. Therefore, Descartes was an epistemological foundationalist: he found the basis for his theories in the famous *cogito ergo sum*, and from geometry he borrowed the method of trusting in what he can "see" in a clear and distinct manner.[28]

This foundational view turned out to be utopian however, and this was clearly demonstrated in the twentieth-century reflection over the methods and limits of science. On the one hand, the philosophical project of the Vienna Circle, which assumed that science was firmly based on observable facts and developed its theoretical constructs with the help of the logic of induction,[29] ended in disaster. This failure was neatly summarized by Karl Popper, who claimed that the high tower of human knowledge had been raised above a swamp; if this construction begins to wobble, we just drive the piles a bit deeper, with no guarantee that we will ever reach the bottom.[30] On the other hand, an opposite strategy, one that strove to place human knowledge within the framework of indefeasible general laws, also turned out to be lacking something. This idea was dear to David Hilbert, who in his Hamburg lectures of 1923 presented the vision of "the world equations," enabling to deduce all the known as well as yet unknown empirical facts.[31] Meanwhile, as demonstrated by Popper, Lakatos, Kuhn, Feyerabend, and others, our theories can never be treated as more than working hypotheses, which at any given time may turn out to be false.[32]

The spectacular failure of the foundational projects testifies to the imperfection of the cognitive tools at our disposal. Neither the bottom-up strategy, taking the concrete (empirical observations) as the indefeasible point of departure of all cognitive activities, nor the top-down approach, which urges us to solve problems on the basis of infallible abstract theories, can serve as a self-sufficient, reliable method of thinking. Thinking is necessarily non-foundational, requiring both the concrete and the abstract. It is true not only in the empirical sciences, but also in other areas of experience, including the law. However, it is worth it to go beyond this general declaration and illustrate in a more detailed way why both strategies, the bottom-up and the top-down, fail so dramatically in legal reasoning.[33]

Let us begin with a thought experiment. Imagine that our legal system consists of previously decided cases only; it contains no general rules or principles. Let us further assume that the courts have decided the following four cases so far:

(*Pinkerton* case) Pinkerton was a guest in *The What Cheer House* inn. He had with him a certain amount of money, which he left in the inn's safe in accordance with the inn's regulations. Pinkerton was informed about the existence of the regulations

[28]   Cf. Brożek, 2016b, pp. 115–118.
[29]   Carnap, 1928.
[30]   Cf. Popper, 2005, p. 94.
[31]   Kragh, 2015, pp. 80–81.
[32]   Cf. Godfrey-Smith, 2003.
[33]   Cf. Brożek, 2017b.

at the beginning of his stay. His money was stolen. During the trial, the owner of *The What Cheer House* was unable to provide sufficient evidence that they could not have foreseen the theft or prevented it. The court decided that the innkeeper is liable for the loss incurred by the plaintiff.

(*Binkerton* case) Binkerton was a guest in *The Cheerful Inn*. He had with him a certain amount of money, which he left in a locked room. The inn had an internal regulation pertaining to valuables, which required to lock them in a safe; however, Binkerton was never informed about it. His money was stolen. During the trial, the owner of *The Cheerful Inn* was able to provide sufficient evidence that they could not have foreseen the theft or prevented it. The court decided, however, that the innkeeper is not liable for the loss incurred by the plaintiff.

(*Tinkerton* case) Tinkerton was a guest in *Under the Tinker Tree* inn. He had with him a certain amount of money, which he left in the inn's safe in accordance with the inn's regulations. He was not informed about the regulation, but accidently discovered it when reading the inn's notice board. His money was stolen. During the trial, the owner of *Under the Tinker Tree* was unable to provide sufficient evidence that they could not have foreseen the theft or prevented it. The court decided that the innkeeper is liable for the loss incurred by the plaintiff.

(*Finkerton* case) Finkerton was a guest in *The Finnish Heaven* inn. He had with him a certain amount of money, which he left in a locked room. The inn had no regulations on how to keep valuables, and Finkerton was informed about this fact. His money was stolen. During the trial, the owner of *The Finnish Heaven* was able to provide sufficient evidence that they could not have foreseen the theft or prevented it. The court decided that the innkeeper is not liable for the loss incurred by the plaintiff.

Further, let us imagine that, on the basis of the four cases described above, we are to decide upon another case:

(*Winkerton* case) Winkerton was a guest in *Under the White Eagle* inn. He had with him a certain amount of money, which he left in the inn's safe. The inn had no regulations on how to keep valuables, and Winkerton was informed about this fact. His money was stolen. During the trial, the owner of *Under the White Eagle* was unable to provide sufficient evidence that they could not have foreseen the theft or prevented it.

What should the judgment be in Winkerton's case? Is the innkeeper liable for his loss or not? The problem is that the four cases decided previously – Pinkerton's, Binkerton's, Tinkerton's, and Finkerton's – give rise to the formulation of different sets of abstract rules (separate "technical ladders," as Llewellyn would call them) that may help in Winkerton's case. Let us observe that the decisions in the four precedents follow logically from (among others!) each of the following abstract rules:

(Rule 1) The innkeeper is liable for the theft of the valuables of their guests only if the items have been deposited in the inn's safe.
(Rule 2) The innkeeper is liable for the theft of the valuables of their guests only if the following three conditions have been met: the items have been deposited in

the inn's safe, there exists an internal regulation regarding how to keep valuables, and the innkeeper is unable to provide sufficient evidence that they
could not have foreseen the theft or prevented it.

(Rule 3) The innkeeper is liable for the theft of the valuables of their guests only if
the following two conditions have been met: there exists an internal regulation
regarding how to keep valuables, and the innkeeper is unable to provide
sufficient evidence that they could not have foreseen the theft or prevented it.

(Rule 4) The innkeeper is liable for the theft of the valuables of their guests only if
the following two conditions have been met: the items have been deposited in
the inn's safe, and the innkeeper is unable to provide sufficient evidence that
they could not have foreseen the theft or prevented it.

The assumption that the four precedents "contain" Rules 1 or 4 leads to the conclusion that in the new case (Winkerton's) the innkeeper is liable for the loss incurred
by his guest; however, if we adopted the view that the legal norm "embodied" in the
four precedents is best expressed by Rule 2 or Rule 3, our conclusion would be
different: the owner of *Under the White Eagle* is not liable for Winkerton's loss.

It must be stressed that this ambiguity is not a coincidence or an outcome of
a cunning selection of cases. Our analysis can easily be generalized in accordance
with Quine's thesis pertaining to the underdetermination of a theory by facts.[34]
Quine claims that any amount of past evidence in physics (empirical observations) is
consistent with more than one theory. To put it differently: any theory is under-
determined by all possible observations.[35] In the same way, an arbitrary number of
individual legal decisions in concrete cases – all *possible* such decisions – does not
determine one, unique set of rules of behavior. It follows that there can be no legal
system, in which there are no abstract rules. For purely *logical* reasons, a lawyer
cannot rely exclusively on the bottom-up strategy.

However, the problems surrounding the bottom-up approach reach much deeper.
From the logical point of view, each particular situation is infinitely characterizable
(i.e. it has (countably) infinitely many features). When describing the Pinkerton
case, we have pointed out to the following facts: (1) that he was a guest in *The What
Cheer House*; (2) that he deposited a certain amount of money in the inn's safe; (3)
that in the inn, there was an internal regulation on how to keep valuables; (4) that he
was informed about the existence of the regulation; (5) that the money was stolen;
and (6) that during the trial the owner of *The What Cheer House* was unable to
provide sufficient evidence that they could not have foreseen the theft or prevented
it. We were not interested, however, in any other facts of the case: what was
Pinkerton's hair color; what was the color of the walls in his room; who was the
manufacturer of the safe; whether the owner of *The What Cheer House* was an
experienced innkeeper; what was the weather at the time when the theft occurred;

[34] Cf. Quine, 1970.
[35] Ibid., pp. 178–179.

etc. From the infinitely many features of the case we have chosen but a few. Why those and not others?

In order to answer this question, it is reasonable to examine the actual *Pinkerton* v. *Woodward* case, which was decided by the California court in 1867, in the midst of the Gold Rush.[36] Pinkerton, together with three fellow travelers, was heading back home with some amount of gold dust. They decided to stay overnight in *The What Cheer House* inn, owned by Woodward. The gold, according to the regulations of the house, was deposited in the safe. Unfortunately, it was subsequently stolen. The question before the court was whether Woodward was liable for the loss incurred by Pinkerton. Woodward pointed out that since in *The What Cheer House* there is a restaurant, he is the owner of a lodging house, not an inn. This distinction was an important one, since innkeepers in US law were treated as public servants and, in contraposition to the owners of lodging houses, were responsible for the losses of their guests "as insurers" (i.e. according to the principle of strict liability).

It should be noted that Woodward highlighted a certain feature of the case (the fact that in *The What Cheer House* he runs a restaurant), which at first glance seems inessential. It is one of the infinitely many aspects of the considered situation, just like Pinkerton's hair color, that are in no way linked to the theft of the gold dust. The point is, however, that according to Woodward running a restaurant defined the nature of his business, which in turn determined the principles governing his liability. This example illustrates that the choice of the relevant features of a legal case – just a few from among infinitely many – is dictated by a theory. In *Pinkerton* v. *Woodward*, the theory in question consisted of the set of principles of liability in US law. Furthermore, this conclusion can be generalized: it is impossible to give a description of facts in a legal case outside of the context of an abstract theory. By formulating the short descriptions of four imaginary cases – Pinkerton's, Binkerton's, Tinkerton's, and Finkerton's – we have committed a "methodological crime." We chose a few from among infinitely many features of those cases, ignoring the fact that the choice, without some abstract theory dictating it, is purely arbitrary. Thus, the fact that it is impossible to think exclusively in the bottom-up was not only for logical but also *classificatory* reasons.

Let us now imagine a completely different situation. We have a legal order that, instead of concrete, previously decided cases, consists of one abstract rule alone:

(R) Anyone who by a fault on their part causes damage to another person is obliged to remedy it.

Let us consider what challenges transpire when one attempts to decide Winkerton's case on the basis of Rule (R). Winkerton was a guest in *Under the White Eagle* inn, where he deposited a certain amount of money in a safe. The inn had no regulations on how to keep valuables. Unfortunately, someone broke into the safe and stole

---

[36] *Pinkerton* v. *Woodward* (1867), 33 Cal. 557.

Winkerton's money. The question is whether the innkeeper is liable for Winkerton's loss. In other words, and in the context of Rule (R), have they caused damage to their guest "by a fault on their part"?

It is easy to imagine that the owner of the *Under the White Eagle* could be surprised by Winkerton's claim. Ultimately, they did not commit the theft, and Rule (R) clearly states that the damage should be remedied by the person who caused it. The innkeeper had nothing to do with the thieves' actions – they knew nothing about the thieves' intentions, did not help them to get to the safe, offered them no assistance in leaving *Under the White Eagle* quietly. However, why shouldn't we assume that one may cause damage to someone else by *failing* to do something? For example, a failure to help an older lady who suffered a heart attack in the middle of the street does not constitute an action but nevertheless causes damage. Thus, one may argue, even if the innkeeper was not working together with the thieves, they might have contributed to the damage suffered by Winkerton by failing to do a number of things; for example, they might have forgotten to lock the door to the office where the safe was located, failed to change the preset safe code, or decided to cut costs and bought the cheapest safe, one easily tackled by an experienced thief.[37]

The innkeeper has one more line of defense. They can point out that, while they have failed to do a number of things (indeed, they should have locked the door to the office), they did not do it "by a fault on their part" – their failure was not intentional but rather resulted from absentmindedness. However, this argument is also unclear. Can we speak of "fault" when someone only acted intentionally? When the innkeeper does not consider at all that their behavior may facilitate the theft or even encourage it, while any reasonable man could easily see it, speaking of "fault" is not exaggerated. A similar conclusion applies to a situation when the innkeeper is aware of the potential risk of harm but believes, groundlessly, that nothing bad will happen. Both negligence and recklessness may be considered forms of fault.[38]

This short analysis underscores one of the limitations of the top-down approach, that is of carrying out legal reasoning on the basis of abstract rules alone. Such rules are necessarily vague, they involve such expressions as "cause damage," or "by a fault," which makes it impossible to apply them in an algorithmic or automatic way. Vagueness of linguistic expressions may be defined as follows: although typically there is no doubt whether a certain object or event should be referred to with that expression, there exist borderline cases (i.e. objects and events in relation to which a competent user of the given language cannot decide, whether they "fall under" a certain expression or not). When one ponders whether Person X did something "by fault," no doubt will transpire in cases such as a premeditated murder or burglary. Similarly, when a surgeon acted with due care and according to the rules

---

[37]   Cf. Hodgson & Lewthwaite, 2007; Beever, 2007.
[38]   Cf. Hodgson & Lewthwaite, 2007.

of their art, but the patient nevertheless died on the operating table, there would be no room for speaking of the surgeon's fault. However, there will be cases when the expression "Person X did it by fault" will give rise to doubt and controversy; hence, the concept of "fault" is a vague one.

One may argue that a reasonable way to avoid the troubles caused by vagueness is to formulate legal rules in a much more concrete manner than the extremely general Rule (R). For example, one may consider using the following norm:

(R′) An innkeeper is liable for the loss incurred by their guests through a theft of their valuables, when the innkeeper themselves committed the act, conspired with the persons who committed it, or contributed to it through recklessness or negligence.

One will quickly realize, however, that this new formulation is also filled with vague expressions: "innkeeper," "loss," "valuables," "conspiracy," "contribute," "negligence," or "recklessness." Although it is easy to point out some typical situations, in which the innkeeper's behavior may be described as "negligent" or to be sure that a very expensive watch is a valuable item, it is equally easy to imagine situations, in which the use of those expressions will be surrounded with doubt.

There exists one more reason that makes thinking on the basis of abstract rules problematic. The creation of an absolutely precise concept – at least outside of the exact science of mathematics – is simply impossible. This point was masterfully demonstrated by Friedrich Waismann, who observed that linguistic concepts are open textured.[39] Waismann asks us to imagine a substance that has all the physio-chemical characteristics of gold, but emits a new, unknown kind of energy. Should we still call it "gold"? Undoubtedly, we would need to make some decision here. However, this problem makes us realize that the application of any concept, even as precise as "gold," is never fully determined: there may always be a situation in which doubt emerges. Although, with our current state of knowledge, a competent user of English should not hesitate in deciding whether a given substance is "gold" (which means that the concept is not vague), we can always imagine a set of circumstances undermining this certainty. In other words, open texture is "potential vagueness."

To illustrate this point, let us assume that Rule (R′), establishing the liability of innkeepers for the theft of valuable items belonging to their guests, is unproblematic at least in one dimension: we know what the word "innkeeper" means and we apply it with the same kind of certainty that accompanies people, equipped with chemical knowledge and the best instruments, establishing that a given substance is gold. From the contemporary perspective, we may assume that innkeepers are entrepreneurs who run hotels, hostels, motels, lodging houses, and bed-and-breakfast establishments. The problem is that some changes in social reality (here: in the hotel industry) may take an unexpected turn, making the term "innkeeper" vague again.

---

[39] Cf. Waismann, 1951.

For example, what about an entrepreneur who offers a short stay in small cabins at airports? Such cabins have no bathrooms and other amenities typically found in hotels. The guests do not pay for the accommodation in a daily scheme, but on an hourly basis. Moreover, the space they get is no more than four square meters, which is twice less than the smallest existing hotel rooms. An answer to the question of whether the operator of the airport cabins is an innkeeper is far from easy.

Both vagueness and open texture constitute *the semantic reason* for the insufficiency of the top-down strategy. With general and abstract rules only, we are unable to decide in every single legal case. A question can always emerge on how to understand this or that abstract expression; this requires us to make a decision (e.g. whether the given entrepreneur should be considered an innkeeper) that does not follow logically from the rule itself. Moreover, this problem can manifest itself at every level of abstractness. Even the development of an extremely complicated system of relatively concrete rules of behavior cannot safeguard us from vagueness and open texture, since they constitute immanent features of language.[40]

The limitations of the top-down strategy are closely linked to another feature of the law. As Holmes, Pound, and other legal realists repeatedly stressed, it is impossible to create a system of abstract rules foreseeing all the situations that may take place in social life. The existing legal orders offer a remedy for this problem: the legislator, in addition to rules, takes advantage also of legal principles. Principles, similarly to rules, are abstract norms of conduct, but at the same time they have some peculiar characteristics. Robert Alexy claims that they require "that something be realized to the greatest extent possible given the legal and factual possibilities."[41] A good example is Article 5 of the Constitution of the Republic of Poland, which says inter alia that "the Republic of Poland shall ... ensure the protection of the natural environment pursuant to the principles of sustainable development."

An intriguing aspect of legal principles is that they do not ascribe precisely determined rights and duties to a well-defined group of people. At the same time, they have some normative force: one can cite them as the legal basis for deciding particular cases. From the logical point of view, legal principles constitute the so-called improper group obligations. Such an obligation is placed upon a group of people who are required to see to it that a certain state of affairs obtains; however, it suffices that only a subset of the group acts in the required way.[42] For example, if students ought to prepare the blackboard before the lecture, the obligation will be fulfilled if only one of the students does so. Thus, improper group obligations are *multiply realizable*: the desirable state of affairs (e.g. a clean blackboard) can be achieved in many ways, and the regulation does not select one of them as being legally required. Similarly, Article 5 of the Polish Constitution expresses an improper group obligation of all the addressees of the law – the requirement to protect the

[40] See Hart, 1949.
[41] Alexy, 2002, p. 47.
[42] Cf. Horty, 2001.

natural environment. This goal may be achieved in a number of ways (e.g. by utilizing plastic bottles or introducing a ban on producing them). Such issues are usually decided in legal statutes and other acts. However, the crucial point lies elsewhere: in any legal order in which there are principles expressing improper group obligations, it is impossible to avoid the problem of multiple realizability. In other words, a system of abstract norms, which includes legal principles (optimization criteria), does not univocally determine all the rights and duties of concrete persons. This is *the constructional reason* for the insufficiency of the top-down strategy.

Let us summarize our findings so far. I have argued that thinking "from the concrete to the abstract," according to the bottom-up approach, has serious limitations and cannot be an exclusive method of solving legal problems. There are two different reasons why this is so: the logical (an arbitrarily large set of previously decided cases is consistent with many different theories), and the classificatory (the determination of the legally relevant features of a concrete case is relative to the accepted theory). I have also attempted to show that the road from abstract to the concrete, applying the top-down strategy, faces unsurmountable obstacles. On the one hand, abstract rules are vague and open textured, constituting the semantic reason for the insufficiency of the top-down way of thinking; on the other hand, one needs to bear in mind the constructional reason: legal orders include improper group obligations, and hence do not univocally determine all rights and duties of all persons. From these observations it follows that legal thinking must necessarily take advantage of both strategies: it is simultaneously bottom-up and top-down.

This conclusion is coherent with the findings of the previous chapters. Thinking, which is rooted exclusively in the concrete, devoid of abstraction and theorization, cannot efficiently deal with the problems we encounter. But abstract theories and the infallible method of deduction alone are also insufficient. The abstract conceptual scheme of law is not precise enough to capture all the aspects of the complex social life that may turn out to be important. The structure of legal thinking is necessarily concrete-abstract.

4.3 A THINKING MANUAL

One of the most intriguing philosophical works of the twentieth century was Paul Feyerabend's *Against Method*.[43] If one had to summarize the theses of methodological anarchism defended by Feyerabend in two words, no other choice would remain but to say "anything goes." Despite all appearances to the contrary, it is not a simple and straightforward slogan. Feyerabend is not trying to say that everything is equally acceptable or justified; rather, he believes that "everything may be useful": it is a grave mistake to exclude some methods or ways of thinking a priori

---

[43] Cf. Feyerabend, 1993.

from the toolbox of science. There is no universally valid method, embodying Rationality with a capital "R." The most absurd theory or procedure, one that is inconsistent with mainstream science and seemingly unreasonable, may lead to creative discoveries and, in time, become a fully reasonable element belonging to the mainstream.

Feyerabend's methodological precept is quite difficult to follow. Our minds have a natural tendency to stick to well-tested solutions and become quickly accustomed to using a particular set of tools for thinking. We love endorsing "isms," which give us both the feeling of cognitive safety and of belonging to a group. This does not alter the fact, however, that Feyerabend is right. In thinking, also in the law, "anything may be useful," since thinking is not based on unshakable foundations and requires us to constantly move between the abstract and the concrete. We may take advantage of all the logically valid schemes of reasoning, such as the legal syllogism, but also of logically invalid arguments. Simple legal topoi in the form of a single sentence may be useful, just like complex and highly unified theories. One may find wisdom and inspiration in doctrinal considerations, as well as in judicial opinions.

Of course, not all of these tools will be equally useful in all contexts. Much will depend on the kind of problem we are dealing with, and the tradition to which it belongs. It is hard to imagine that a common-law lawyer could simply refer to the theories developed by the German legal scholars of the nineteenth century: Karl Friedrich von Savigny, Rudolf von Ihering, or Bernhard Windscheid. Their conceptions not only disregard the nature of the common law, they also see legal problems differently, or better yet: see different legal problems. The same question (e.g. pertaining to the liability of innkeepers) may be an expression of two diametrically different problems. It will be understood in one way by a US lawyer, and in another by a German. These differences may be quite substantial, but it is not the case that the tools for thinking developed within one tradition are completely useless in another. Under the relevant circumstances, "anything may be useful."

This methodological pluralism is conditioned by the complex architecture of the legal mind; it does not exclude the possibility, however, of formulating some principles of thinking, which could be useful for dealing with any kind of problem irrespective of legal culture and tradition. Of course, these principles must be very general and pertain to the fundamental aspects of human cognitive abilities only. Further, they cannot form a well-defined procedure leading to a correct answer to any question. They can, however, make us think better, increasing the likelihood of finding efficient solutions to problems.

In this section, I formulate six such principles: of experience, caution, exemplification, variability, unification, and contrast. Their application will be illustrated with the use of the already mentioned example, which constitutes a locus classicus of legal philosophy. This imagined case was first introduced by Herbert Hart:

A legal rule forbids you to take a vehicle into the public park. Plainly this forbids an automobile, but what about bicycles, roller skates, toy automobiles? What about airplanes? Are these, as we say, to be called "vehicles" for the purpose of the rule or not?[44]

Hart's example has played an important role in many legal-philosophical discussions pertaining to both the nature of legal language and to legal ontology,[45] and although it has been analyzed in dozens of ways – or maybe because of that – it constitutes a perfect point of reference for the theses formulated here.

The first of the principles I wish to describe reads as follows:

(Principle of experience) One should educate one's intuition through conscious attempts to solve actual and imagined legal problems, as well as through the analysis of the existing solutions to such problems.

Antonio Damasio observes that

the quality of one's intuition depends on how well we have reasoned in the past; on how well we have classified the events of our experience in relation to the emotions that preceded and followed them; and also on how well we have reflected on the successes and failures of our past intuitions. Intuition is simply rapid cognition with the required knowledge partially swept under the carpet, all courtesy of emotion and much past practice.[46]

A well-shaped intuition is a powerful tool: it delivers optimal or close-to-optimal answers to the questions we face while engaging our cognitive resources in a minimal way. It is a precisely tuned cognitive mechanism, which is based on an enormous knowledge about the world gathered in the process of individual development. An expert in a field (e.g. in the law) is able to make decisions unconsciously, ones that are hard to improve upon even with the help of the most complex conscious reasoning.

This can be illustrated with Hart's example. When a person who has had nothing to do with the law hears the rule "Vehicles are not allowed into the public park" and we ask them whether one can ride a bicycle in the park, two things may happen. First, there may emerge a strong intuition prompting a concrete solution (e.g. that one can use bicycles in the park). This intuition will not be rooted in the law, but in everyday observations (e.g. of seeing people riding bicycles in parks). Second, the question may generate some confusion, resulting from the emergence of two conflicting intuitions. One of these intuitions would be based on past experience (parks are places for active rest such as bicycle riding); the other would result from the meaning of the rule (after all, bicycles *are* vehicles, aren't they?). A lawyer might also experience one of the two intuitive reactions: either suggesting an obvious answer or leading to the clash of two intuitions and, in consequence, to confusion. These

---

44 Hart, 1958, p. 607.
45 Cf. Schauer, 2008.
46 Damasio, 2006, pp. xviii–xix.

reactions, however, would be an outcome of quite different experiences than in the case of the layperson. A strong intuition suggesting that one can ride bicycles in the park would most likely result from some past practice (e.g. a typical understanding of the word "vehicle" in the given legal system, which encompasses cars and motor- cycles, but not bicycles). In turn, the emergence of two conflicting intuitions will bring some level of confusion, but it will also launch (often unconsciously) some interpretive procedures (e.g. looking for the goals of the regulation in question). To put it differently, the intuition of a lawyer and of a layperson function in the same way: they immediately provide a provisional answer of how to deal with the encoun- tered problem. However, these intuitive judgments are based on different experi- ences and lead to different outcomes. A lawyer will unconsciously incorporate the case at hand into a broader context of legal knowledge; a layperson, on the other hand, will only unconsciously assess the case against the backdrop of their com- monsense worldview.

The second principle – also pertaining to the functioning of intuition – may be formulated in the following way:

(Principle of caution) Intuitive judgment can be trusted in a limited way.

Whenever one encounters a problem, the mechanism of intuition suggests a solution based on one's previous experience. Usually, these solutions will be quite accurate, even if they are not optimal. However, especially when the problem at hand is atypical or quite abstract (e.g. pertaining to probability), it is reasonable to control one's intuition. Yet this is no easy task since intuitive judgments are strong and persistent, while our minds are constructed in such a way that they prefer quick cognitive closure rather than long and tiresome mental effort.[47]

In the "vehicle in the park" case, intuition may lead us astray in a number of ways, especially when we have had to deal with similar problems, which had always been solved in the same way or when we had learned to understand certain expressions in a particular way (e.g. that "vehicle" includes cars and motorcycles but not bicycles or scooters). In such circumstances a very strong, experience-based intuition emerges. Meanwhile, it may turn out that it is not the best solution to the considered problem. For example, it may transpire that in some areas of law (e.g. tax law) bicycles should not be counted among vehicles, while in a regulation pertaining to public parks it is better to assume that bicycles are vehicles.

The next principle is:

(Principle of exemplification) Abstract reasoning should be illustrated with con- crete examples.

Thinking with the use of abstract concepts may be extremely efficient, but the problem is that such thinking easily turns into the empty, meaningless manipulation

---

[47]   Cf. Webster & Kruglanski, 1994.

of linguistic expressions. In order to safeguard oneself from it, one needs to stay in touch with the concrete. When interpreting an abstract legal rule, it is not enough to paraphrase it. One should imagine some examples of its application, borderline cases, and counterexamples. Only in this way may one reach some level of certainty regarding the understanding of legal provisions or doctrinal theories. Moreover, exemplifications, while increasing understanding, bring something more to the table: they enable the activation of intuitions, which in turn make it possible to quickly, if not always accurately, assess the contemplated interpretation of a rule or its application.

It is easy to see how this works on the basis of our Hartian example. If one confined oneself to some manipulations of the "no vehicles in the park" rule – for example by paraphrasing it into "It is forbidden to enter the park in any vehicle equipped with any propulsion mechanism," or even "It is forbidden to enter the park in a vehicle equipped with an engine" – one could not claim that one understands the rule "perfectly well." Moreover, such abstract paraphrases would evoke no intuitions. Only after imagining a number of situations – of a person, who considers whether they can enter the park in a car, on a bicycle, or on roller-skates – could one have a more comprehensive understanding of the interpretative work at hand and afford intuition its spontaneous functioning.

The fourth rule is:

(**Principle of variability**) While mentally simulating concrete cases one should alter various aspects of the imagined situations.

When we use mental simulations, it is easy to imagine typical cases that lead to predictable intuitive reactions. Therefore, there exists some risk that abstract conceptual constructs will be understood in a standard way, disregarding both the complexity of the problem at hand and the limits of intuitive cognition. The best way to deal with this danger is to make relatively small adjustments to what we mentally simulate and register the transformations of the evoked intuitions. This strategy is also useful in those cases when there is no clear initial intuition of how to deal with a problem and we attempt to stimulate our minds to find an insight.

The principle of variability was masterfully applied by Lon L. Fuller in his commentary to Hart's example with the rule prohibiting vehicles from entering public parks.[48] Let us recall that according to Hart the rule certainly applies to some situations; one would have no doubt that cars are banned from entering the park, since cars are vehicles. In this context, Fuller poses the following question: "what . . . if some local patriots wanted to mount on a pedestal in the park a truck used in World War II, while other citizens, regarding the proposed memorial as an eyesore, support their stand by the 'no vehicle' rule?"[49] There is no doubt that a truck is a vehicle; but it would be absurd to assume that a World War II truck cannot be

---

[48] Fuller, 1958.
[49] Ibid., p. 663.

transported into the park to be placed there as a memorial, since it "violates" the Hartian rule. A strong intuition, which urges us to interpret the word "vehicle" in such a way that it refers to trucks, has its limitations. Let us have a look at another modification of our imagined situation, namely an ambulance carrying a seriously injured person. Every second counts, and the closest way to the hospital is through the park. Would the ambulance passing through the park be a violation of the "no vehicle" rule? Or let us consider still another situation: We do not count bicycles among vehicles (at least in the context of our rule). What would happen if a bicycle was equipped with an electric engine? Can it enter the park? Should the rider abstain from engaging the engine while driving through the confines of the park? The principle of variability, when reasonably applied, increases our understanding of the problem at hand, helping to determine the limits of our intuitive judgments and paving the way for insights.

The fifth principle reads:

> **(Principle of unification)** When constructing a theory, one should try to make it embrace as large a class of cases as possible and to achieve the highest possible degree of coherence.

Were there no general norms pertaining to the entire branches of the law, and only quite concrete legal institutions with no interconnections between them, we would end up with a very fragmented legal system, or more precisely with many discon-nected mini-systems. If legal doctrine made no attempt to reconstruct and system-atize the catalogue of the general principles of private, criminal, or administrative law, a lawyer's fate would boil down to casuistic discussions of particular, separate legal cases. If canons of statutory interpretation essentially varied depending on the kind of problem one is facing, legal decisions would become unpredictable and incomprehensible. Unified theories are useful, since they generate a coherent view of the (relevant fragment of the) world, thereby increasing our global understanding. The principle of unification warns us also against introducing ad hoc hypotheses (i.e. modifying theories by embedding some exceptions into them in order to solve a particular problem or demonstrate that it is in fact a pseudoproblem). Finally, one needs to remember that the principle of unification is connected to a certain danger: it may lead to constructing a theory that is so abstract that it loses any connection with everyday experience. Although it generates perfect global understanding, it may become "locally" incomprehensible.

In the context of the "vehicle in the park" case, one may develop a theory, according to which vehicles are all means of transport equipped with any type of engine (and hence bicycles, scooters, or children toys are not vehicles). If this theory served only to provide an interpretive framework for the "no vehicle in the park" rule, it would be worse (i.e. it would lead to a smaller degree of unification) than a similar theory introducing a uniform understanding of the term "vehicle" in the entire legal system or an entire branch of law. As Fuller demonstrated, such an understanding of the concept would also be imperfect, as it would include the World War II truck that is to be placed in the park to serve as a memorial. However, to say that vehicles are all means of transport equipped with an engine of any type with the exception of World War II trucks would be a classical ad hoc modification – it would help to deal with a particular problem, but it would also decrease the degree of unification of the theory we use. A better way would be to follow Fuller's suggestion that the understanding of the "no vehicles in the park rule" should involve the rule's goal; if it is the safety of pedestrians, the truck mounted on a pedestal would not violate the regulation, while professional bicycle riders, practicing for the Tour de France, would be breaking it.

The final principle is:

> **(Principle of contrast)** One should consider alternative solutions to the given problem, developing different, mutually incompatible hypotheses, even if some of them seem inadequate.

The strength of the principle of contrast is visible at three different levels. Firstly, it enables a better understanding of the problem and uncovering of the hidden assumptions one makes while attempting to solve it. A comparison of two different interpretations of a statutory or contractual provision, or of alternative ways to solve a hard case, makes it easier to recognize mental habits (e.g. insisting on a particular understanding of some legal concepts) and modify them. It is often the only way to secure an optimal answer to a legal question. Secondly, the principle of contrast is a heuristic device: it suggests new, often unintuitive solutions. Third and finally, the principle comes with some capacity of persuasion. If one solves a legal problem with a hypothesis that prevailed in comparison with other competing hypotheses, such a solution may be deemed justified.

Let us once again consider the Hartian example. When pondering the meaning of the term "vehicle," one can formulate, among others, two competing definitions: that vehicles are all the means of transport equipped with any type of engine or that a vehicle is any means of transport that can potentially be dangerous for pedestrians. The comparison of these two solutions makes us see clearly two important aspects of the Hartian problem. The first definition is based on the assumption that linguistic intuitions should be respected; ultimately, legal provisions should be formulated in such a way as to be comprehensible for the addressees of the law, and hence in our interpretation we cannot depart too much from the ordinary understanding of the term "vehicle." The second solution is diametrically different: it urges us to take into account the goal of the "no vehicle in the park" rule, and not its literal meaning. This tension between semantics and pragmatics, lying at the heart of the problem, comes to the fore only when both solutions are formulated and compared. If we limited ourselves to the first (semantic) approach, we could indefinitely debate whether the term "vehicle" pertains to cars and motorcycles only, or if it includes also bicycles and wheelchairs equipped with electric engines; however, we would remain blind to the goal of the regulation. It should also be clear that irrespective of which of the competing solutions is ultimately selected (and it is quite possible that we would find and accept still another one), the outcome of our mental activities is a well-justified decision, since it has been chosen from a larger pool of possible solutions through comparison and elimination.

Let me repeat that the presented principles of legal thinking (of experience, caution, exemplification, variability, unification, and contrast) do not amount to an infallible procedure that guarantees success. Rather, they constitute a general thinking manual that can be used in many ways, depending on the nature of the case at hand, its context (e.g. the legal tradition), and goals (e.g. judge's as opposed to legal council's or legislator's). The principles teach us how to consciously use the mental tools that are at our disposal.

4.4 JUSTIFICATION

One of the crucial conceptual distinctions in the philosophy of science is that between the context of discovery and the context of justification.[50] When one considers the context of discovery, one is interested in all the mechanisms leading to generating new ideas and hypotheses. In the context of justification, on the other hand, the key question is how to demonstrate that one's hypothesis is sound. It may seem that these two aspects of thinking have little to do with one another. Let us recall a passage from Hutcheson's lecture quoted in Chapter 1: "all of us have known judges who can make the soundest judgments and write the dullest opinions on them; whose decisions were hardly ever affirmed for the reasons which they gave. Their difficulty was that while they had the flash, the intuitive power of judgment, they could not show it forth."[51] They were, in other words, doing extremely well in the context of discovery, but were very bad when it came to the context of justification.

The thinking manual described in Section 4.3 (i.e. the principles of experience, caution, exemplification, variability, unification, and contrast), together with hundreds of argument schemes, concepts, and theories elaborated in each legal tradition, form a rich inventory of methods for generating solutions to legal problems; they are not designed, however, to justify legal decisions. For example, it would be quite difficult to show that the principle of experience ("Intuitive judgment can be trusted in a limited way") or of variability ("While mentally simulating concrete cases one should alter various aspects of the imagined situations") can in any way contribute to the justification of a court ruling. At the same time, one must remember that strict philosophical distinctions are rarely anything more than analytical tools. To say that there exist two separate contexts of thinking, discovery

---

[50]   The distinction was introduced by Reichenbach, 1938.
[51]   Hutcheson, 1929, p. 287.

and justification, marks an important shift in perspective rather than describing any unbridgeable gap between two distinct mental procedures.

Justification is public;[52] its primary goal is to defend one's view against the counterarguments and doubts raised by others. As such, it necessarily involves only those means of thinking that can be made public. In other words, justification does not directly take advantage of intuition or imagination; it is a linguistic enterprise. One can be capable of reliable intuitive judgments, deep insights, or surprising plays of imagination, and yet constantly fail to meet the justification criteria. However, it should be observed that there are some precepts in the thinking manual that are directly linked with justification. The principle of unification, which urges one to construct comprehensive and highly coherent theories, may produce fully justified outcomes. In turn, the principle of contrast, asking us to work with mutually incompatible hypotheses to choose the best one, also comes with justificatory force: a hypothesis that has prevailed in a comparison with some competing solutions may be deemed justified. In both cases, justification is a by-product of the idea-generating mechanism. Also, as we shall see, both principles are connected to different views of justification. However, the point is that there are close ties between at least some tools used in the context of discovery and the methods of justification.[53]

Moreover, justification is something one can learn. Legal training is not limited to the techniques for finding answers to legal questions; to the contrary, it is very much centered on how to justify a claim so that it fits into the legal system or is useful in persuading a judge. A lawyer who has undergone intensive training during their legal studies and has been practicing law for many years would usually have enough experience to pass sound intuitive judgments on what works as justification and what does not. In this way, the criteria for justification become "embodied" in one's unconscious decision-making mechanisms.

The debate revolving around the concept of justification is usually presented as pertaining to a choice between two fundamentally different approaches: foundationalism and coherentism.[54] Both come in various, often quite different forms. However, it is not impossible to characterize them in a general way, which does justice to the essential ideas behind both stances. Foundationalists claim that there exists a designated kind of statements or beliefs, which provide an unshakable ground for any justification; a hypothesis is justified if it is possible to show that it can be inferred from those foundations.[55] Thus, each and every version of foundationalism consists of two elements: the set of basic beliefs and the set of rules of inference. A belief is justified if it is a basic belief or it can be "obtained" from basic beliefs with the use of inference rules. Of course, there are many ways in which basic beliefs are understood (e.g. as empirically grounded or assumed as axioms), as well as

---

[52] Cf. Goldman, 1988.
[53] See also Hoyningen-Huene, 1987.
[54] Cf. Audi, 1988.
[55] Cf. Bonjour, 1985.

different conceptions of inference (deduction, induction, etc.). For example, one of the most famous foundational projects in the philosophy of science, developed by the members of the Vienna Circle in the 1920s, posited that science is founded on the so-called observational statements, and justified scientific theories are constructed on this basis with the use of the logic of induction.[56]

Coherentism, in turn, is a view that a belief is justified if it belongs to a coherent set of beliefs. But when is a set of beliefs coherent? This question has been answered in a number of ways.[57] There is no doubt that coherence implies consistency: an inconsistent set of sentences is incoherent. However, mere consistency is not enough to speak of anything more than a minimal level of coherence. A collection of legal cases that have nothing to do with one another (e.g. one can reconstruct no ratio decidendi governing all or some of the cases), even if consistent, would have no claim to being highly coherent. In other words, a set of beliefs may be said to be coherent (to a degree), if the beliefs in it are connected in some logical way.[58]

Thus, it seems that there are two competing views of justification. On the one hand, a belief may be said to be justified if it follows from some basic or fundamental beliefs; on the other, a belief is justified if it "fits together" with other beliefs one already accepts. It is not surprising that the main division line in the discussion pertaining to justification lies between foundationalism and coherentism. The question has been usually posed against the backdrop of the methodology of the empirical sciences. There, the crucial problem is the status of empirical observations. Foundationalists claim that they have a special role to play: science is an edifice constructed upon facts, and theories are but generalizations of the observed phenomena. Coherentists, in turn, disagree: they value theory and see knowledge as a large network of interconnected beliefs, where no particular statement, even if based on direct observations, is given priority over others; what matters is the overall quality of the network, not the source of its particular nodes. An extreme coherentist would be happy to repeat after Hegel that "if facts contradict theory, so much the worse for the facts."[59]

The problem is that once we look at the scientific practice – at what really *works* in science – any rigid distinction between foundationalism and coherentism immediately collapses. Full-blooded foundationalism is nothing more than a fairy-tale for well-behaved children. No one has ever seen a "naked fact," an observation that is not mediated by some theory. Without theory one would not even know where to

---

[56]   See Schlick, 1959.
[57]   Cf. Hage, 2013.
[58]   A more precise definition – albeit not the only possible one – may be based on the following three criteria: (1) an inconsistent set of sentences is incoherent; (2) the increase of the number of nontrivial inferential connections between the sentences of a set increases the coherence of the set; (3) the increase of the level of unification of a set of sentences increases the coherence of the set. Cf. Bonjour, 1985.
[59]   This slogan was attributed to Hegel by Walter Benjamin in Benjamin, 1998, p. 46.

look and what to observe.[60] Pure coherentism is not the answer either. To say that the goal of science is to construct perfect theories characterized by this or that constellation of formal properties would miss the point entirely. Scientists strive to explain and predict empirical phenomena. The fact that their theories are "mathematically beautiful" (i.e. they possess some desirable formal properties) is undoubtedly a source of an intense aesthetic experience and sometimes additional evidence that a more truthful model of reality has been stumbled upon (although equally often "formal beauty" has led the physicists astray).[61] Yet the ultimate goal of science is to explain and predict empirical facts; the most coherent theory, which does this job badly, is far inferior to an almost incoherent one that has the requisite explanatory and predictive power.[62]

This shows that the controversy between foundationalism and coherentism is considerably exaggerated. On the one hand, one cannot seriously claim that some set of beliefs is so fundamental that it can never be modified or rejected; on the other hand, it is unreasonable to assume that all our beliefs are equally easy to change. A pure version of foundationalism (that there is indeed a set of unshakable beliefs that serve as the basis for justifying other beliefs) is impossible to uphold in most contexts. The same is true of a pure form of coherentism (that beliefs are equally easy to reject and that the only source of justification is the "fitting in" of a belief into a greater, coherent whole). In fact, these "pure forms" constitute two extremes in a continuum; they are two sides of the same coin.[63] A workable criterion of justification in the empirical sciences must lie somewhere in between them.[64]

This is even more clearly discernible in the law. A purely foundational view of justification is useless in legal reasoning. The only candidates for "legal basic beliefs" are statutory rules or precedents. However, any lawyer knows that statutory rules may be interpreted in different ways, derogated from the legal system or replaced overnight; precedents, in turn, can be reconstructed and understood in more than one way, or overruled. It is easy to understand why people believe in the foundational model of justification when it comes to empirical inquiries. Our cognitive inertia and mental habits make it hard to realize that there are no such things as "naked," theory-neutral facts. However, the law is different; it undergoes a constant change, both legislative and interpretive. In such a setting, there is no place for "pure" foundationalism. The extreme version of coherentism does not fare much better. The law is a tool for regulating social behavior, and as such needs to be highly predictable. Legal rights and duties must be relatively stable in order to serve as

[60] For a more detailed critique of foundationalism, see Hasan & Fumerton, 2018.
[61] Cf. Hossenfelder, 2018.
[62] For a more detailed critique of coherentism, see Olsson, 2017.
[63] It should be noted, however, that adopting the conception of the so-called integrated coherentism, where everything, including logic and the standards for belief revision, is subject to assessment (and hence a set of positions is integratedly coherent if and only if it satisfies the standards included in the set of positions itself), would make foundationalism a special case of coherentism. Cf. Hage, 2013.
[64] Cf. Haack, 1993.

a reference framework for our daily decisions. Therefore, some law-related beliefs (e.g. pertaining to the general principles of criminal liability) should be more difficult to modify than others (e.g. a local ordinance on the use of bicycles in public parks). "Pure" coherentism is not a viable option as a criterion of legal justification.

It does not mean, however, that a combination of foundationalism and coherentism is the only option available to lawyers when the problem of justification is considered. The law and other normative domains bring to the fore a different possibility: dialecticism. On this view, a belief is justified if the arguments in its favor prevail over the arguments backing a competing stance. This dialectical dimension is clearly visible in any legal debate: judicial opinions, trial transcripts, and legislative documents are filled with arguments pro and contra a given conception. When one considers this justificatory practice from the most general perspective, it involves no traces of either foundationalism or coherentism. No beliefs are designated as "basic" or "unmodifiable"; no "fitting in" within a broader context is, per se, a criterion for accepting or rejecting arguments.

It is interesting that this view of justification, which today plays out its role in the normative sphere, used to be the conception of choice in empirical investigations before the birth of modern science with perhaps its most famous embodiment being the medieval scholastic method. The method – so nicely put to work in many medieval treatises, and in particular in the works of Thomas Aquinas – consisted in stating a question (*quaestio*), enumerating arguments in favor of a particular answer (*videtur*), arguments against it (*sed contra*), and finally weighing the arguments and deciding what the answer should be (*respondeo*). Interestingly, recent historical studies reveal that one of the more important sources of the scholastic method can be traced back to Islamic law: Islamic religious lawyers in the tenth century used a method called *al-khilaf*, which perfectly matches the procedure applied later by medieval thinkers in Western Europe. It reached the Latin philosophers through their Arabic predecessors.[65]

The idea that justification is provided by the strongest argument is quite simple. However, the problem is how to assess which argument is the strongest. In other words: when does one argument prevail over the other? The best way to approach this issue is to take advantage of the conception of argumentation developed by Chaim Perelman. He distinguishes between two kinds of audiences: particular and universal. A particular audience is any given group of people that needs to be persuaded; the universal audience, in turn, is a thought-construct, consisting of all rational human beings. It is the audience that determines the criteria for the acceptance of arguments.

It is easy to see that the strength of arguments may be evaluated differently by particular audiences. Thus, it is impossible to say in general what kinds of arguments may be efficient when dealing with a particular audience. Logical validity may be

---

[65] Cf. Makdisi, 1974.

important to some but disregarded by others; empirical adequacy may be valued by one group of people, but completely ignored by another comprising of Hegelians, who will always choose theory over facts; coherence will be welcome by some audiences, and dismissed by others. Importantly, arguing in front of a particular audience will often involve much more than an appeal to reason; in particular, it may take advantage of human unconscious and emotional reactions. From this perspective, arguments presented to a particular audience may frequently aim at generating intuitive judgments or activating imagination. The classical art of rhetoric recognized this fact. Among the typical forms of arguments, Greek and Roman authors include *argumentum ab exemplo* (from example) and *a simile* (from similarity or analogy) – both of them, as I have tried to argue in Chapter 2, are methods of inducing mental simulations, which may give us access to unconscious content (intuition).

The universal audience is different. As Perelman puts it, it consists of "all of humanity, or at least all those who are competent and reasonable."[66] Let us briefly consider this characterization. It must be repeated, first and foremost, that the universal audience is a thought-construct. In reality, it is impossible to argue in front of "all of humanity." What Perelman has in mind is the process of developing arguments *as if* one faced the universal audience. Second, in such a setting idiosyncrasies, individual obsessions, self-serving goals, or atypical emotional reactions are unimportant: among "all of humanity" they cancel out. Therefore, argumentation produced for the universal audience is objective: it must necessarily be based on what people share, and ignore how they differ. It follows that the universal audience will be prone to accept arguments that take advantage of logically valid forms of reasoning, coherent theories, and empirically established facts. The move from a particular audience to the universal one is a road from the subjective to the objective; from the emotional to the logical; from the concrete to the abstract; from the intuition- and imagination-based to the language-based; and, finally, from the pragmatic to the ideal. Of course, these are not sharp distinctions. Rather, actual rational argumentation will take place in the space between two extremes: one, where the justification criteria are completely arbitrary and hang together with a particular audience, and the other, which sets forth ideal standards for acceptance of arguments (as embodied in the idea of the universal audience).

Argumentation in the law will also always oscillate between these two extremes. When involved in negotiations between two parties, or presenting a case in front of a jury, a lawyer has a very particular audience to consider, where psychological tricks and an appeal to self-interest may be far more important than logical validity or empirical adequacy. When arguing in front of a professional judge who is trained (to a certain extent, at least) in identifying logical fallacies and assessing the objective strength of arguments, the development of a line of argumentation more appealing

[66] Perelman, 1982, p. 14.

to the universal audience will be needed; however, the ultimate goal will be to act in the best interest of the client. Judges will need to use an even more objective argumentation standard, since their task is to persuade higher court judges and the public at large. Similarly, a doctrinal study should be filled with arguments designed for a universal audience since they are aimed at a largely anonymous group of experts.

In light of this, one can speak of two diametrically different views of justification in the law. One of them is pragmatic or dialogue-based: a justified belief or decision is the one that fares best in comparison with competing options. The comparison may be carried out according to various criteria: from purely arbitrary and subjective (in the case of a particular audience) to purely objective (in the ideal case of the universal audience). The other conception is formal or theory-based: a justified belief is the one that fits best within a broader theoretical context. Here also, there is no unique criterion of justification, but a number of different options, from the purely foundational to the fully coherentist.

Moreover, both conceptions of justification are linked in an interesting way. Let us consider the following thought experiment. We are arguing in front of a group of people who make their decisions in a purely random way (e.g. by throwing dice). This is an extreme case of a particular audience: its assessment of the quality of arguments is fully accidental. Let us further imagine that this extreme case occupies one (the left) end of a line. By moving along the line toward its right end, we encounter audiences who display more stable patterns of argument assessment. For example, there may be a group of people who accept any argument based on a passage from Nietzsche; or an audience that is persuaded by any claim following from the precept to promote the well-being of a particular social group such as bus drivers or white adult Christians. The further we move right, the more objective the acceptance standards are. It means that the argumentation structure becomes more complex, some sets of beliefs are designated as more important (foundational) than others, and formal criteria (consistency, unification) gain influence. At the same time, individual preferences, group interests, and mere whims are valued less and less. Still, the particular audiences belonging to the section of the line located close to its right end may tend to accept quite different arguments; some may be more foundational, others more coherentist. However, the importance of formal as opposed to merely pragmatic criteria for justification will become more and more apparent. Finally, at the far right end of the line, we will have the universal audience. Arguably, such an audience will be ready to accept only such a solution to the problem that follows from a complete and final theory of the world; a theory, it should be added, that is purely foundational (no beliefs belonging to the final theory can ever be rejected), but at the same time fully coherent. On the one hand, it shows the ideal character of the universal audience; on the other hand, it uncovers an interesting relationship between foundational and coherentist views of knowledge.

Importantly, lawyers do not have to choose between the pragmatic and the formal conceptions of justification but rather the actual justification criteria are determined by the given legal culture and tradition, as well as the type of problem one is dealing with. Generally speaking, justification in the common law is more dialectical than in civil law;[67] at the same time, judges in both traditions tend to use more objective justification criteria in comparison to advocates, who for obvious reasons explore more contextual justification standards. Therefore, there is no ultimate conception of legal justification. Rather, there is a justification space determined by the opposition of the foundational–coherentist on the one hand, and the particular–universal on the other.

Finally, our analysis thus far has said nothing about the content of a justified legal belief or decision. We have concentrated on the form and context of legal reasoning, underscoring that the structure of a legal argument contributes to the quality of the final decision. But it is not impossible that a decision that "fits together" with some previously accepted theses, follows from a set of basic beliefs, or is acceptable by a particular audience (even consisting of experts) is also unjust or at least may be regarded as such. Formal and quasi-formal features alone – consistency, logical validity, coherence, or dialectical strength – do not guarantee fairness. Of course, one may point out that if a legal decision is endorsed by the universal audience (i.e. the set of "all those who are competent and reasonable"), it will be fair and just. However, as I emphasized, the universal audience is only an ideal, a mere thought-construct. One can try to imagine what arguments would be acceptable by such an entity but can never say with any degree of certainty that one knows what arguments these are. In real life, less ideal and more operable justification standards are available. The downside is that using these standards may lead us to a "local maximum" (i.e. to a decision that is fully coherent with some accepted beliefs, but that can be improved when the substantive dimension of legal rationality is taken into account alongside the pragmatic and the formal features of reasoning). For example, a claim based on the communist view of the law may display the required features (e.g. be acceptable by a particular audience such as a higher court, or be highly coherent with the political agenda of the ruling party), but at the same time be simply unjust. This is precisely the subject matter of the chapter that follows.

---

[67]   Cf. Hadfield, 2006.

5

Substance

This chapter discusses two aspects of rationality in the law, namely the constructive and the ecological. I will begin with a short outline of Kant's practical philosophy since it constitutes a perfect point of reference for the subsequent considerations: it helps to bring to the fore two opposing dimensions of rationality – the ideal and the factual. I proceed to discuss the attempts to construct elaborate standards of rational thinking in law and morals, identifying their strengths and weaknesses, and exposing their role as "signposts" directing and organizing our cognitive efforts. Then, I contrast constructive rationality with its ecological counterpart – a view that practical decisions must be a good "fit" for the social environment. Such an approach makes it possible to discuss an oft-neglected dimension of legal thinking: the limits of the implementation of our elaborate, rational constructs into legal practice. I conclude with an answer to the question pertaining to the relationship between the two kinds of rationality. I defend the claim that the role of the theoretical constructs is to generate variation, while social ecosystems serve as a selection mechanism. The resulting view is a comprehensive picture of the legal mind, its mechanisms, the normative precepts guiding it, and the legal environment in which it functions.

5.1 KEEPING UP WITH KANT

Immanuel Kant was a creature of dull habit and impressive self-constraint, as illustrated by his daily routine. He would get up early at 5:00 a.m., woken by his servant, Martin Lampe, an old soldier who was instructed to be persistent so that Kant would not oversleep. After drinking a cup or two of weak tea, he would smoke a pipe of tobacco – the only one on any given day. Then he would work on his lectures and treaties. At 7:00 classes would begin, lasting till 11:00. Before lunch, Kant would still find some time for writing; after lunch there was time for a walk and some rest in the company of his friend Green. Before going to sleep, he would do some more light work and read.[1]

[1] Kuehn, 2001, p. 222.

Sometime in the autumn of 1791, Kant's routine was disrupted by a letter he received from a young Austrian noblewoman, Maria von Herbert. Kant was apparently moved by what she had to say and used some of his precious time in the spring of 1792 to write a reply. Von Herbert approached him with a personal yet deeply ethical question. She began in a dramatic fashion: "Great Kant, . . . I call to you for help, for comfort, or for counsel to prepare me for death."[2] And she continued:

> I loved someone who, in my eyes, encompassed within himself all that is worthwhile, so that I lived only for him, everything else was in comparison just rubbish, cheap trinkets. Well, I have offended this person, because of a long drawn out lie, which I have now disclosed to him, though there was nothing unfavorable to my character in it, I had no vice in my life that needed hiding. The lie was enough though, and his love vanished.[3]

Having found herself in such a pitiful situation, von Herbert sees no sense in living and thinks of committing suicide. What prevents her from taking this ultimate step is Kant's philosophy. However, although she "read the metaphysic of morals, and the categorical imperative, . . . it doesn't help a bit. Her reason abandons her just when she needs it."[4] And hence she turns to Kant himself for any help he can provide.

One would expect that Kant will show his young correspondent some genuine compassion. At the very least, one would expect a powerful argument to the effect that suicide is not a way out of love-related problems. Meanwhile, Kant concentrates on something else. He offers an exercise in conceptual analysis, distinguishing between reticence and dishonesty. While, he says, one is entitled to some lack of frankness, lying is "a serious violation of a duty to oneself; it subverts the dignity of humanity in our own person, and attacks the roots of our thinking."[5] It follows that von Herbert's friend was justified in "having wavered his affection for her." Kant also offers some kind of consolation; he believes that the "just indignation" of von Herbert's friend will diminish with time and his coldness will be transformed "into a more firmly grounded love."[6] If this does not happen, however, it will only mean that the affection was shallow in the first place and would have disappeared anyway. A comforting disjunction, indeed.

The following year saw von Herbert write another letter to Kant. She informed him, among other things, that she finds her life empty, "superfluous and unnecessary."[7] For Maria, there is no reason to stay alive; yet, she hopes that Kant will provide such a reason: "I ask you, because my conception of morality is silent here, whereas it speaks decisively on all other matters. And if you cannot give me the answer I seek, I beg you to give me something that will get this intolerable emptiness

[2] Kant, 1999, p. 379.
[3] Ibid., p. 379.
[4] Ibid., p. 380.
[5] Ibid., p. 412.
[6] Ibid., pp. 412, 413.
[7] Cf. ibid., p. 451.

out of my soul."[8] In short: von Herbert exhibits all the symptoms of a deep depression. At the same time, Kant learned from J. B. Erhard what her "lie" was: she had concealed from her friend that she had been abused and betrayed by a previous lover.[9] Despite knowing this, Kant chose not to answer Maria's second letter. The story had a very sad ending: ten years later Maria von Herbert committed suicide.

Kant was not von Herbert's therapist; he had no obligation to care for her. However, his letter and subsequent silence are very telling. The exchange between Kant and the young woman was a clash between human tragedy and painstaking conceptual analysis; between the intricacies of real life and the solemnity of an abstract theory; between disturbing emotions and cold reason. It was also a short dialogue on the nature of morality, where von Herbert turned out to be completely lost, and Kant remained an emotionless moralist, as emotionless as his daily routine.

Indeed, Kant forcefully rejects the idea that morality has anything to do with emotions. He assumes, in the spirit of Pietism, the denomination of his upbringing, that our ethical experience is that of universally binding norms, which should be followed not because of some external criteria, but simply because they are moral norms. It is with this in mind that we should consider Kant's narrative. The first question he poses is whether our passions or feelings should have any bearing on our moral behavior. His answer is firmly in the negative: emotions cannot give rise to objective moral obligations, as they are contingent. It is enough to look around to realize that different people cherish different things, tend to follow different precepts, and entertain different feelings. Because of that, Kant rejects so-called hypothetical imperative as the source of moral obligation. The hypothetical imperative reads: "If you set an end Z, perform whatever actions are indispensably necessary means to the attainment of Z that lie in your power." In connection to it, Kant notes:

> All practical principles which presuppose an object (matter) of the faculty of desire as the ground of determination of the will are empirical, and can furnish no practical laws. By the matter of the faculty of desire I mean an object the realization of which is desired. Now, if the desire for this object precedes the practical rule, and is the condition of our making it a principle, then I say (in the first place) this principle is in that case wholly empirical, for then what determines the choice is the idea of an object, and that relation of this idea to the subject by which its faculty of desire is determined to its realization. Such a relation to the subject is called the pleasure in the realization of an object. This, then, must be presupposed as a condition of the possibility of determination of the will. But it is impossible to know *a priori* of any idea of an object whether it will be connected with pleasure or pain, or be indifferent. In such cases, therefore, the determining principle of the choice must be empirical, and, therefore, also the practical material principle which presupposes it as a condition.[10]

---

[8] Ibid., p. 452.
[9] Cf. ibid., p. 454.
[10] Kant, 1909, pp. 107–108.

In short, then, Kant's argument is that passions and desires cannot provide the foundations for morality as, being empirical, they are neither universal nor necessary, and so lack the two characteristic features of genuine moral obligation. Instead, Kant proposes his famous categorical imperative, which in one of its versions is: "Act only in accordance with that maxim through which you can at the same time will that it become a universal law."[11]

The crucial difference between the categorical and the hypothetical imperatives is that the former, unlike the latter, is unconditional. Reflecting on this, Kant writes:

> If I think of a hypothetical imperative in general, I do not know in advance what it will contain until the condition is given to me. But if I think of a categorical imperative, then I know right away what it contains. For since the imperative contains besides the law only the necessity that the maxim should conform to the law, but the law contains no condition to which it is limited, then there is nothing remaining in it but the universality of a law, to which the maxim of the action is to conform, and which conformity alone the imperative really represents as necessary.[12]

The categorical imperative displays, therefore, the required necessity and universality.

Yet, Kant's conception comes with some nuances, which must be underscored here in order to draw a complete picture of his view of morality. Let us pause for a moment and consider again the content of the categorical imperative: "Act only according to that maxim through which you can at the same time will that it should become a universal law." Kant also offers other equivalent, as he claims, formulations, for example, "So act as if the maxim of your action were to become through your will a universal law of nature";[13] or "Act so that you use humanity, as much in your own person as in the person of every other, always at the same time as end and never merely as means."[14] Let us deem them, respectively, the universal law formulation, the law of nature formulation, and the humanity as an end formulation. It is striking that Kant considers them equivalent, for he says, in effect, that imagining a system of rational, universal rules of conduct is the same as imagining a perfect world in which moral norms function in the same way as the laws of physics; or a world in which humanity is cherished through all our actions.

In the previous paragraph I have used the word "imagine" twice. This is by no means accidental. Indeed, all the formulations of the categorical imperative can be taken as short instructions to use one's imagination: to conceive a moral system that one would accept as universally binding; to think of a set of moral rules as if they had the ontological status of the laws of physics; or to consider a universe where all our

---

[11] Kant, 2002, p. 37.
[12] Ibid., p. 37.
[13] Ibid., p. 38.
[14] Ibid., pp. 46–47.

rule-governed actions are aimed, at least partially, to endorse humanity as a central value. In other words, different versions of the categorial imperative are tools for engaging one's abilities of mental simulation. Take the law of nature formulation of the imperative and consider whether lying should be prohibited. How to do this? Well, one needs to imagine a world in which people are unable to lie, since the non-lying rule has a status of a deterministic law of physics. This certainly is a powerful, even if not detailed, image; it has a huge advantage over remaining at the level of linguistic constructions, where one can only keep repeating ad nauseam: "Act only according to that maxim . . .," "Act only according to that maxim . . .." Kant acknowledges this fact and places imagination at the heart of his theory. Its role is to provide synthesis, that is to serve as a bridge between abstract concepts, such as the ones used in the formulation of the categorical imperative, and perceived particular events and objects. He famously says:

> Synthesis in general (*überhaupt*) as we shall hereafter see, is the result of the power of imagination, a blind but indispensable function of the soul, without which we would have no knowledge whatsoever, but of which we are scarcely ever conscious.[15]

The problem is that Kant is far from clear as to how imagination does the trick of synthesizing the particular into the general. Imagination remains a crucial but somewhat mysterious ability that operates at the borders of consciousness and is indispensable for the generation of knowledge.

Kant is also not blind to the power of emotions and desires in human behavior. In particular, he believes that factors external to reason play an important role in the practice of following legal norms. For him, any act of lawgiving has the following form: "Do (or do not do) x because y." The first part of this formula is the law itself, while the second is an incentive. Furthermore, there are two kinds of incentives: internal and external. The former are those that are provided by the law itself ("do one's duty because it is one's duty"). The latter "must be drawn from sensibly dependent determining grounds of choice, inclinations and aversions, and among these, from aversions; for it is a lawgiving, which constrains, not an allurement, which invites."[16] This is what distinguishes ethics from law: while ethics is concerned with self-obligation, which require internal incentives, law is defined by the use of external incentives, and hence by the competence to impose obligations on others. In other words, ethics concerns principles that cannot legitimately be enforced by coercion and law concerns principles that are permissibly enforced by coercion. Consequently, ethics and law have different purposes: the former secures moral or inner freedom, the latter freedom of interaction in a society.

One may rightly maintain, therefore, that law is distinct from ethics. It is not, however, an instance of strict separation. As Kant observes:

15   Kant, 1929, p. 112.
16   Kant, 1991, p. 46.

Thus ethics commands that I still fulfill a contract I have entered into, even though the other party could not coerce me to do so; but it takes the law ... and the duty corresponding to it from the doctrine of right, as already given there. Accordingly the giving of the law that promises agreed to must be kept lies not in ethics but in *ius*. All that ethics teaches is that if the incentive which juridical lawgiving connects with that duty, namely external constraint, were absent, the idea of duty by itself would be sufficient as an incentive.[17]

This passage indicates the following. First, as acting ethically means acting out of duty, and legal obligations are duties, there is an ethical obligation to act according to legal (or externally coerced) duty. Second, it follows that in the case of a contract there are two different duties to fulfill, both arising not from ethics but from law (*Ius*): there is a legal duty to fulfill the contract (because of the external incentives) and an ethical duty to fulfill it (because it is a duty). Therefore, one can say that "the juridical precedes the ethical" or that law is relevant for ethics, for all legal duties are also ethical duties.

Having said that, a more important aspect of the relationship between ethics and law must be stressed. I have been deliberately using the word "ethics" instead of "morality," since for Kant the sphere of the moral comprises both ethics and law (whenever I have used the word "morality" in relation to Kant's philosophy, I am referring to both ethics and law). Therefore, Kant's ambitious program of the metaphysics of morals has to be seen as foundational for both ethics and law. It is well known, however, that it is ethics that is at the core of Kant's considerations in both the *Groundwork* and in the *Critique of Practical Reason*. Hence, the question arises as to whether the foundations of moral reasoning as encapsulated in the categorical imperative only apply to ethics or also rather to law.

It has been argued that one should distinguish between the general categorical imperative,[18] which applies both to ethics and law, and specific versions thereof, which concern both spheres separately. Let us recall again our previous formulation of the imperative: "Act only according to that maxim through which you can at the same time will that it should become a universal law." This formulation concerns only ethics, as it includes the term "maxim." By this Kant means a material rule used to guide a person in particular situations about what to do. It thus provides a kind of bridge between a person's inner disposition and outer action. "Because the aspect of motive, of morality, is embedded in the concept of a maxim ..., the general categorical imperative is acquired as soon as the expression 'maxim' is replaced by that of 'principle,' which is neutral as far as morality is concerned and signifies arbitrary, not necessarily self-decreed principle. The required general form of the categorical imperative therefore reads: 'Act only according to principles which can be conceived and willed as universal law.'"[19] Consequently, in addition to the

[17] Ibid., p. 47.
[18] Cf. Höffe, 1989.
[19] Ibid., p. 156.

categorical imperative of ethics there exists a version of the categorical imperative for law, which reads: "Act externally only in agreement with principles which can be conceived and willed as a universal law."[20] The difference between the formulations of the categorical imperatives adequate for ethics and law lies in two facts. The "legal" imperative requires of us to act externally according to certain principles. This formulation marks an important feature of acting rationally in the domain of law, a feature that has already been mentioned: "juridical duties are precisely those where the incentive need not be duty – it may, for example, be the threat of coercion connected to the law by the legislative authority which promulgates it."[21] In other words, the "ethical" imperative requires us to fulfill our duties out of duty, while the motivation of acting is irrelevant with regard to the "legal" imperative. Still, "the categorical imperative of Law refers only to duties to others and not to duties to oneself."[22] This is understandable as the purpose of the domain of law is to secure the freedom of interaction in a society.

These considerations enable us to address the question of what is the role of the emotions in Kant's conception of practical reason. To put it succinctly (and here I deviate from Kant's complex terminology): Kant distinguishes between the criterion for determining the content of moral (i.e. ethical and legal) precepts and the adequate motive for following those precepts. In both ethics and law, the content of the rules of conduct is determined through the categorical imperative: they should be such that they "can be conceived and willed as universal law." A norm of conduct, be it ethical or legal, is justified only if it is universalizable. As regards motives, however, acting ethically is purely rational – here, one acts ethically if one does so "out of duty." In the law, however, motives may be purely psychological: fear, pleasure, happiness, etc.

Let us illustrate this point with the exchange between Kant and von Herbert. Kant observes that lying is "a serious violation of a duty to oneself; it subverts the dignity of humanity in our own person, and attacks the roots of our thinking."[23] Therefore, lying is incompatible with the categorical imperative (in the quoted sentence Kant invokes the humanity as an end formulation thereof). Moreover, the obligation not to lie is an ethical rather than legal duty (i.e. it is "a duty to oneself"). Thus, to fulfill it one needs not only conformity to the categorical imperative, but also acting with proper motivation. If one does not lie (therefore complying with the content of the categorical imperative) because of various emotions (fear, love, disgust, etc.), one is not acting ethically!

In his reply to von Herbert, Kant says:

Ask yourself whether you reproach yourself for the imprudence of confessing, or for the immorality intrinsic to the lie. If the former, then you regret having done your duty. And why? Because it has resulted in the loss of your friend's confidence. This

---

[20] Ibid., p. 156.
[21] Kant, 1991, p. 46.
[22] Höffe, 1989, p. 156.
[23] Kant, 1999, p. 412.

regret is not motivated by anything moral, since it is produced by an awareness not of the act itself, but of its consequences. But if your reproach is grounded in a moral judgment of your behavior, it would be a poor moral physician who would advise you to cast it from your mind.[24]

It transpires that, according to Kant, von Herbert's suffering is well deserved. If by telling her friend the truth she acted "out of duty," being aware of the "immorality intrinsic to her lie," her actions were ethical, but the pain is easily explainable as a reminder of what she had done. If, however, she regrets disclosing the lie because of the consequences, her action was not ethical in the first place: it was compatible with the categorical imperative, but lacked proper motivation. Thus, she can either be commended (and left suffering) or be condemned (and left suffering all the same).

There is one more dimension, in which Kant believes moral action to be connected to emotions. In *The Groundwork of the Metaphysics of Morals* he speaks of a peculiar feeling of respect or reverence (*Achtung*), which accompanies a decision determined by the categorical imperative. However, the feeling in question is very peculiar. Kant says: "the immediate determination of the will through the law and the consciousness of it is called respect, so that the latter is to be regarded as the effect of the law on the subject and not as its cause."[25] Thus, respect is an outcome of recognizing, on the basis of the categorical imperative, what is the morally required action, and not a factor influencing such a recognition. In other words, according to the prevalent interpretation, respect does not play a motivational role in moral action.[26]

This is a very peculiar position. The contemporary moral psychology would be at pains trying to identify the Kantian respect with any feeling or emotion that is typically considered as morally relevant. Traditionally, the catalogue of moral emotions includes anger, elevation, guilt, compassion, shame, embarrassment, disgust, gratitude, and contempt;[27] Kant's respect seems to be more similar to epistemic emotions, in particular to revelation, characteristic of *"Heureka* moments"*: it is not something that motivates us to act in one way or another, but accompanies a positive change (e.g. increase of coherence) in our belief system.[28]

The resulting picture is of a very demanding standard of practical rationality. There are two main aspects thereof. When it comes to determining the content of rational moral (i.e. ethical and legal) rules, Kant is quite clear: moral precepts are rational (just, fair, justified) as long as they comply with the categorical imperative. No other considerations can contribute to our decision-making process in the sphere of the practical. To be moral agents, "our own lawgivers," we must exercise

[24] Ibid., p. 412.
[25] Kant, 2002, p. 17.
[26] Reath, 1989, pp. 287, 290.
[27] Cf. Haidt, 2003.
[28] Hurley et al., 2011, p. 78ff.

autonomy in relation to our own interests and desires, as well as the influence of others. The second issue is motivation. In the case of ethics, moral action must be undertaken "out of duty"; otherwise, it is not moral action. In the law, the admissible motives may be differentiated, including emotions such as fear or embarrassment. From this point of view, legal action is easier than ethical; but it is not easy, since it requires compliance with the categorical imperative. As we have seen, Kant recognizes that decision-making in the practical sphere involves much more than the manipulation of abstract rules of conduct. It requires imagination and is accompanied by various emotions, including those that can be deemed "epistemic." In other words, Kant provides us with a very broad and comprehensive picture of the cognitive and motivational mechanisms responsible for moral thinking and action. Nonetheless, the high standard of the categorical imperative remains at the very heart of his view. Indeed, it is difficult to keep up with Kant.

5.2 THE SUPREME COURT OF CONSTRUCTIVISM

Thinking, including legal thinking, is an extremely complex process, based on the cooperation of three different mechanisms: unconscious decision-making (i.e. intuition and insight), mental simulation (both unconscious and conscious, i.e. imagination), and linguistic constructions. These mechanisms, as we have seen, are not mutually independent – they work together through various interactions: intuition, based on past experience, automatically suggests solutions to the encountered problems, which may in turn become the subject of conscious deliberation with the use of mental simulations and language; imagination on the one hand helps to activate intuitions and achieve insights, while on the other hand enabling understanding of linguistic expressions; finally, thinking in language is a kind of auxiliary construction or framework, which must be filled in with concrete simulations and intuitions.

Importantly, legal thinking, which takes advantage of these mechanisms, must be non-foundational. Solving legal problems is not based on identifying some irremovable foundations – premises, which cannot be rejected – and applying them through infallible methods of reasoning. Because of several different reasons – the logical, the classificatory, the semantic, and the constructional – legal thinking is a permanent "play" between the linguistic abstraction and the imagined concrete, augmented by unconscious intuitions and insights. It also transpires that in order to make this play more efficient, one should take advantage of six principles: of experience, caution, exemplification, variability, unification, and contrast.

It should be noted that speaking of the six principles belongs to a different layer of reflection over legal thinking than the reconstruction of the architecture of the legal mind. The principles are normative precepts, which suggest how legal thinking ought to be carried out, and not how it potentially can be carried out. Relying on the experience embodied in one's unconscious mind; being cautious in relation to the intuitive judgments, especially when confronted with an atypical issue; imagining particular instantiations of abstract concepts; taking advantage of a series of slightly different mental simulations; developing a unified theory; and working with competing hypotheses are good ways to increase the likelihood of solving any legal problem. The question is, however, what does it mean to solve such a problem: which solutions are acceptable or justified? An answer to this question is also normative in character, and has two separate but interconnected aspects.

As we have seen in the previous chapter, there is the dimension of justification. The legal justification space is determined by two concepts: of theory-based (formal) and dialogue-based (pragmatic) justification. According to the first conception, a justified legal belief belongs to a theory, which has certain formal characteristics (it is highly coherent and is based, to some extent, on a set of beliefs that are regarded as more fundamental than others). The dialogical view of justification, in turn, favors beliefs that survive the comparison of competing arguments. Here, one can speak of two extreme forms of justification (as embodied by the idea of a particular audience and of the universal audience). Together, the theory-based and the dialogue-based approaches delimit a space of potential justification standards; the choice of a particular standard hangs together with the legal tradition as well as the type of problem one is dealing with. However, these criteria for justification are not sufficient. It is easy to imagine a solution to a legal problem that "fits" within a broader context or is highly persuasive, but at the same time violates the rudimentary sense of justice and fairness. A substantive ingredient is missing, one supplied by the theories of practical rationality.

Theories of rationality (justice, fairness) developed by philosophers have a constructive character.[29] They aim at developing the rules of reasoning or acting, which should be observed in order to think or act rationally (in a just or fair way). This strategy has been employed in the most important moral and legal-theoretic conceptions: from Kant's theory of practical reason, through Bentham and Mill's utilitarianism, to the twentieth-century variations on the Kantian and utilitarian themes in the philosophy of law: Kelsen's normativism,[30] Robert Alexy's theory of the rational legal discourse,[31] and the economic analysis of law.[32]

Let us return to Kant's practical philosophy. As already noted, Kant claimed that rational decisions (in the sphere of law and ethics) need to be compatible with the categorical imperative: "Act only in accordance with that maxim through which you can at the same time will that it become a universal law."[33] The imperative may look innocent: it is but a short rule, one that we instinctively tend to accept. It endorses no particular obligations, only determining the general framework for arriving at

---

[29] Cf. Smith, 2008, p. 26ff.
[30] Cf. Kelsen, 2011; Kelsen, 1967.
[31] Cf. Alexy, 2009.
[32] Cf. Posner, 2007.
[33] Kant, 2002, p. 37.

rational moral and legal decisions. However, the innocence is an illusion. Let us consider in more detail what Kant requires of us. For example, imagine Judge Kantius, who is always able to interpret legal provisions and issue rulings in accordance with the categorical imperative. What kind of man is he?

First, Kantius is flawless when it comes to developing and manipulating abstract conceptual constructs. If, as Kant claims, universalizability is the essence of practical rationality, our judge needs to master highly abstract norms of conduct. In order to do so, the language they use must be abstract, but also free from troublesome features which usually come with abstraction, and in particular: vagueness and open texture. Judge Kantius is therefore the embodiment of Leibniz's dream: he is equipped with an abstract tool for thinking about the law that is as perfect as the language of mathematics.[34]

Second, our judge must always make decisions in the context of the entire legal system. At the first glance, it may seem that the categorical imperative is easily applicable to simple, isolated problems. For example: when Judge Kantius considers the interpretation of the rule "Vehicles are not allowed into the public park," he only needs to determine which of the possible interpretations of the provision could be "willed as a universal law." The problem is that in order to make such a determination one needs to take into account all the possible situations, in which the given interpretation would potentially be applicable; after all, the resulting understanding of the rule must be universal "as if" it was a law of physics. Judge Kantius should not only consider whether cars, motorcycles, or bicycles can enter the park. His universal rule must pertain to children toys, trucks serving as war memorials, wheelchairs equipped with electric engines, passenger planes, restored Spitfires that served during World War II, ambulances carrying seriously injured persons, etc. Moreover, Kantius should also consider how the given understanding of the rule is related to other legal rules (and all their potential interpretations); if the outcome is "a universal law," it is not allowed that another equally universal rule would give rise to a different conclusion. For example, if we assume that the rule prohibiting vehicles from entering the park should be interpreted so that an ambulance carrying a seriously injured person cannot drive through the park, we need to make sure that some other legal norm (e.g. one prescribing that human life and health should be protected by the law) will not give rise to a different decision. Judge Kantius is a true intellectual Hercules:[35] adjudicating any particular case, he takes into account the entire legal system, seeing to it that the decision he makes will not violate the consistency of the system. In a sense, deciding a case, he decides all possible cases.

Third and finally, Judge Kantius is fully autonomous in his decision-making. His decisions are based on reason and reason alone. He is deaf to the voices of other

---

[34] Cf. Leibniz, 1989.
[35] Cf. Dworkin, 1986, pp. 266–275.

people, capable of ignoring his intuitions, and can separate himself from his strongest emotions. He is, in fact, a perfect inferential machine, capable of drawing conclusions in an infallible way. Of course, as I have already argued, like any Kantian moral subject Judge Kantius may take advantage of imagination or experience emotions. However, neither his mental simulations nor emotional reactions influence the content of his judgment. Imagination is used as an auxiliary tool for arriving at a justified decision. Emotions, on the other hand, perform an aesthetic rather than practical function: when one establishes a rule of behavior consistent with the categorical imperative, the process is accompanied by the feeling of respect. Other emotions, such as fear or guilt may also enter the stage as motivational factors when following legal rules. But it must be stressed again that they do not influence the content of those rules. Moreover, arguably, Judge Kantius's duty to adjudicate legal cases is not only a legal duty, but also a moral one; if so, he can fulfill it only if he acts purely "out of duty," completely detached from any emotions.

Judge Kantius is therefore a kind of superhero, and his cognitive abilities exceed by orders of magnitude what a typical Smith or Jones can do. People are not equipped with a perfect language free from vagueness and open texture; they are unable to develop a complete and coherent system of norms, yielding a unique right answer to any legal problem; and they do not possess the level of self-control required for the Kantian exercise of autonomy.

The construction of an unachievable ideal as the standard of practical rationality is characteristic also of other theoretical conceptions developed within the Kantian tradition. A case in point is Robert Alexy's theory of legal discourse. In a nutshell, he claims that rational (fair, just, or justified) decisions are those that can be outcomes of a discussion carried out according to certain rules classified into six groups. The basic rules include, inter alia:[36] "No speaker may contradict him or herself"; "Every speaker may only assert what he or she actually believes"; and "Different speakers may not use the same expression with different meanings." The rationality rules, in turn, are: "Every speaker must give reasons for what he or she asserts when asked to do so, unless he or she can cite reasons which justify a refusal to provide a justification"; "Everyone who can speak may take part in discourse"; "Everyone may problematize any assertion"; "Everyone may introduce any assertion into the discourse"; and "Everyone may express his or her attitudes, wishes, and needs." The third group comprises the rules for allocating the burden of argument: "Whoever proposes to treat a person A differently from a person B is obliged to provide justification for doing so"; "Whoever attacks a statement or norm which is not the subject of the discussion must state reason for so doing"; or "Whoever has put forward an argument is only obliged to produce further arguments in the event of counterarguments." The fourth group includes argument forms such as the legal syllogism. The fifth group are justification rules, which

[36] Alexy, 2009, pp. 187–206.

include, among others: "The consequences of every rule for the satisfaction of the interests of each and every individual must be acceptable to everyone"; "Every rule must be openly and universally teachable"; "The moral rules underlying the moral views of a speaker must be able to withstand critical testing in terms of their historical and individual genesis"; "The actually given limits of realizability are to be taken into account." Finally, the sixth group comprises the transition rules from the practical to other discourses: theoretical, linguistic-analytical, and discourse-theoretical.

As we can see, Alexy's conception is far from trivial or self-evident. In particular, it is debatable if, and to what extent, it represents a reformulation of the Kantian conception of practical rationality. Is it really the case that following the Alexian rules of discourse would always result in decisions that are compatible with the categorical imperative? However, it is quite easy to see that the rules determine a procedure that can never be fully realized. Let us consider two of these rules: "Everyone who can speak may take part in discourse" or "Everyone may introduce any assertion into the discourse." If followed to the letter, these rules would jeopardize any actual debate, turning it into a never-ending story. In other words, a discussion carried out in full compliance with all the rules Alexy formulates is an unachievable ideal. A clerk to Judge Kantius, who embraces the Alexian view of practical rationality, is also a superhuman: in his briefs for Kantius he is able to masterfully craft an argumentative structure, which includes the formulation and evaluation of all potential arguments and counterarguments for any claim that is in any way relevant in the given case.[37]

But we are destined to fail not only trying to live up to the Kantian standards, but also in other cases. In fact, any constructivist view of rationality is beyond our grasp. Next to Judge Kantius, we have his archenemy, Judge "Happy" Benthamius. "Happy" is capable of interpreting and applying the law according to the highest rule of utilitarianism of the "greatest happiness for the greatest number of people" (or, to put it in more contemporary terms, by maximizing the social utility function).[38] This task requires very precise language, since in ordinary language such terms as "happiness" or "utility" are vague. Judge "Happy," similarly to his Kantian counterpart, must also be able to think in a holistic way, since it is the legal system as a whole, and not individual decisions, that is to promote happiness (social utility). Moreover, in addition to the perfect normative knowledge, "Happy" must be extremely competent when it comes to the knowledge of facts and empirical laws, as he should be able to predict all the consequences of his decisions. Finally, he has an enormous power of self-control: he follows only the principle of maximizing social utility, ignoring all other potential sources of inspiration or persuasion, from emotional reaction to alternative theories. He does so by engaging in error-free, complex

---

[37] For a more detailed discussion of Alexy's theory of argumentation, see Brożek, 2007; Pavlakos, 2007; Borowski et al., 2017.

[38] Bentham, 1977, p. 393. See also Burns, 2005.

calculations with the use of abstract symbolic systems (e.g. rational choice theory). Judge "Happy" is another superhuman.

Among our superheroes one must also include other judges, who may be lesser celebrities, but have too many unusual qualities to resemble mortal lawyers. For example, let us consider Rudolf von Positivismus, trained in the tradition of the German positivism.[39] He believes that the law is what the statute says, and the role of the judge is to apply legal provisions according to the infallible, deductive schemes of reasoning. Positivismus, similarly to Judge Kantius and Judge "Happy" Benthamius, works with a perfect language, where there is no vagueness and open texture; he faces no problems when reconstructing a coherent and complete legal system; and his decisions are based on the norms of the positive law and nothing more[40] – he is capable of disregarding anything else, including moral and religious precepts, psychological pressure applied by the family members, and supplications of friends and acquaintances. The same is true of the great enemy of Rudolf von Positivismus – Giovanni Iusnaturale. It is argued[41] that he can solve any legal case by applying the methods of deductive logic to the highest norm of the natural law: *bonum est faciendum et prosequendum, et malum vitandum*, good is to be done, and pursued and evil avoided.[42] This is no small accomplishment since according to a well-established reading of Thomas Aquinas the precepts of the natural law are expressible only in analogical terms, which are not subject to standard logical analysis.[43] It seems, therefore, that Giovanni Iusnaturale must have very special cognitive capacities, exceeding the abilities of normal human beings, including the great philosophers of the Middle Ages. He can state the norms of natural law in a precise, unequivocal language, while the rest of us are limited to our imperfect analogies.

Why do we create these superheroes? Why populate the Supreme Court of Constructivism with Judge Kantius, Judge "Happy" Benthamius, Rudolf von Positivismus, or Giovanni Iusnaturale? Perhaps, as Friedrich August von Hayek suggests, we are led there by the fatal conceit of reason. Seduced by Cartesian rhetoric, we have found ourselves believing in "a form of rationalism [that] not only discards tradition, but claims that pure reason can directly serve our desires without any such intermediary, and can build a new world, a new morality, a new law, even a new and purified language, from itself alone."[44]

There is a simple answer to this challenge. We keep developing unachievable standards of rationality not because we believe in the power of reason but because in our struggles with the world we need signposts. The constructivist super-judges do

---

[39] Cf. Larenz, 1991; Wróblewski, 1992.
[40] Cf. Stelmach & Brożek, 2006, pp. 8–9.
[41] Cf. Kalinowski, 1967.
[42] Aquinas, 1947, I.II.94.2.
[43] Cf. Krąpiec, 1975, p. 229.
[44] Hayek, 1992, pp. 48–49.

not embody an instruction of how a lawyer should think; rather, they are an element of legal mythology.[45] Without such myths our behavior would be no more than a series of more or less accidental actions. As Kant put it, we need *foci imaginarii*,[46] imaginary focal points at the horizon, to assist us in finding our way in the difficult terrain of legal reflection. We let Kantius, "Happy" Benthamius, Positivismum, and Iusnaturale inhabit the legal Olympus because we desperately need role models.

How do such myths function? First and foremost, they provide us with a kind of cognitive scaffolding, organizing our efforts to solve legal problems. For example, when following in the footsteps of Judge Kantius, one would not be interested in things such as utility maximization or reconstructing the legislative intent; rather, one would "see" the legal problem through the prism of universalizability, looking for a solution that is acceptable "as if" it followed from a universal law. To this end, one would engage in a play of imagination aimed at constructing a perfect world, in which each and every action is a "celebration" of the humanity in ourselves and other people. A follower of Judge "Happy" Benthamius would adopt a completely different perspective. Their goal would be to "translate" the legal problem – irrespective of whether it concerns business, domestic affairs, or criminal activity – into the conceptual scheme of utilitarianism. Every aspect of the case would be expressed in the language of gains and losses, and the task at hand would be considered one of optimization: finding a solution that maximizes gains and minimizes losses, given the values of some additional parameters (e.g. the amount of risk or the estimation of the level of uncertainty). To put it differently: any constructivist standard of rationality comes with auxiliary constructions and a set of preferred tools for thinking. The former are all the theoretical structures connected to the given view of rationality in the law. A detailed reformulation of the Kantian ideal (such as Alexy's theory of legal discourse) or important conceptual distinctions in the utilitarian tradition (e.g. between act utilitarianism and rule utilitarianism) constitute such auxiliary constructions. Each constructivist conception of rationality is also associated with some typical tools for thinking. For example, Kantians would rely both on some use of imagination and on conceptual analysis as well as deductive logic, while the defenders of utilitarianism would take advantage of rational choice theory or game theory.

The second function of the constructivist myths is to serve as a solution sieve. As I have tried to show, these standards of rationality are so ideal that they cannot determine which answers to legal questions are justified. However, they may provide negative selection: it will usually be easy to say that some potential solution to a legal problem is not acceptable since it does not meet the chosen ideal. Of course, it still leaves a number of solutions that are possibly acceptable; but any substantial reduction of the solution space is a very useful thing.

---

[45] Cf. Kołakowski, 1989.
[46] Kant, 1929, p. 533.

It follows that the constructivist myths, while far from providing a precise, step-by-step procedure for arriving at the solution to a legal problem, constitute approximation mechanisms. They equip us with conceptual structures and reasoning tools that hugely facilitate legal thinking and make it resemble to a degree the unachievable ideals embodied by our superhero judges. We can never be sure that our judgments are utility-maximizing or fully universalizable; but we can say that we come close to these standards, or at least much closer than without the help of the mythological scaffolding.

There is, however, an important disadvantage of using such constructivist conceptions of rationality. The myths they form are so powerful that it makes it difficult for us to see beyond them. At some point, one is willing to concede as a fact that "rationality wars" are indeed fought between two superpowers, Kantianism and utilitarianism, with occasional interference of smaller and less known forces. Meanwhile, there is much more to rationality than the constructivist approach. Let us take a closer look at this alternative.

5.3 GOING ECO

Asset allocation is an intriguing economic problem, with the crux of it being how to construct the investment basket in order to maximize return and minimize risk. In 1952, Harry Markowitz provided a solution to this problem by designing a rule known as the mean-variance portfolio, which (among other things) won him the Nobel Prize in 1990. Interestingly, Markowitz himself used a different strategy, the simple 1/N rule: invest equally in each of the N alternatives. Even more interestingly, research showed that this simple rule of thumb usually performs much better, and almost never significantly worse, than the mean-variance portfolio as well as 13 other sophisticated asset allocation policies, based on advanced mathematics and an in-depth analysis of existing market data.[47]

This is tremendously surprising. Rational agents who aim at maximizing their utility function should take advantage of reasoning tools that were specifically designed to promote this particular goal. The mean-variance portfolio, or a similar model, should be their instrument of choice. Meanwhile, it turns out that the actual economic environment is too complex (involving too many options) and too unpredictable to be handled with a perfectly designed and precise but fragile tool. A simple, coarse method is at least as useful, but much easier to apply.

Let us have a look at another example. Arguably, giving consent to become an organ donor is a rational course of action from the Kantian perspective. At the same time, Kantians value autonomy: our decisions must be autonomous to count as moral. Hence, a reasonable way to design legal regulations pertaining to organ donation should be the following: the law makes it possible to become an organ donor, but the

---

[47] Cf. Todd et al., 2012, p. 4.

decision whether to do so or not lies in the hands of individuals. They must clearly express their consent; otherwise, there would be doubts as to whether an autonomous decision in this matter has been made at all. This approach has been adapted by the German legislature. As a result, only 12 percent of Germans are potential organ donors while, in contrast, in neighboring Austria the corresponding rate is 99 percent. This difference is easy to explain. In Austrian law the consent required for organ donation is presumed. There is a default in the Austrian regulation stipulating that every individual agrees to become an organ donor. If an individual is not happy with this solution, they have to submit an official form to the Austrian Federal Health Institute. In Germany, on the other hand, an explicit consent is required, which also must be submitted in writing to the relevant authorities.[48]

This may seem like a trivial story, but it conveys a powerful message. It is not the case that Germans are poor Kantians and Austrians see their every action through the prism of the categorical imperative. In fact, like all people, they very rarely reflect at any length on their moral choices. They just stick to the default, be it non-consent (as in Germany) or consent (as in Austria). For a legislator who believes in the fairness of organ donation, the German choice of legal mechanisms is simply a bad one: it makes false assumptions with regard to how people actually think and behave.

These two illustrations show that purely constructive considerations can lead us astray. A decision made exclusively on the basis of some ideal standard of rationality much too easily turns out to be an inefficient solution. There are two potential sources of this failure: the environment and the human mind. On the one hand, environments may be too complex or unpredictable to succumb to highly sophisticated decision-making tools designed by the constructivists; on the other hand, our minds are often not prepared or willing to utilize such complicated tools, preferring simple heuristics. The point has been nicely summarized by Herbert Simon who observed: "human rational behaviour . . . is shaped by a scissors whose two blades are the structure of task environments and the computational capabilities of the actor."[49]

In this context, psychologists, economists, and philosophers are speaking of the so-called ecological rationality.[50] The concept is not easy to define, as its understanding changes from field to field, and sometime even from author to author. However, the differences notwithstanding, there are some quite general characteristics of this kind of rationality. First and foremost, it involves no general procedure of decision-making or a standard to be followed. We would say that the cognitive mechanisms utilized by the human mind are ecologically rational if the decisions we make "fit into," or "are well adjusted to," the environment in which we act; conversely, a social institution is ecologically rational if it is so shaped as to match our decision-making abilities and tendencies.[51]

---

[48]   Cf. ibid., pp. 409–410.
[49]   Simon, 1990, p. 7.
[50]   Cf. Smith, 2008; Todd et al., 2012.
[51]   Smith, 2008, p. 36ff.

Let us consider both aspects of ecological rationality in some detail. From the constructivist perspective, a decision is rational if it logically follows from a set of previously established premises; or, more generally, it is rational as long as it is arrived at through applying a certain procedure. It is the procedure, and not the decision itself, that makes the decision rational. With the shift from the constructivist to the ecological approach, this is no longer the case. The mode in which the decision is made becomes irrelevant; the key question is how the decision "fares" in the given environment. This paves the way for contemplating the (ecological) rationality of intuitive (unconscious) decisions. Indeed, much literature on ecological rationality revolves around the unconscious mechanisms of decision-making. Most notably, Gerd Gigerenzer argues that "fast and frugal" heuristics, constituting the mind's "adaptive toolbox," are ecologically rational.[52] As illustrated in Chapter 1 with the examples of availability, representativeness, and anchoring and adjustment heuristics, such mental "shortcuts" may lead to irrational decisions. However, this happens only under specific circumstances, when one is faced with an atypical problem, involving abstract reasoning or probability assessment. In a typical environment, heuristics do their job quite well. It shows their ecological as opposed to constructive rationality. Various heuristics that have been identified and tested to date – recognition, fluency, take-the-best, tallying, satisficing, one-bounce rule, gaze, default, tit-for-tat, imitate the majority, imitate the successful and others[53] – have one common denominator: while failing to meet the high standards of elaborated theories of rationality, they are able to operate in complex and unpredictable environments producing acceptable, if suboptimal, outcomes.

Importantly, there is no closed catalogue of heuristics; various theorists make different suggestions in this respect. It should also be stressed, as already noted in Chapter 1, that there is no agreement as to the exact shape of the neural mechanism or mechanisms responsible for unconscious, heuristic decisions. Undoubtedly, it is an evolved capacity, and when we use this term, "we refer to a product of nature and nurture – a capacity that is prepared by the genes of a species but usually needs experience to be fully expressed."[54] The ability to make intuitive yet ecologically rational decisions in a given domain is, to a large degree, an outcome of extensive training. The human brain (and mind) comes equipped in some inborn, "hardwired" capacity for heuristic decision-making processes, which are tailored for the environment, in which the brain evolved; however, the capacity can be activated only when filled with a sufficient amount of experience. With regard to everyday matters, the experience is quickly accumulated by everyone; but in more specialized aspects of social life (e.g. in the law) ecologically rational intuitive decisions may occur only after an extensive training in the given area of expertise.

[52] Todd et al., 2012, p. 7ff; Gigerenzer, 2004.
[53] Ibid., pp. 9–10.
[54] Ibid., p. 11.

Let us now turn to the institutional dimension of ecological rationality. A social institution is ecologically rational if its design is sufficiently attuned to the way people make decisions.[55] An impressive institutional framework (e.g. a set of detailed regulations pertaining to the protection of environment), which is fully compatible with some constructivist standard (e.g. the utilitarian precept of maximizing the social utility function), may still turn out to be practically useless if it fails to generate the required kind of social behavior. This failure may have different sources; but the principal among them is not taking into account the actual mechanism of decision-making. As experimental research in psychology shows, people are neither perfect utility-maximizers nor fully autonomous Kantian subjects.[56] Only a relatively small part of the decisions we make every day are conscious,[57] and even less than that – well-reasoned.[58] Therefore, a legal institution that is too demanding with regard to the kind of decisions required by the law may well be destined to fail or produce unexpected and undesirable outcomes.

This can be illustrated by the discussion pertaining to the concept of the declaration of will. In the continental tradition, entering into a binding contract requires the parties to "manifest their will in a sufficient way." According to the classical, nineteenth-century doctrine, the declaration of will is

> an outcome of a process in which two important stages can be distinguished. First: the stage of internal will formation. It starts with a motive, the idea of declaring an intent. Then there is the motivational phase, where the idea is properly verified, and when that happens, a decision, i.e. an act of internal will, is reached. After that only one element is needed for the successful declaration of will, which is the manifestation of the will to the external world. This is yet another stage in the decision-making process, usually called the external will.[59]

This description of decision-making could easily be included in any tome on the history of psychology reporting how, in the eighteenth and nineteenth centuries (especially in the German tradition), the decision-making processes were imagined. The two basic components of this vision can be described as rationalism and voluntarism: it was thought that man was able to make a free and conscious decision in a purely rational manner.[60] In other words, it was assumed that emotional factors do not in principle influence the decision-making processes. It was, therefore, a Kantian theory, both in essence and origins. And, of course, it was incompatible with how people actually make decisions.

It quickly transpired that the conception of the declaration of will is troublesome for two different reasons.[61] On the one hand, we do not have direct access to the

---

[55] Smith, 2008, p. 36.
[56] Cf. Brożek & Janik, 2019 and the literature cited therein.
[57] Cf. Bargh & Morsella, 2008.
[58] Cf. Newell & Shanks, 2014.
[59] M. Pyziak-Szafnicka, 2009, p. 628.
[60] Cf. Ihering, 1877; Zyzik, 2018.
[61] Cf. Kessler, 1975, p. 1071ff.

mental processes of other people. Therefore, it is impossible to establish "the actual will" of any person. Moreover, they can always, and often truthfully, claim that the declaration they made was influenced by strong emotions, and hence cannot count as a declaration of will. This led to the adoption of a much more objectivizing approach, where the crucial element in determining one's will was the interpretation of its declaration (the "external will") from the perspective of a "rational recipient" of the declaration (i.e. according to some communally shared standards). On the other hand, the overemphasis of the rational aspect of decision-making made the theory of the declaration of the will somewhat blind to the irrational factors at play. It is clearly visible in the area of consumer law, where big companies are only too eager to exploit the more vulnerable sides of the human psyche. In order to remedy this, some jurisdictions assume explicitly that the addressees of the law (consumers) often act unreasonably, under the influence of emotional impulses, recklessly and immaturely.[62] Consequently, they are granted special protection (e.g. a right to withdraw from the contract or an extended guarantee). In both cases – of objectivization as well as the special treatment of consumers – the law has deviated from the constructive assumptions of the theory of the declaration of the will, opting instead for solutions more receptive to the actual mechanisms of decision-making. The theory has become more ecologically rational.

It should by now be perfectly clear that the introduction of the notion of ecological rationality may have far-reaching consequences for our understanding of the functioning of the law. First, it provides an explanation why some legal decisions are considered good, even if they do not come with a detailed and commonly acceptable justification; conversely, it also explains why some other decisions, perfectly defendable against the background of the highest criteria of constructive rationality, turn out to be poor. As Judge Hutcheson put it in the already quoted passage, "all of us have known judges who can make the soundest judgments and write the dullest opinions on them";[63] but we also know refined theoreticians, who make elaborated and well-justified proposals of virtually no practical merit.

Second, the perspective provided by the concept of ecological rationality leads to interesting insights regarding the design of legal institutions. The traditional way of thinking about the way the law influences human behavior – in terms of the threat of punishment on the one hand and positive incentives on the other – turns out to be severely limited. The legislator cannot think of the addressees of the law as mere felicity calculators, since pleasure and pain are not the only coins acceptable in the trade of social interactions. Human decision-making is a complex process, taking place in the framework where such factors as emotions, the way of presenting and structuring of information, or the way of introducing incentives (e.g. prohibitions as opposed to "nudges")[64] are of vital importance.

---

[62] Cf. Mark, 2016.
[63] Hutcheson, 1929, p. 287.
[64] Cf. Thaler & Sunstein, 2019.

The adoption of the concept of the ecological rationality is also relevant for the ongoing debates in legal and moral philosophy. Let me illustrate this with an example. One of the most popular and intriguing conceptions of practical rationality discussed today may be termed "Reasons First."[65] It is advocated, in different versions, by Joseph Raz, John Skorupski, Thomas Scanlon, or Mark Schroeder, and posits that the irreducible concept of reason is central to any successful explanation of rationality and normativity. But what are reasons? According to Raz, they are certain facts that "constitute a case for (or against) the performance of an action."[66] The fact that I am hungry is a reason for eating something; the fact that my uncle is seriously ill is a reason to visit him; the fact that I have made a promise to a colleague to help them paint their house is a reason to do it.

It is not our power of rational thinking that makes facts into reasons; rather, "they are reasons because rational creatures can recognize and respond to them."[67] In other words, reasons are "out there"; they exist independently of whether they are identified as such or not. Moreover, as Raz repeatedly observes, finding an appropriate response to a reason does not necessarily involve our rational faculties or abilities – it is possible to do it "without the mediation of rational power."[68] As Raz puts it, "with experience we learn to identify and respond to reasons instinctively, though in ways that depend on and presuppose, first, reliance on past reflection, and second, the monitoring presence of rational powers that control and stand ready to correct misidentifications or misdirected responses."[69]

These two aspects of the "Reasons First" conception (i.e. the realist stance toward reasons as independently existing facts and the possibility to respond to reasons in an instinctive yet experience-based way), mark the extent to which this conception deviates from the constructivist accounts of practical rationality, such as Kantianism or utilitarianism. For example, for Kant, an action is rational (just) if it complies with the categorical imperative; there is no fact – whether we term it a reason or not – that would have any bearing on such a compliance. Moreover, an action is moral only if its motive is to act out of duty; otherwise, even if its substance is compatible with the categorical imperative, the action cannot be deemed moral. From this perspective, no moral action can be instinctive, since such actions lack the required motivation.

It is interesting to ask what motivated Raz's (and others') rejection of the traditional approach to practical rationality and the conceptual shift to realism about reasons. The explanation lies in the poverty of rule-based accounts of law and morality.[70] As we have seen in Chapters 3 and 4, even the most sophisticated systems of moral or legal rules fail at some point: there will be cases for which the system

---

[65] Cf. Wedgwood, 2015.
[66] Raz, 2011, p. 36.
[67] Ibid., p. 86.
[68] Ibid., p. 85.
[69] Ibid., p. 86.
[70] Cf. Scanlon, 2004.

produces no straightforward answers. At the same time, these are situations where our intuition, supported or unsupported by additional reasoning, may be quite clear. This strongly suggests that the normative world is much richer than any system of moral or legal rules. If so, a natural step is to say that reasons (i.e. certain facts independent of our valuations but possessing some normative force) simply exist, and the construction of a sophisticated system of moral or legal rules constitutes a mere approximation of the complexity of the normative world.

The strength of this argument diminishes as soon as the concept of ecological rationality is introduced. It explains how it is possible to have a rich normative world without adopting the realist stance in relation to reasons. Indeed, it is possible to treat something as rational, even though it fails to meet the standards of constructive rationality. At the same time, one does not need to dispense altogether with the notion of constructive rationality, which, in the "Reasons First" approach, is ascribed a secondary or derivative role. According to the conception advanced here, both ecological and constructive rationalities are important. The pressing question is, however, what is their relationship. I will address this problem in Section 5.4.

5.4 VARIATION AND SELECTION

Our journey so far has taken us through the labyrinth of practical rationality. It is, indeed, a labyrinth. Despite hopes and occasional claims to the contrary, it seems impossible to develop a simple standard or procedure that would serve as the ultimate grounds for assessing the strength and quality of legal or moral arguments. However, it should come as no surprise. Essentially the same story can be told in relation to rationality in the sphere of theoretical reflection, in particular – in the empirical sciences. The relatively simple criteria of empirical justification as defended by the members of the Vienna Circle (verification) or Karl Popper (falsification), turned out to be gross idealizations. The actual scientific practice is much more complex. One cannot simply follow in the footsteps of Moritz Schlick, Rudolf Carnap, and other Viennese philosophers and claim that the laws of physics (or some other science) are justified through the application of the logic of induction. No matter how many times a law is verified (i.e. it is successful in predicting the course of events), there is always a possibility that it will fail in some future cases. Also, one cannot be a fierce Popperian critic, rejecting a scientific theory whenever it fails to produce reliable predictions. Equipped with such an extreme form of falsificationism, science would never reach its current state. Historians of science are quick to point out that virtually all the important theories have suffered some form of falsification; instead of rejecting them outright, scientists kept working with them, introducing little modifications or wondering whether the encountered anomalies should really be treated as falsification.[71] This failure of simple solutions

---

[71] Kuhn, 1962; Lakatos, 1978; Laudan, 1981.

to the rationality problem is a testimony to a deep truth: our minds are imperfect, often erring instruments, which have to deal with a very complex and sometimes all too puzzling reality.

Of course, confronted with this complexity we have no other choice but to simplify. It transpires that this has been a successful strategy in science, albeit far from perfect. It is equally readily applied in law and other normative considerations. We construct relatively simple standards of conduct in the hope that they will determine answers to any question; invariably, it turns out that no such efficient procedures exist. On the one hand, constructive theories of rationality we develop are ideal in the sense that they require of the decision-maker to do things no human being is capable of: employing a perfect, univocal language, considering entire normative systems and all possible questions while solving a particular problem, and distancing oneself completely from one's emotions. What remains is to approximate these ideals to some extent. On the other hand, our abstract constructs often do not match the environment for which they are designed. A decision reached through the process of painstaking rational analysis or an institution developed in a comfortable armchair by applying highly idealized assumptions and abstract methods, may easily turn out to be little more than a theoretical exercise with no practical value.

Constructive rationality has an additional feature: it should always be written in the plural form. There is not one, but many constructive rationalities. Kantianism and utilitarianism, in their classical forms, are two most notorious examples; but there are many more. Some of them are global theories, establishing rationality standards for the entire sphere of practical reasoning (e.g. the virtue-based, Aristotelian account);[72] others are local, designed to guide us in a more or less narrow field of reflection (e.g. the view of rationality in the law as encapsulated in the continental positivism). Some belong to a well-defined philosophical tradition (e.g. variations on Kant's practical philosophy such as Robert Alexy's theory),[73] others are "patchworks," combining elements from different traditions.[74] Crucially, these various rationalities are not relegated to graduate textbooks. They are actively applied in the important contemporary legal and moral debates pertaining to the most difficult problems, from euthanasia to wealth redistribution. By guiding our imagination and the development of theoretical constructions they help us produce highly differentiated solutions to the encountered problems. This abundance of options is a testimony not only to human creativity, but also to the idea-generating power of constructive rationalities.

In contrast, ecological rationality is much less spectacular. It is at work in the background, hidden but constantly testing our bold conjectures against the hard reality of the social environment. But what exactly is the social environment?

---

[72]   Cf. in the legal context Farelly & Solum, 2007.
[73]   Cf. Alexy, 2009.
[74]   Cf. Brożek, 2007.

Roughly speaking, it consists of three different but interconnected elements. First, the fitness of legal decisions is determined by the features of the physical world. A new regulation pertaining to the protection of the environment (e.g. introducing some minima regarding the production of energy from renewable sources) will have the desired effects only in as much as the science behind the regulation is sound and correctly applied. Second, social environment is co-shaped by the architecture of the human mind. We have strong inbuilt cognitive tendencies, which decisively influence our collective behavior. A precedent altering the principles of contractual liability will successfully shape the future social interactions only if it is understandable to the legal subjects and does not go against our deeply seeded intuitions. Human intuition is characterized by a certain inertia: it is not easy to change our intuitive reactions, the way things "are done" in our community; it must always take much time. Third and finally, social environment is also co-determined by the institutions we have developed over hundreds of years. As I have observed in Chapter 3, it is extremely difficult – if at all possible – to build new legal institutions from scratch. An introduction of a legal regime pertaining to intellectual property, which has nothing to do with the traditional conceptions of ownership, would most likely be destined to fail as a "misfit"; at the very least, the new regulations would quickly be accommodated (interpreted) in such a way as to resemble the well-known institution of "regular" property.

These observations lead to the conclusion that constructive and ecological rationalities are not mutually incompatible; they are not competing, but rather complementary accounts of practical rationality. The best way to describe their interaction is by using two evolutionary concepts: "variation" and "selection."[75] Constructive rationality is a mechanism for generating potential solutions to the encountered problem; the solutions are often significantly different, creating a pool of options not dissimilar to a pool of genes. Of course, genes change through random mutations, while the standards of constructive rationality guide us in intentional efforts to successfully deal with the problem at hand. Since not all options are equally good, and there is no decisive theoretical criterion to choose from among them, they are ultimately selected when implemented within a social environment. Those which turn out to be ecologically rational survive; others are dispensed with but not necessarily forgotten. They become a part of a large theoretical background of our cognitive efforts. All these points are well summarized by Vernon L. Smith, who observes:

> In cultural and biological coevolution, order arises from mechanisms for generating variation to which is applied mechanisms for selection. Reason is good at providing variation, but poor at selection; that is, constructivism is a powerful engine for generating variation, but it is far too narrowly limited and inflexible in its ability to comprehend and apply all the relevant facts in order to serve the process of

[75] Cf. Smith, 2008.

selection, which is better left to ecological processes that implicitly weights more versus less important influences.[76]

Let us illustrate the interaction between the constructive and the ecological rationalities with an example. In Chapter 3, I described a fundamental contemporary debate pertaining to the legal status of autonomous artificial agents. Such agents already exist in the form of autonomous vehicles or weapon systems. However, it is likely that in the not so distant future we will develop general purpose autonomous agents, specialized in no particular task, but capable of making unsupervised decisions in many types of problems. We can even imagine that they will look and behave like humans. The question is, how to regulate their legal status. Should they be considered full-blooded legal agents or rather mere tools in the hands of human subjects?

At the constructive level, one can tackle this problem in a number of ways. Let us consider two extreme approaches. The first is deeply rooted in the Kantian tradition. As we remember, for Kant legal and moral agency is inextricably linked with two characteristic features of the human mind: autonomy of will and rationality. A genuine moral or legal agent is capable of making decisions that are based solely on reason (guided by the categorical imperative); no other factors, including self-interest or strong emotions, have any bearing on the decision-making process. In addition, the process itself is an expression of human dignity and takes humanity as an end in itself. From this perspective, the question whether intelligent machines can be included into the category of moral or legal agents seems to have a straightforward answer: no, artificial agents are neither rational nor equipped with any kind of will; they also lack the dignity of a human being. Therefore, it becomes clear that the legal status of autonomous artificial agents must be regulated in a different way from that of a human agent. How exactly? The simplest solution, but arguably not the only one, would be to treat autonomous artificial agents as typical legal objects (i.e. as entities over which legal subjects [natural or legal persons] may hold rights). Alternatively, one can treat this special kind of machines like animals: while they are not legal agents (they have no genuine rights and duties, and have no criminal or contractual liability), they enjoy a special protection.

The second extreme approach to the considered problem is pure instrumentalism: legal regulations, including legal agency, are mere tools for realizing social goals. Therefore, legal personhood may be conceptualized in any way that helps to achieve these goals. There are no absolute conditions of legal agency; autonomous will, rationality, intentionality, consciousness, or self-awareness are not needed to ascribe legal personhood to someone or something. A rock, a river, an insect, a corporation, or an autonomous vehicle can be included in the pool of legal agents if, and only if, it would contribute to the realization of the goals of the regulation. In other words, the instrumental approach sees nothing wrong in granting autonomous

---

[76] Ibid., p. 38.

artificial agents rights and duties, and holding them criminally or contractually liable, as long as this is what seems to be required for the law to do its job of regulating social interactions in the desired way.

Let us observe that both these conceptions – the conservative one favored by the Kantians and the liberal one endorsed by the instrumentalists – when worked out in detail, may turn out to be highly coherent solutions to our problem, centered around a well-defined standard of constructive rationality. Yet they are completely different, offering opposite answers to the question of whether autonomous artificial agents should be granted legal rights and duties and have criminal or contractual liability. Moreover, there exists no independent constructive criterion for choosing from among them. The supporters of both approaches can exchange more or less persuasive arguments and occasional sarcasm, but the fact is that there is no theoretical end to such a controversy. The solutions must be applied in practice, and it is where ecological rationality enters the stage.

It is difficult to make an a priori assessment as to the practical usefulness of the conservative and liberal approaches to the legal status of the autonomous artificial agents. However, past experience and the general knowledge about the functioning of the legal systems makes it possible to speculate. Arguably, the conservative solution would not be flexible enough. When we think about autonomous artificial agents, what comes to mind are self-driving cars or autonomous weapon systems. They are, indeed, things rather than anything else. The problem of tort or criminal liability for the actions of these machines is easily solved: if a self-driving car injures a pedestrian, the responsibility lies with the owner of the car or its manufacturer. But this is a short-sighted approach: the question is not what to do with self-driving cars or weapon systems, but with the future artificial agents, which will most likely be by orders of magnitude more autonomous (and therefore resembling human decision-makers) than anything that has been developed so far. In such an imagined environment, the conservative solution may be of little value. While self-driving cars pose a foreseeable liability risk to their owners or producers, since they are limited to performing a specialized function, a general-purpose autonomous machine would be a different kind of beast. It would potentially create so many unpredictable situations that their owners could forcefully and reasonably argue that they cannot be liable for the actions of such artificial intelligences. Under such circumstances, the conservative solution would not be ecologically rational.

The liberal solution, on the other hand, by granting legal agency to autonomous machines, would probably meet a different set of problems. The concept of agency is deeply rooted in folk psychology, the conceptual scheme that we use to understand and predict the behavior of ourselves and other people. Central to this understanding is a model view of agency involving, at least, intentionality and freedom of choice. From this perspective, it would be hard to accept ascribing criminal liability to entities that are neither intentional nor free in their choice; such a regulation would be confusing and, most likely, highly inefficient.[77] A good indication that this would indeed be the case can be found in the problems surrounding the criminal liability of corporations. In some jurisdictions (e.g. in Germany), a legal person cannot be subjected to criminal proceedings; in other legal systems (e.g. in France or in Poland), the criminal responsibility of legal entities is possible, but only under the condition that an individual physical person, who committed the act "on behalf" of the legal person, is identified. This clearly shows that the idea of the legal responsibility of legal persons is not a natural extension of the folk-psychological view of human agency: even if we allow legal persons to be charged with criminal offences, much is done to link it to the actions of individual human beings.[78] It follows that it would be difficult to treat autonomous artificial agents as genuine authors of their actions. The liberal solution may not be ecologically rational since it is at odds with the way we think about the world and our behavior in it.

* * *

We are finally in a position to draw a comprehensive, albeit somewhat sketchy, picture of the functioning of the legal mind. Lawyers have a number of mental tools at their disposal that are connected to the functioning of three mechanisms: intuition, imagination, and thinking in language. When I refer to intuition, I have in mind all the unconscious mechanism of decision-making, including intuition and insight. Although operating unconsciously, they nevertheless have a number of features that make it possible to efficiently use and, to an extent, control them. In particular, intuitive decisions are usually based on past experience; this leads to the conclusion that they are quite reliable, unless one is faced with unusual circumstances (e.g. a problem requiring statistical analysis or abstract reasoning). Imagination, or more precisely mental simulation, is also a powerful tool for thinking. It links intuition with language, evoking and educating intuitive responses and enabling understanding of concrete linguistic expressions. More fundamentally, it enables us to test and evaluate our hypotheses with little cost. Linguistic constructions, in turn, provide us with a scaffolding – or, better, many different scaffoldings designed over generations for particular tasks – which help to organize our experience and gain better understanding of the complex world we inhabit. Crucially, all three mechanisms – intuition, imagination, and language – must be used simultaneously and in concert for our thinking efforts to bear fruit.

The architecture of the legal mind, with its interacting elements, makes the process of thinking non-foundational. It necessarily involves the application of two different strategies: top-down and bottom-up. The former urges us to solve problems beginning with abstract theories; the latter identifies particular cases as a point of departure. Because of four different reasons – the logical, the classificatory, the semantic, and the constructional – neither strategy is self-sufficient. They must be

[77]   Cf. Brożek & Jakubiec, 2017.
[78]   Cf. Khanna, 1996.

used together; it follows that legal reasoning is neither purely rule-based nor case-based.

Within this non-foundational framework, one can formulate a number of precepts or normative criteria, which guide us in solving legal problems. The criteria belong to three different although interconnected levels. The first may be called the level of discovery. Here, a number of principles may be formulated that increase the likelihood of finding a solution to the problem at hand. They are the principles of experience, caution, exemplification, variability, unification, and contrast. It must be stressed that these precepts as such are "blind" to the quality of the hypotheses they generate. Their application does not guarantee that the outcome is justified, fair, or just. Rather, they take into account the nature of the mental mechanisms of intuition, imagination, and thinking in language, and demonstrate how to use them in order to expand the pool of potential answers to the question at hand and identify some crucial features of these answers (e.g. that they evoke conflicting intuitive responses), etc.

The second level is justificatory. The concept of justification is strictly connected to the emergence of language and the two dimensions of justification – the pragmatic or the dialogue-based, and the formal or the theory-based – correspond to two important ways in which language shapes human thinking. On the one hand, language is a means of communication and persuasion. From this perspective, a justified belief is the one that is acceptable to an audience. An audience, in turn, may be conceptualized in two opposite ways: as particular or universal. On the other hand, language is also a tool for constructing unified theories. Hence, a belief may be said to be justified if it "fits" into a theory, and here also there are two different normative standards: foundationalism and coherentism. The former urges us to accept only those beliefs that follow logically from a "foundation" (i.e. a set of unchangeable beliefs); the latter, in turn, makes it possible to reject any belief, taking the overall formal quality of the entire set of beliefs as the only criterion of justification. These two dimensions of justification – the pragmatic and the formal – determine the justification space. Importantly, both views meet at an extreme and ideal case, where one has a complete theory of the world. Such a theory would be maximally coherent and fully foundational, as well as acceptable by the universal audience.

The third normative level is substantive rationality or justice. It is populated by the conceptions of constructive rationality, such as Kantianism or utilitarianism. Their characteristic feature is that they are (more or less) ideal standards. It means that they cannot be completely realized; rather, they function as signposts, which organize and direct our thinking efforts but can never be fully met. In other words, in the actual attempts at solving a legal problem, they can only be approximated. It must also be stressed that there is no one, unique constructive standard. There are competing, incompatible views of substantive rationality: they essentially differ when it comes to the choice of thinking tools, heuristic procedures, and justification criteria. In consequence, they usually lead to quite different outcomes. However, it is anything but a flaw. The role of constructive rationality is to generate variation; only a wide range of potential solutions to a legal problem may ultimately enable finding the good one.

As I have emphasized, the three normative layers of legal thinking – the discovery, the justificatory, and the substantive – are conceptually different but interconnected with regard to content. For example, one's intuition, shaped by long instruction and practice, may incorporate some aspects of both justification procedures (e.g. the tendency to produce solutions that are highly coherent with the existing legal knowledge) and substantive considerations (e.g. the tendency to produce solutions compatible with the categorical imperative or the positivist conception of law). Similarly, the principle of contrast operating at the level of discovery has tremendous persuasive potential: a solution selected by comparison with a number of alternatives may be easily acceptable by a reasonable audience. Also, the view of justification as encapsulated in the concept of the universal audience has a substantive dimension. It has been vigorously argued that a claim acceptable by the universal audience must also be compatible with the categorical imperative.

Another crucial feature of the three normative levels of legal thinking is that they constitute a kind of hierarchy. The discovery level is at the bottom: it consists of different tools for generating answers to legal questions. The justificatory level is the first "overlay": it directs our problem-solving activities but also imposes some serious limitations on them. Not every solution produced at the discovery level can meet the criteria for pragmatic or formal justification. Finally, the substantive level is the second overlay: it provides us with yet more guidance and stricter limitations.

The legal mind, taking advantage of the mechanisms of intuition, imagination, and thinking in language, operating within the non-foundational framework for problem-solving, and aided – and limited – by the three normative layers, must ultimately face the hard reality of social environment. Here, it often transpires that the most sophisticated solutions, fully justified and supported by some ideal standard of constructive rationality, become utter failures. They may turn out to be ecologically irrational, while a simple intuitive judgment – the first thing that comes to the lawyer's mind – may become the sought-after solution to the considered problem. However, one should never conclude that our complex theories, our much-discussed rationality standards, and heuristic tools are useless. Without them, we would never generate enough variation for ecological selection to work properly. It is, perhaps, the most ingenious ability of the legal mind; a mind that is anchored in tradition and susceptible to the inertial force of intuition, yet nevertheless sometimes capable of raising itself to the level of a superhero judge or a constructivist legislator and develop a solution that becomes an integral part of the legal bloodstream.

Conclusion

Severe Poetry

Giambattista Vico was undoubtedly one of the most intriguing thinkers of modern times, despite perhaps being too fierce a critic of the fashionable philosophies of his time to be held in high regard by his contemporaries.[1] In an era dominated by worship at the high altar of reason, he emphasized the pivotal role of the senses and the imagination, in brave opposition to Descartes and his acolytes. Some of Vico's claims sound surprisingly familiar to evolutionists and cognitive scientists. For example, when considering "the first people," who had only learned to use language, he describes them as "all robust sense and vigorous imagination," with "a metaphysic not rational and abstract like that of learned men, but felt and imagined . . .. Their minds were not in the least abstract, refined, or spiritualized, because they were entirely immersed in the senses, buffeted by the passions, buried in the body."[2] Elsewhere he can be seen to observe, somewhat in the spirit of the embodiment paradigm, that "words are carried over from bodies and from the properties of bodies to express the things of the mind and spirit."[3]

According to Vico, the Cartesian method, based on truths that we can "see in a clear and distinct way" and the infallible, deductive schemes of reasoning, conceal the real nature of the human psyche. It is not the sterile, ahistorical mind of the geometer, but resembles more the sensual mind of a poet, full of fantasies and immersed in the currents and tides of history; a mind that – from time to time, and in some fields of reflection only – is capable of contemplating pure mathematical abstractions. Our crucial cognitive power has little to do with the construction of logically valid syllogisms; it is called *ingengno*, an ability that is central to the imagination, one which makes it possible to detect similarities between particular things and events.[4]

Vico was not only a philosopher but also a lawyer. When considering the history of Roman law, he appreciated the essential role that imagination, unconstrained by the

[1] Cf. Mali, 1992.
[2] Vico, 1948, pp. 104, 106.
[3] Ibid., p. 70.
[4] Cf. Grnatella, 2015.

precepts of logic, had played in its development. Roman law was not a creation of analytic minds but rather a realm of metaphor and fiction. As Vico put it:

> ancient jurisprudence was throughout poetic. By its fictions what had happened was taken as not having happened, and what had not happened as having happened; those not yet born as already born; the living as dead; and the dead as still living . . . . It introduced so many empty masks without subjects, *iura imaginaria*, rights invented by imagination. It rested its entire reputation on inventing such fables as might preserve the gravity of the laws and do justice to the facts. Thus all the fictions of ancient jurisprudence were truths under masks.[5]

And, he added, "all ancient Roman law was a serious poem, represented by the Romans in the forum, and ancient jurisprudence was a severe poetry."[6]

Terming a province such as law to be "poetry" may seem a serious abuse of reason. One might coquettishly reply: "Poetry? Perhaps, but of the worst kind." Less malicious commentators would likely say that if law can be described as poetry, then everything is poetry – geography, physics, microeconomics – since we use the imagination in all areas of reflection. However, I believe that Vico's metaphor is much more profound. What law and poetry have in common is not only the use of imagination, but the "how" and "why" of doing it. The key word in this context is *gravitas*, gravity: both lawyers and poets are preoccupied with issues of existential importance. The gravity of this goal would be completely lost in an axiomatic system or abstract considerations. Without the imagination, embedding thinking in the concrete, and evoking intuitions and emotions, law and poetry would become pure but empty forms.

The legal mind, as I have tried to show in this book, has a complex architecture. Three mechanisms – of intuition, imagination, and thinking in language – must work together if we want to solve legal problems successfully. The imagination plays a designated role in this structure, since it constitutes a bridge between unconscious intuitions and abstract conceptual constructions. Such a perspective paves the way for potentially groundbreaking research and new theoretical hypotheses. For example, one may ask whether and how lawyers should use thought experiments. One can also consider, given the importance of mental simulations for the understanding of language, what is the nature of legal interpretation. Still, there is the intriguing problem of legal abstraction: its mechanisms, functions, and limits. Yet another question pertains to the rationality of legal thinking, and in particular the interaction between two types of rationality: the constructive and the ecological. Some of these issues have been addressed, even if only partially, in this book. But it is only the beginning: each answer generates fresh problems and opens up new, fascinating fields of reflection upon the severe poetry of law.

---

[5]   Vico, 1948, p. 350.
[6]   Ibid., p. 350.

Bibliography

Alexander, L. & Sherwin, E., 2008. *Demystifying Legal Reasoning*. Cambridge: Cambridge University Press.

Alexy, R., 2002. A *Theory of Constitutional Rights*. Oxford: Oxford University Press.

    2005. Arthur Kaufmanns Theorie der Rechtsgewinnung. In: U. Neumann, W. Hassemer, & U. Schroth, eds. *Verantwortetes Recht: Die Rechtsphilosophie Arthur Kaufmanns*. Stuttgart: Franz Steiner, pp. 47–66.

    2009. A *Theory of Legal Argumentation*. Oxford: Oxford University Press.

Angelelli, I., 2004. Adventures of abstraction. *Poznań Studies in the Philosophy of the Sciences and the Humanities*, 82, pp. 11–35.

Antognazza, M., 2009. *Leibniz: An Intellectual Biography*. Cambridge: Cambridge University Press.

Aquinas, T., 1947. *The Summa Theologica*. New York: Benziger Bros.

Aristotle, 2006. *Meteorology*. Digireads.com.

Atria, F., 2001. *On Law and Legal Reasoning*. Oxford: Hart Publishing.

Audi, R., 1988. Foundationalism, coherentism, and epistemological dogmatism. *Philosophical Perspectives*, 2, pp. 407–422.

Bargh, J., 2017. *Before You Know It: The Unconscious Reasons We Do What We Do*. New York: Atria.

Bargh, J. & Morsella, E., 2008. The unconscious mind. *Perspectives on Psychological Science*, 3, pp. 73–79.

Barrow, J. D., 1991. *Theories of Everything: The Quest for Ultimate Explanation*. Oxford: Clarendon Press.

Barsalou, L., 1999. Perceptual symbol systems. *Behavioral and Brain Sciences*, 22, pp. 577–660.

    2008. Grounded cognition. *Annual Review of Psychology*, 59, pp. 617–645.

    2009. Situating concepts. In: P. Robbins & M. Aydede, eds. *The Cambridge Handbook of Situated Cognition*. Cambridge: Cambridge University Press, pp. 236–263.

    2010. Grounded cognition: Past, present, and future. *Topics in Cognitive Science*, 2, pp. 716–724.

Barsalou, L. & Wiemer-Hastings, K., 2005. Situating abstract concepts. In: D. Pecher & R. Zwaan, eds. *Grounding Cognition: The Role of Perception and Action in Memory, Language and Thinking*. Cambridge: Cambridge University Press, pp. 129–163.

Bartha, P., 2013. Analogy and analogical reasoning. In: E. Zalta, ed. *The Stanford Encyclopedia of Philosophy*. https://plato.stanford.edu/archives/fall2013/entries/reasoning-analogy/.

Beever, A., 2007. *Rediscovering the Law of Negligence*. Oxford: Hart Publishing.

Benjamin, W., 1998. *The Origin of German Tragic Drama*. New York: Verso.

Bentham, J., 1843. *The Works of Jeremy Bentham*. Vol. 3. Edinburgh: W. Tait.

    1977. *A Comment on the Commentaries and a Fragment on Government*. In: J. H. Burns & H. L. A. Hart, eds. *The Collected Works of Jeremy Bentham*. Oxford: Oxford University Press.

Bergen, B., 2012. *Louder Than Words: The Science of How the Mind Makes Meaning*. New York: Basic Books.

    2016. Embodiment, simulation and meaning. In: N. Riemer, ed. *The Routledge Handbook of Semantics*. London: Routledge, pp. 142–157.

Blackstone, W., 1830. *Commentaries on the Laws of England*. Vol. 3, 17th ed. London: Richard Taylor.

Bonjour, L., 1985. *The Structure of Empirical Knowledge*. Cambridge, MA: Harvard University Press.

Borghi, A., Binkofski, F., Castelfranchi, C., Cimatti, F., Scorolli, C., & Tummolini, L., 2017. The challenge of abstract concepts. *Psychological Bulletin*, 143, pp. 263–292.

Borghi, A. & Binkofsky, F., 2014. *Words as Social Tools: An Embodied View on Abstract Concepts*. Dordrecht: Springer.

Borowski, M., Paulson, S., & Sieckmann, J.-R., eds., 2017. *Rechtsphilosophie und Grundrechtheorie: Rober Alexys System*. Tübingen: Mohr Siebeck.

Brandom, R., 1994. *Making It Explicit*. Cambridge, MA: Harvard University Press.

Brewer, S., 1996. Exemplary reasoning: Semantics, pragmatics, and the rational force of legal argument by analogy. *Harvard Law Review*, 109, pp. 923–1028.

Brożek, B., 2007. *Rationality and Discourse*. Warsaw: Wolters Kluwer.

    2011. Beyond interpretation. In: J. Stelmach & R. Schmidt, eds. *Krakauer-Augsburger Rechtsstudien: Die Grenzen der rechtsdogmatischen Interpretation*. Warsaw: Wolters Kluwer, pp. 19–28.

    2013a. Philosophy and neuroscience: Three modes of interaction. In: J. Stelmach, B. Brożek & Ł. Kurek, eds. *Philosophy in Neuroscience*. Kraków: Copernicus Center Press, pp. 16–57.

    2013b. *Rule-Following: From Imitation to the Normative Mind*. Kraków: Copernicus Center Press.

    2014a. *Granice interpretacji*. Kraków: Copernicus Center Press.

    2014b. The emotional foundations of law: On Petrażycki's legal theory. *Rivista di filosofia del diritto*, 2, pp. 279–288.

    2015. On tû-tû. *Revus*, 27, pp. 15–23.

    2016a. Explanation and understanding. In: B. Brożek, M. Heller, & M. Hohol, eds. *The Concept of Explanation*. Kraków: Copernicus Center Press, pp. 11–42.

    2016b. *Myślenie: Podręcznik użytkownika*. Kraków: Copernicus Center Press.

    2017a. The troublesome person. In: V. Kurki & T. Pietrzykowski, eds. *Legal Personhood: Animals, Artificial Intelligence, and the Unborn*. Dordrecht: Springer, pp. 3–13.

    2017b. Two faces of legal reasoning: Rule-based and case-based. In: D. Krimphove & G. Lentner, eds. *Law and Logic: Contemporary Issues*. Berlin: Duncker & Humblot, pp. 67–79.

    2018. Analogical arguments. In: G. Bongiovani, ed. *Handbook of Legal Reasoning and Argumentation*. Dordrecht: Springer, pp. 365–386.

Brożek, B. & Hohol, M., 2014. *Umysł matematyczny*. Kraków: Copernicus Center Press.

    2015. *Umysł matematyczny*. Kraków: Copernicus Center Press.

Brożek, B. & Jakubiec, M., 2017. On the legal responsibility of autonomous machines. *Artificial Intelligence and Law*, 25, pp. 293–304.

Brożek, B. & Janik, B., 2019. Can artificial intelligences be moral agents? *New Ideas in Psychology*, 54, pp. 101–106.

Brożek, B. & Kurek, Ł., 2018. Folk psychology and explanation. In: B. Brożek, J. Stelmach & Ł. Kwiatek, eds. *Explaining the Mind*. Kraków: Copernicus Center Press, pp. 149–170.

Burns, J., 2005. Happiness and utility: Jeremy Bentham's equation. *Utilitas*, 17, pp. 46–61.

Byrne, R., 1988. The early evolution of creative thinking: Evidence from monkeys and apes. In: S. Mithen, ed. *Creativity in Human Evolution and Prehistory*. London: Routledge, pp. 110–124.

Cairns, J. & Plessis, P. D., eds., 2010. *The Creation of the Ius Commune: From Casus to Regula*. Edinburgh: Edinburgh University Press.

Carnap, R., 1928. *Der logische Aufbau der Welt*. Leipzig: Felix Meiner.

Churchland, P., 2012. *Plato's Camera: How the Physical Brain Captures a Landscape of Abstract Universals*. Cambridge, MA: MIT Press.

Clark, A., 2005. Word, niche, and super-niche: How language makes minds matter more. *Theoria*, 54, pp. 255–268.

   2006. Language, embodiment, and the cognitive niche. *Trends in Cognitive Sciences*, 10, pp. 370–374.

Clarke, D., 1997. *Philosophy's Second Revolution. Early and Recent Analytic Philosophy*. Chicago: Open Court.

Damasio, A. R., 2006. *Descartes' Error: Emotion, Reason, and the Human Brain*. London: Vintage.

   2018. *The Strange Order of Things*. London: Vintage.

Damasio, A. R., Everitt, B. J., & Bishop, D., 1996. The somatic marker hypothesis and the possible functions of the prefrontal cortex. *Philosophical Transactions: Biological Sciences*, 351, pp. 1413–1420.

Damasio, A. R., Tranel, D., & Damasio, H., 1991. Somatic markers and the guidance of behaviour: Theory and preliminary testing. In: H. Levin, H. Eisenberg, & A. Benton, eds. *Frontal Lobe Function and Dysfunction*. New York: Oxford University Press, pp. 217–229.

Danziger, K., 1990. *Constructing the Subject. Historical Origins of Psychological Research*. Cambridge: Cambridge University Press.

Dennett, D., 2013. *Intuition Pumps: And Other Tools for Thinking*. New York: W.W. Norton.

Dewey, J., 1924. Logical method and the law. *Cornell Law Review*, 10, pp. 17–27.

Dorfman, J., Shames, V., & Kihlstrom, J., 1996. Intuition, incubation, and insight. Implicit cognition in problem solving. In: G. Underwood, ed. *Implicit Cognition*. New York: Oxford University Press, pp. 257–296.

Dove, G., 2011. On the need for embodied and dis-embodied cognition. *Frontiers in Psychology*, 1, doi:10.3389/fpsyg.2010.00242.

   2014. Thinking in words: Language as an embodied medium of thought. *Topics in Cognitive Science*, 6, pp. 371–389.

   2015. Three symbol ungrounding problems: Abstract concepts and the future of embodied cognition. *Psychonomic Bulletin & Review*, 23, pp. 1109–1121.

Dworkin, R., 1968. Is law a system of rules? In: R. Summers, ed. *Essays in Legal Philosophy*. Berkeley: University of California Press, pp. 25–60.

   1975. Hard cases. *Harvard Law Review*, 88, pp. 1057–1109.

   1986. *Law's Empire*. Cambridge, MA: Harvard University Press.

   2013. *Taking Rights Seriously*. London: Bloomsbury Academic.

Eckhardt, B. von, 1996. *What Is Cognitive Science?* Cambridge, MA: MIT Press.

Enough, B. & Mussweiler, T., 2001. Sentencing under uncertainty: Anchoring effects in the courtroom. *Journal of Applied Social Psychology*, 31, pp. 1535–1551.

Eskridge, W., 1987. Dynamic statutory interpretation. *University of Pennsylvania Law Review*, 135, pp. 1479–1555.

Farelly, C. & Solum, L., eds., 2007. *Virtue Jurisprudence*. New York: Palgrave Macmillan.

Feyerabend, P., 1993. *Against Method*. New York: Verso.

Feynman, R., 1965. New textbooks for the 'new' mathematics. *Engineering and Science*, 28(6), pp. 9–15.

Fine, C., 2006. Is the emotional dog wagging its rational tail, or chasing it? Unleashing reason in Haidt's social intuitionist model of moral judgment. *Philosophical Explorations*, 9, pp. 83–98.

Finnis, J., 1980. *Natural Law and Natural Rights*. Oxford: Clarendon Press.

Fischer, J. & Ravizza, M., 2000. *Responsibility and Control: A Theory of Moral Responsibility*. Cambridge: Cambridge University Press.

Franklin, S. & Graesser, A., 1997. Is it an agent, or just a program? A taxonomy for autonomous agents. In: J. Muller, M. Wooldridge, & N. Jennings, eds. *Intelligent Agents III: Agent Theories, Architectures, and Languages*. Berlin: Springer, pp. 21–35.

Friedman, M., 1974. Explanation and scientific understanding. *Journal of Philosophy*, 71, pp. 5–19.

Fuller, L., 1958. Positivism and fidelity to law: A reply to Professor Hart. *Harvard Law Review*, 71, pp. 661–669.

   1969. *The Morality of Law*. New Haven, CT: Yale University Press.

Gadamer, H.-G., 2007. Text and interpretation. In: R. E. Palmer, ed. *The Gadamer Reader*. Evanston, IL: North Western University Press, pp. 156–191.

Galili, I., 2009. Thought experiments. Determining their meaning. *Science & Education*, 18, pp. 1–23.

Galton, F., 1880. Statistics of mental imagery. *Mind*, 5, pp. 301–318.

Gigerenzer, G., 2001. The adaptive toolbox. In: G. Gigerenzer & R. Selten, eds. *Bounded Rationality: The Adaptive Toolbox*. Cambridge, MA: MIT Press, pp. 37–50.

   2004. Fast and frugal heuristics: The tools of bounded rationality. In: D. Koehler & N. Harvey, eds. *Blackwell Handbook of Judgment and Decision Making*. Oxford: Wiley-Blackwell, pp. 62–88.

   2007. *Gut Feelings. The Intelligence of the Unconscious*. New York: Penguin.

Gigerenzer, G. & Gaissmaier, W., 2011. Heuristic decision making. *Annual Review of Psychology*, 62, pp. 51–82.

Gilmore, G., 1951. Book review: The Bramble Bush. *Yale Law Journal*, 60, pp. 1251–1253.

Gladstone, W., 2010. *Studies on Homer and the Homeric Age*. Cambridge: Cambridge University Press.

Glenberg, A. M. & Kaschak, M. P., 2002. Grounding language in action. *Psychonomic Bulletin & Review*, 9, pp. 558–565.

Godfrey-Smith, P., 2003. *Theory and Reality: An Introduction to the Philosophy of Science*. Chicago: University of Chicago Press.

Goldman, A., 1988. Strong and weak justification. *Philosophical Perspectives*, 2, pp. 51–69.

Gopnik, A., 2000. Explanation as orgasm and the drive for causal understanding. In: F. Keil & R. Wilson, eds. *Cognition and Explanation*. Cambridge, MA: MIT Press, pp. 299–324.

Grabowski, A., 2013. *Juristic Concept of the Validity of Statutory Law*. Berlin: Springer.

Grnatella, M., 2015. Imaginative universals and human cognition in the new science of Giambattista Vico. *Culture and Psychology*, 21, pp. 185–206.

Guthrie, C., Rachlinski, J., & Wistrich, A., 2000. Inside the judicial mind. *Cornell Law Review*, 86, pp. 777–830.

Haack, S., 1993. *Evidence and Inquiry*. Oxford: Blackwell.

Hacking, I., 1975. *Why Does Language Matter to Philosophy?* Cambridge: Cambridge University Press.

Hadfield, G., 2006. The quality of law in civil code and common law regimes: Judicial incentives, legal human capital and the evolution of law. *American Law & Economics Association Annual Meetings*, 40, pp. 1–44.

Hage, J., 2013. Three kinds of coherentism. In: M. Araszkiewicz & J. Savelka, eds. *Coherence: Insights from Philosophy, Jurisprudence and Artificial Intelligence*. Dordrecht: Springer, pp. 1–32.

2017. Theoretical foundations for the responsibility of autonomous agents. *Artificial Intelligence and Law*, 25, pp. 255–271.

Haidt, J., 2001. The emotional dog and its rational tail: A social intuitionist approach to moral judgement. *Psychological Review*, 108, pp. 814–834.

2003. The moral emotions. In: I. Davidson, K. Scherer, & H. Goldsmith, eds. *Handbook of Affective Sciences*. Oxford: Oxford University Press, pp. 852–870.

Harper, R., 1904. *The Code of Hammurabi*. Chicago: University of Chicago Press.

Hart, H. L. A., 1949. The ascription of responsibility and rights. *Proceedings of the Aristotelian Society*, 49, pp. 171–194.

1958. Positivism and the separation of law and morals. *Harvard Law Review*, 71, pp. 593–629.

Hasan, A. & Fumerton, R., 2018. Foundationalist theories of epistemic justification. In: E. Zalta, ed. *The Stanford Encyclopedia of Philosophy*. https://plato.stanford.edu /archives/fall2018/entries/justep-foundational/.

Hastie, R., Schkade, D.A., & Payne, J., 1999. Juror judgments in civil cases: Effects of plaintiff's requests and plaintiff's identity on punitive damage awards. *Law and Human Behavior*, 23, pp. 445–470.

Hayek, F. A., 1992. *The Fatal Conceit: The Errors of Socialism*. New York: Routledge.

Heller, M., 2008. Przeciw fundacjonizmowi. In: *Filozofia i wszechświat*. Kraków: Universitas, pp. 82–103.

2013. *Philosophy of Chance: A Cosmic Fugue with a Prelude and a Coda*. Kraków: Copernicus Center Press.

Hodgson, J. & Lewthwaite, J., 2007. *Tort Law*. Oxford: Oxford University Press.

Höffe, O., 1989. Kant's principle of justice as categorical imperative of law. In: *Kant's Practical Philosophy Reconsidered*. Dordrecht: Kluwer Academic Publishers, pp. 149–167.

Holmes, O., 1881. *The Common Law*. Chicago: American Bar Association.

1897. The path of the law. *Harvard Law Review*, 10, pp. 457–478.

Horty, J., 2001. *Agency and Deontic Logic*. Oxford: Oxford University Press.

Hossenfelder, S., 2018. *Lost in Math: How Beauty Leads Physics Astray*. New York: Basic Books.

Hoyningen-Huene, P., 1987. Context of discovery and context of justification. *Studies in History and Philosophy of Science Part A*, 18, pp. 501–515.

Hurley, M., Dennett, D., & Adams, R., 2011. *Inside Jokes: Using Humor to Reverse-Engineer the Mind*. Cambridge, MA: MIT Press.

Hutcheson, J., 1929. The judgment intuitive: The role of the "hunch" in judicial decision. *Cornell Law Review*, 14, pp. 274–288.

Hutchison, A., 2014. The Whanganui River as a legal person. *Alternative Law Journal*, 39, pp. 179–182.

Ihering, R. von, 1877. *Der Zweck im Recht*. Leipzig: Breitkopf & Hartel.

James, W., 1884. What is an emotion? *Mind*, 9(34), pp. 188–205.

Jamrozik, A., McQuire, M., Cardillo, E., & Chatterjee, A., 2016. Metaphor: Bridging embodiment to abstraction. *Psychonomic Bulletin & Review*, 23, pp. 1080–1089.

Johnson, A., Coleman-Norton, P., & Bourne, F., 1961. *Ancient Roman Statutes*. Austin: University of Texas Press.

Jung-Beeman, M., Bowden, E. M., Haberman, J., Frymiare, J. L., Arambel-Liu, S., Greenblatt, R., Reber, P. J., Kounios, J., 2004. Neural activity when people solve verbal problems with insight. *PLoS Biology*, 2(4), e97.

Kahneman, D., 2011. *Thinking, Fast and Slow*. New York: Farrar, Straus and Giroux.

Kahneman, D. & Klein, G., 2009. Conditions for intuitive expertise. *American Psychologist*, 64, pp. 515–526.

Kahneman, D. & Tversky, A., 1972. Subjective probability: A judgment of representativeness. *Cognitive Psychology*, 3, pp. 430–454.

Kalinowski, G., 1967. *Le Problème de la vérité en morale et en droit*. Lyon: E. Vitte.

Kant, I., 1909. *Kant's Critique of Practical Reason and Other Works on the Theory of Ethics*. London: Longmans, Green & Co.

  1929. *Critique of Pure Reason*. London: Macmillan.

  1991. *The Metaphysics of Morals*. Cambridge: Cambridge University Press.

  1999. *Correspondence*. Cambridge: Cambridge University Press.

  2002. *Groundwork of the Metaphysics of Morals*. New Haven, CT: Yale University Press.

Karremans, J., Stroebe, W., & Claus, J., 2006. Beyond Vicary's fantasies: The impact of subliminal priming and brand choice. *Journal of Experimental Social Psychology*, 42, pp. 792–798.

Kaufmann, A., 1986. Vorüberlegungen zu einer juristischen Logik und Ontologie der Relationen: Grundlegung einer personalen Rechtstheorie. *Rechtstheorie*, 17, pp. 257–276.

Kay, P. & Kempton, W., 1984. What is the Sapir-Whorf hypothesis? *American Anthropologist*, 86, pp. 65–79.

Kay, P. & Regier, T., 2006. Language, thought and color: Recent developments. *Trends in Cognitive Sciences*, 10, pp. 51–54.

Kelsen, H., 1967. *Pure Theory of Law*. Berkeley: University of California Press.

  2011. *General Theory of Law and State*. Clark, NJ: Lawbook Exchange.

Kensinger, E., 2009. Remembering the details: Effects of emotion. *Emotion Review*, 1, pp. 99–113.

Kessler, F., 1975. Some thoughts on the evolution of the German Law of Contracts: Part I. *UCLA Law Review*, 22, pp. 1066–1072.

Khanna, V., 1996. Corporate criminal liability: What purpose does it serve? *Harvard Law Review*, 109, pp. 1477–1534.

Kołakowski, L., 1989. *The Presence of Myth*. Chicago: University of Chicago Press.

Kossowska, M., 2005. *Umysł niezmienny*. Kraków: Wydawnictwo Uniwersytetu Jagiellońskiego.

Kossowska, M. & Hiel, A. V., 2003. The relationship between need for closure and conservative beliefs in Western and Eastern Europe. *Political Psychology*, 24, pp. 501–518.

Kounios, J. & Beeman, M., 2014. The cognitive neuroscience of insight. *Annual Review of Psychology*, 66, pp. 71–93.

Kozhevnikov, M., 2007. Cognitive styles in the context of modern psychology: Toward an integrated framework of cognitive style. *Psychological Bulletin*, 133, pp. 464–481.

Kozhevnikov, M., Kosslyn, S., & Shephard, J., 2005. Spatial versus object visualizers: A new characterization of visual cognitive style. *Memory & Cognition*, 33, pp. 710–726.

Kragh, H., 2015. *Higher Speculations. Grand Theories and Failed Revolutions in Physics and Cosmology*. Oxford: Oxford University Press.

Krąpiec, M., 1975. *Człowiek i prawo naturalne*. Lublin: Towarzystwo Naukowe KUL.

Kruglanski, A., 1989. The psychology of being "right": The problem of accuracy in social perception and cognition. *Psychological Bulletin*, 106, pp. 395–409.

Kuehn, M., 2001. *Kant: A Biography*. Cambridge: Cambridge University Press.

Kuhn, T., 1962. *The Structure of Scientific Revolutions*. Chicago: University of Chicago Press.

Kulesza, J., 2007. O pojmowaniu zaniechania w polskiej nauce prawa karnego. *Czasopismo Prawa Karnego i Nauk Penalnych*, 11(2), pp. 19–52.

Kupiszewski, H., 2013. *Prawo rzymskie a współczesność*. Bielsko-Biala: Od.Nowa.

Lakatos, I., 1978. *The Methodology of Scientific Research Programmes*. Cambridge: Cambridge University Press.

Lakoff, G. & Johnson, M., 1980. *Metaphors We Live By*. Chicago: University of Chicago Press. 1999. *Philosophy in the Flesh*. New York: Basic Books.

Lakoff, G. & Núñez, R., 2000. *Where Mathematics Comes From*. New York: Basic Books.

Landriscina, F., 2009. Simulation and learning: The role of mental models. *Journal of E-Learning and Knowledge Society*, 5(2), pp. 23–32.

Langevoort, D., 1998. Behavioral theories of judgment and decision-making in legal scholarship: A literature review. *Vanderbilt Law Review*, 51, pp. 1499–1529.

Larenz, K., 1991. *Methodenlehre der Rechtswissenschaft*. Berlin: Springer.

Laudan, L., 1981. A confutation of convergent realism. *Philosophy of Science*, 48, pp. 19–49.

Leibniz, G., 1989. Dissertation on the art of combinations. In: *Philosophical Papers and Letters*. Dordrecht: Kluwer Academic Publishers, pp. 73–84.

Levinas, E., 1973. *The Theory of Intuition in Husserl's Phenomenology*. Evanston, IL: Northwestern University Press.

Levy, N., 2006. The wisdom of the pack. *Philosophical Explanations*, 9, pp. 99–103.

Lillard, A., 1998. Ethnopsychologies: Cultural variations in theories of mind. *Psychological Bulletin*, 123, pp. 3–32.

Llewellyn, K. N., 2012. *The Bramble Bush: On Our Law and Its Study*. New Orleans: Quid Pro.

Mach, E., 1973. On thought experiments. *Philosophical Forum*, 4, pp. 134–147.

Magee, B., 1997. *Confessions of a Philosopher*. New York: Random House.

Makdisi, G., 1974. The scholastic method in medieval education: An inquiry into its origins in law and theology. *Speculum*, 49, pp. 640–661.

Mali, J., 1992. *The Rehabiitation of Myth: Vico's 'New Science'*. Cambridge: Cambridge University Press.

Mark, V., 2016. The consumer in European regulatory private law: A functional perspective on responsibility, protection and empowerment. In: D. Leczykiewicz & S. Weatherill, eds. *The Image(s) of the Consumer in EU Law: Legislation, Free Movement and Competition Law*. Oxford: Hart Publishing, pp. 381–400.

Maryniarczyk, A., ed., 2009. *Universal Encyclopedia of Philosophy*. Lublin: Polskie Towarzystwo Tomasza z Akwinu.

McCaffery, E., Kahneman, D., & Spitzer, M., 1995. Framing the jury: Cognitive perspectives on pain and suffering awards. *Virginia Law Review*, 81, pp. 1341–1420.

McCrea, S., 2010. Intuition, insight, and the right hemisphere: Emergence of higher socio-cognitive functions. *Psychology Research and Behavior Management*, 3, pp. 1–39.

McLeod, I., 2013. *Legal Method*. London: Palgrave Macmillan.

McNammara, D., Kintsch, E., Songer, N., & Kintsch, W., 1996. Are good texts always better? Interaction of text coherence, background knowledge, and levels of understanding in learning from text. *Cognition and Instruction*, 14, pp. 1–43.

Mednick, S., 1962. The associative bases of the creative process. *Psychological Review*, 69, pp. 220–232.

Mercier, H. & Sperber, D., 2017. *The Enigma of Reason*. Cambridge, MA: Harvard University Press.

Morris, M. & Peng, K., 1994. Culture and cause: American and Chinese attributions for social and physical events. *Journal of Personality and Social Psychology*, 67, pp. 949–971.

Newell, B. & Shanks, D. R., 2014. Unconscious influences on decision making: A critical review. *Behavioral and Brain Sciences*, 37, pp. 1–19.

Nørretranders, T., 1999. *The User Illusion: Cutting Consciousness Down to Size*. New York: Penguin.

Olsson, E., 2017. Coherentist theories of epistemic justification. In: E. Zalta, ed. *The Stanford Encyclopedia of Philosophy*. https://plato.stanford.edu/archives/spr2017/entries/justep-coherence/.

Paivio, A., 2013. *Mind and Its Evolution: A Dual Coding Theoretical Approach*. New York: Psychology Press.

Pardo, M. & Patterson, D., 2013. *Minds, Brains, and Law: The Conceptual Foundations of Law and Neuroscience*. Oxford: Oxford University Press.

Pavlakos, G., ed., 2007. *Law, Rights, and Discourse: The Legal Philosophy of Robert Alexy*. Oxford: Hart Publishing.

Peer, E. & Gamliel, E., 2013. Heuristics and biases in judicial decisions. *Court Review*, 49, pp. 114–118.

Perelman, C., 1982. *The Realm of Rhetoric*. Norte Dame, IN: Notre Dame University Press.

Petrażycki, L., 1959. *Wstęp do nauki o prawie i moralności*. Warsaw: PWN.

    2002. *O pobudkach postępowania i o istocie moralności i prawa*. Warsaw: Oficyna Naukowa.

    , 2011. *Law and Morality*. New York: Routledge.

Pinker, S., 2003. Language as an adaptation to the cognitive niche. *Studies in the Evolution of Language*, 3, pp. 16–37.

    2010. The cognitive niche: Coevolution of intelligence, sociality, and language. *PNAS*, 107, pp. 8993–8999.

Pizarro, D. & Bloom, P., 2003. The intelligence of the moral intuitions: A reply to Haidt. *Psychological Review*, 110, pp. 193–196.

Popper, K., 1972. *Objective Knowledge: An Evolutionary Approach*. Oxford: Oxford University Press.

    1996. *Knowledge and the Body-Mind Problem: In Defence of Interaction*. New York: Routledge.

    2005. *The Logic of Scientific Discovery*. New York: Routledge.

Posner, R., 1976. Blackstone and Bentham. *Journal of Law & Economics*, 19, pp. 569–606.

    2007. *Economic Analysis of Law*. New York: Aspen Publishers.

Pound, R., 1908. Mechanical jurisprudence. *Columbia Law Review*, 8, pp. 605–623.

Pulvermüller, F., Garagnani, M., & Wennekers, T., 2014. Thinking in circuits: Toward neuro-biological explanation in cognitive neuroscience. *Biological Cybernetics*, 108, pp. 573–593.

Pyziak-Szafnicka, M., ed., 2009. *Kodeks cywilny. Część ogólna. Komentarz*. Warsaw: Wolters Kluwer.

Quine, W., 1948. On what there is. *Review of Metaphysics*, 2(5), pp. 21–38.

    1970. On the reasons for indeterminacy of translation. *Journal of Philosophy*, 67(6), pp. 178–183.

Raz, J., 2011. *From Normativity to Responsibility*. Oxford: Oxford University Press.

Reath, A., 1989. Kant's theory of moral sensibility: Respect for the moral law and the influence of inclination. *Kant-Studien*, 80, pp. 284–302.

Reichenbach, H., 1938. *Experience and Prediction: An Analysis of the Foundations and the Structure of Knowledge*. Chicago: University of Chicago Press.

Rescher, N., 1977. *Dialectics: A Controversy-Oriented Approach to the Theory of Knowledge*. Albany: State University of New York Press.

Reyes, R., Thompson, W., & Bower, G., 1980. Judgmental biases resulting from differing availabilities of arguments. *Journal of Personality and Social Psychology*, 39, pp. 2–12.

Ross, A., 1957. Tû-Tû. *Harvard Law Review*, 70, pp. 812–825. Originally published in Danish in 1951.

Salmon, W., 1990. Scientific explanation: Causation and unification. *Critica*, 22(66), pp. 3–23.

Sartor, G., 2008. Legal concepts: An inferential approach. EUI LAW Working Paper No. 2008/03.

Scanlon, T., 2004. Reasons: A puzzling duality? In: R. Wallace, J. Pettit, S. Scheffler, & M. Smith, eds. *Reason and Value: Themes from the Moral Philosophy of Joseph Raz*. New York: Oxford University Press, pp. 231–246.

Schauer, F., 2008. A critical guide to vehicles in the park. *New York University Law Review*, 83, pp. 1109–1134.

   2009. *Thinking Like a Lawyer: A New Introduction to Legal Reasoning*. Cambridge, MA: Harvard University Press.

Schlick, M., 1959. The foundation of knowledge. In: A. Ayer, ed. *Logical Positivism*. New York: Free Press, pp. 209–227.

Scriven, M., 1959. Truisms as the ground for historical explanations. In: P. Gardiner, ed. *Theories of History*. New York: Free Press, pp. 443–475.

Sheehy, B., 2006. Fundamentally conflicting views of the rule of law in China and the West & (and) implications for commercial disputes. *Northwestern Journal of International Law & Business*, 26, pp. 225–266.

Shettleworth, S., 2012. Do animals have insight, and what is insight anyway? *Canadian Journal of Experimental Psychology*, 66, pp. 217–226.

Simon, H., 1956. Rational choice and the structure of environments. *Psychological Review*, 63, pp. 129–138.

   1990. Invariants of human behavior. *Annual Review of Psychology*, 41, pp. 1–19.

Simpson, J. & Weiner, E., eds., 1989. *The Oxford English Dictionary*. Oxford: Oxford University Press.

Smith, V., 2008. *Rationality in Economics: Constructivist and Ecological Forms*. Cambridge: Cambridge University Press.

Smólski, A., 2001. Prawo Archimedesa? – ależ to bardzo proste! *Foton*, 75, pp. 43–50.

Sójka-Zielińska, K., 2010. Idea 'kodyfikacji' w kulturze prawnej europejskiego oświecenia. *Zeszyty Prawnicze*, 10, pp. 7–21.

Sorensen, R., 1992. *Thought Experiments*. Oxford: Oxford University Press.

Stelmach, J., 1991. *Die Hermeneutische Auffasung der Rechtsphilosophie*. Ebelsbach: R. Gremer.

Stelmach, J. & Brożek, B., 2006. *Methods of Legal Reasoning*. Dordrecht: Springer.

Stelmach, J., Brożek, B., & Kurek, Ł., eds., 2017. *The Province of Jurisprudence Naturalized*. Warsaw: Wolters Kluwer.

Stevenson, C. & Soanes, A., eds., 2006. *Oxford Dictionary of English*. Oxford: Oxford University Press.

Taylor, A., 1911. The words eidos, idea in pre-platonic literature. In: A. Taylor, ed. *Varia Socratica*. Oxford: James Parker & Co., pp. 178–267.

Thagard, P., 2005. *Mind: Introduction to Cognitive Science*. Cambridge, MA: MIT Press.

Thaler, R. & Sunstein, C., 2019. *Nudge*. New York: Penguin.

Thomson, J., 1971. A defence of abortion. *Philosophy and Public Affairs*, 1, pp. 47–66.

Tieszen, R., 1989. *Mathematical Intuition: Phenomenology and Mathematical Knowledge*. Dordrecht: Kluwer Academic Publishers.

Todd, P., Gigerenzer, G., & Group, A. R., 2012. *Ecological Rationality: Intelligence in the World*. Oxford: Oxford University Press.

Tomasello, M., 1999. *The Cultural Origins of Human Cognition*. Cambridge, MA: Harvard University Press.
    2003. *Constructing a Language: A Usage-Based Theory of Language Acquisition*. Cambridge, MA: Harvard University Press.
    2008. *Origins of Human Communication*. Cambridge, MA: MIT Press.
Tversky, A. & Kahneman, D., 1974. Judgment under Uncertainty: Heuristics and Biases. *Science*, 185, pp. 1124–1131.
Vico, G., 1948. *The New Science of Giambattista Vico*. Ithaca, NY: Cornell University Press.
Volz, K. & Cramon, D. von, 2006. What neuroscience can tell about intuitive processes in the context of perceptual discovery. *Journal of Cognitive Neuroscience*, 18, pp. 2077–2087.
Waismann, F., 1951. Verifiability. In: A. Flew, ed. *Logic and Language*. Oxford: Blackwell, pp. 35–68.
Wason, P. & Shapiro, D., 1971. Natural and contrived experience in a reasoning problem. *Quarterly Journal of Experimental Psychology*, 23, pp. 63–71.
Webster, D. & Kruglanski, A., 1994. Individual differences in need for cognitive closure. *Journal of Personality and Social Psychology*, 67, pp. 1049–1062.
Wedgwood, R., 2015. The pitfalls of "reasons." *Philosophical Issues*, 25, pp. 123–143.
Weinreb, L., 2005. *Legal Reason: The Use of Analogy in Legal Argument*. Cambridge: Cambridge University Press.
Weisberg, R., 2006. *Creativity*. Hoboken, NJ: John Wiley.
Weiss, G., 2000. The enchantment of codification in the common-law world. *Yale Journal of International Law*, 25, pp. 435–532.
White, J. B., 1985. *The Legal Imagination*. Chicago: University of Chicago Press.
Williams, J., Russell, N., & Irwin, D., 2017. On the notion of abstraction in systemic functional linguistics. *Functional Linguistics*, 4, doi:10.1186/s40554-017-0047-3.
Wittgenstein, L., 1958. *Philosophical Investigations*. London: Basil Blackwell.
    1978. *Remarks on the Foundations of Mathematics*. Cambridge, MA: MIT Press.
Wróbel, W. & Zoll, A., eds., 2004. *Kodeks karny. Komentarz. Część ogólna*. Kraków: Zakamycze.
    2016. *Kodeks karny. Część szczególna. Tom III*. Warsaw: Wolters Kluwer.
Wróblewski, J., 1992. *The Judicial Application of Law*. Dordrecht: Kluwer Academic Publishers.
Wundt, W., 1918. *Grundriss der Psychologie*. Leipzig: Alfred Kröner.
Zajonc, R., 1980. Feeling and thinking: Preferences need no inferences. *American Psychologist*, 35, pp. 151–175.
Zander, T., Öllinger, M., & Volz, K., 2016. Intuition and insight: Two processes that build on each other or fundamentally differ? *Frontiers in Psychology*, 7, doi:10.3389/fpsyg .2016.01395.
Zelden, C., 1989. Regional growth and the federal district courts: The impact of judge Joseph C. Hutcheson, Jr., on Southeast Texas, 1918–1931. *Houston Review*, 11, pp. 67–94.
Zwaan, R. & Kaschak, M. P., 2008. Language in the brain, body, and world. In: P. Robbins & M. Aydede, eds. *The Cambridge Handbook of Situated Cognition*. Cambridge: Cambridge University Press, pp. 368–381.
Zyzik, R., 2018. *Obraz człowieka w teorii oświadczeń woli*. Kraków: WAM.

Index

abduction (abductive reasoning), 59
abstraction, 7, 8, 63, 76, 79, 81, 82, 83, 85, 87, 89, 90,
    92, 94, 96, 121, 144, 146, 166
  as decontextualization, 79
  as generalization, 79
  as omission, 79
Adams v. New Jersey Steamboat Co., case, 57, 58,
    87, 89, 101
Alexy, Robert, 120, 145, 147, 148, 150, 158
analogy, 57, 58, 59, 89, 100, 101, 107, 133
  as a method of the application of law, 100
  as an interpretive device, 100
anchoring effect (anchoring and adjustment
    heuristic), 6, 12, 25, 26, 28, 153
application of law, 1, 3, 13, 102
Aquinas, Thomas, 132, 149
Archimedes, 29, 30
argument, 6, 8, 89, 100, 128, 132, 133, 134, 145,
    147, 157
  a cohaerentia, 100
  a contrario, 3, 100
  a fortiori, 100
  a loco communi, 100
  a loco specifici, 100
  a simile, 3, 100, 133
  ab exemplo, 100, 133
argumentation, 4, 16, 39, 68, 98, 132, 133,
    134, 148
Aristotle, 79, 83, 98
Atkin, James (Lord Atkin), 15
audience, 46, 107, 132, 133, 134, 135, 145,
    163, 164
  particular, 133, 135
  universal, 132, 133, 134, 135, 145, 163, 164
autonomous machine, 104, 161
autonomous weapon system, 161
availability heuristic, 6, 28

Bentham, Jeremy, 92, 93, 94, 96, 113, 145
Blackstone, William, 92, 93, 94, 96

California v. Carney, case, 56, 59
Carnap, Rudolf, 157
Carpenter v. N.Y., N.H. H.R.R. Co., case, 58
categorical imperative, 137, 139, 141, 142, 143, 145,
    146, 147, 148, 152, 156, 160, 164
caution, principle of, 8, 106, 122, 124, 128, 144, 163
Churchland, Paul, 76
Code of Hammurabi, 61, 62, 80, 81
codification, 90, 92, 93
cognitive closure, 36, 37, 124
cognitive mechanism, 4, 123
cognitive niche, 7, 8, 90, 97, 98
cognitive science, 4, 18, 52
cognitive style, 47, 79
coherence, 74, 75, 99, 126, 130, 133, 135, 143
  criteria of, 130
coherentism, 129, 130, 131, 132, 163
common law, 1, 9, 93, 94, 100, 101, 108, 111,
    122, 135
concept, 7, 13, 50, 51, 52, 61, 64, 70, 71, 73,
    74, 76, 80, 82, 83, 84, 110, 119, 124, 128,
    140, 145
  abstract, 50, 51, 52, 61, 82, 84, 124, 140, 145
  concrete, 50, 61
  formation of, 50
  intermediary, 69, 70, 71, 73, 74
  legal, 7, 68, 70, 71, 127
conceptual mapping, 51
conceptual metaphor theory, 51
context of discovery, 128, 129
context of justification, 128
contrast, principle of, 8, 100, 106, 122, 127, 128, 129,
    144, 163, 164
cultural evolution, 86